The Walled Garden

by

Jane Preston

Grosvenor House
Publishing Limited

The right of Jane Preston to be identified as the author of this
work has been asserted in accordance with Section 78
of the Copyright, Designs and Patents Act 1988

The book cover is copyright to Jane Preston

This book is published by
Grosvenor House Publishing Ltd
Link House
140 The Broadway, Tolworth, Surrey, KT6 7HT.
www.grosvenorhousepublishing.co.uk

A CIP record for this book
is available from the British Library

ISBN 978-1-83975-683-2

Introduction

Those of you who are already familiar with Selborne in Hampshire, will realise that I have taken a few liberties with the layout and topography of the village. Nevertheless, visitors will find they can still 'run up' the Zig-Zag; make a wish by the Wishing Stone at the top; cross the Plestor to visit the church; look for the hoopoe in the Gilbert White Memorial Window; walk through the beechwoods on the Hangar; go riding on the Common; visit the Wakes and buy books at the bookshop. There's no point, however, in searching for Westhangar Hall or looking for the Franklin and Halliday gravestones as these exist only in my imagination. The ancient yew-tree in the churchyard was blown down in a gale in the late 1980s but the stump remains.

Heather La Fontaine arrives in Selborne in 1984 to complete and write up the family history of the Franklin family of Westhangar Hall, expecting to spend a few peaceful months in the Hampshire countryside, but soon discovers that almost every member of the household is facing a serious personal crisis. Her plans for the restoration of the neglected Walled Garden become a symbol for the gradual resolution of their problems, while the discovery of encoded entries in an old diary provides Heather with an important, shocking link to her own family history.

Jane Preston, 2021.

*For all those who love gardens, village life
and the English countryside*

Chapter One

Heather drove slowly and carefully through the small market-town of Alton in Hampshire on the alert for road-signs as well as glancing every few seconds in the mirror, trying to ignore the queue of impatient motorists behind her. Too late, she spotted the sign to Selborne and swore silently as she prepared to take the 5-mile detour necessary to approach the village from the other direction.

'They've changed these roads since I lived round here,' she muttered irritably, then was forced to swerve sharply onto the grass verge as a long lorry carrying a load of wooden pallets edged past her far too closely.

Heather knew that Frog, her elderly green Morris Minor, her reliable companion for close on twelve years, was not the speediest of vehicles, but it still turned heads and elicited sympathetic smiles from passers-by, and it held too many memories for her to think of replacing it. Jerome had given her the car not long before he died, his farewell gift.

'Steady, steady,' Heather said to herself, 'there's no rush, you're going to arrive far too early anyway.' She pulled into a long, shady lay-by, both to allow time for the beating of her heart to return to normal – for it had been a close shave – and to take another look at the Ordnance Survey map lying on the passenger-seat beside her. Winding the car-window down a few inches, she sighed with pleasure as the mingled scents of hawthorn, cow-parsley, pink-campion, stitchwort and damp grass wafted into the car while primroses shone from below the hedgerows, thick with snowy blackthorn blossom, the welcoming scents and sights of Hampshire and her childhood

1

home. She remained sitting for a few moments, contemplating the prospect of the new assignment that had so unexpectedly and opportunely come her way with a mixture of apprehension and excitement.

Research into family-history was always bound to throw up interesting, sometimes shocking discoveries as even the most apparently conventional family could harbour secrets of a dark nature of which they were either unaware or most anxious to conceal.

'The thrill of the chase' was how she had described her work to a sceptical friend who had asked, in some bewilderment, how she could possibly enjoy leafing through dusty old documents, tattered letters in near-indecipherable handwriting, frustratingly undated diaries, scribbled family-trees with half the dates missing, recipes for the most unpalatable dishes or, even worse, remedies for dreadful diseases. And where was the pleasure in traipsing through overgrown churchyards, kneeling on wet grass, trying to peer at lichen-covered lettering on old gravestones...and all this for families not even her own?

To Heather, the challenge of bringing forgotten stories back to life was amongst her greatest pleasures. Finding lost links between generations, identifying unnamed sketches of old houses, discovering that that beautifully dressed young woman depicted on a *carte-de-visite,* her whole life ahead of her, was doomed to die young of puerperal fever, or alternatively, to become the mother of nine children of whom only three would survive babyhood, gave her a quiet sense of success.

She expected this job to be quite different from her most recent assignment as part of a small team researching the activities of an archaeological society that had ceased its work years earlier, but whose findings had never been properly written up. Its members had gradually aged and become less able to engage in fieldwork, the funds had dried up and public interest in the uncovering of indifferent Bronze Age artifacts on a patch of derelict farmland had waned. It was only the chance discovery by amateur metal-detectors, of a hoard of rare ancient coins a couple of hundred yards away that had re-vitalised the interest, both of the owner of the land and the British Museum and Heather had been employed to keep records of every scrap of metalwork found as the work re-commenced. After two years, the site had been cleared and closed once more and she'd realised that, although the work had been necessary and rewarding, it was the discovery of the human and domestic affairs of the more recently deceased, to satisfy the curiosity of their live descendants, that afforded her the most enjoyment.

She had been recommended for this new job at Westhangar Hall, near Selborne, by a colleague with whom she'd worked a few years before, whilst cataloguing the disorganised archives of a run-down Stately Home in North Yorkshire. These had been housed in a series of unheated, draughty attics, where Heather reckoned that, over the space of three years, she had inhaled more of the decayed remains of long dead insects, fragments of mouldering paper and the dust of ages than had really been good for her.

Yet here I am, letting myself in for another unspecified length of time, breathing in deadly detritus and cobwebs, but smiled as she re-started Frog and edged slowly onto the road. The brief had been irresistible, a plea from a middle-aged widow, Mrs Franklin, whose husband John had begun the process of assembling the family papers and heirlooms with a view to publishing his results but had died most unexpectedly from a heart-attack, leaving her bereft and the work unfinished.

'I would have liked to carry on the work of my dear husband myself,' The widow had explained, over the phone, a slight catch in her voice, 'but the shock of losing him...at such a comparatively young age...so suddenly... brought on a slight stroke which has affected my eyes and my ability to concentrate, temporarily, I hope. So...although I'll be happy to answer any questions that might crop up, there's very little practical help I could give.'

That will suit me just fine, Heather had thought, let me loose in the archives and I'll be a happy woman. The terms were generous, and she'd have her own accommodation separate from the main house. And now here she was, bowling along a winding lane between high, green banks, well-hedged fields of wheat and barley to her left, meadow and woodland to her right and hardly another vehicle in sight – bliss!

She'd been excited to discover that her destination was to be Hampshire, not far from where she and her brother had spent the greater part of their childhood, living with their grandparents in a village about three miles from the market town of Alton, despatched there initially for safety from dangerous and dirty Manchester during the war. Then, following the separation of their parents in 1948, she and Craig had simply remained where they were, joined eventually by their bitter and unhappy mother. Although they missed their father's presence at first, he had never had much influence on their lives and they'd been happy to continue to have five acres of garden, pasture and woodland surrounding their grandparents' bungalow at their disposal, able to make camps, swing from trees, light fires and cook sausages on sticks, watched with interest by Gran's two cats. Helping to pick fruit, feeding the hens (Grandad ran a small poultry-farm and kept a dozen ducks), even weeding the flower beds and mowing the lawns were all pleasures compared with the restricted lives they had lived in the centre of an industrial, noisy and unhealthy city.

They had both settled well into their new schools and as they grew towards their teens, they would cycle for miles, exploring the country lanes in perfect safety. They'd visited Selborne from time to time, had even read parts of Gilbert White's famous book and would always enter the little church to look at the hoopoe in the stained-glass, Memorial bird-window, hoping one day to spot one for themselves in their grandparents' garden – but they never did.

If they'd brought sandwiches, they would eat them on the Plestor, the patch of green in front of the church, then hide their bikes behind the ancient yew-tree, said to be well over 1,000 years old and wander through the village to the steep footpath called the Zig-Zag that led up the sloping woodlands known as the Hangar, racing each other to reach the Wishing Stone at the top. After solemnly circling the stone three times they'd scamper down again, always a little anxious that their bikes might have been stolen. But in all their years living in Hampshire and visiting Selborne, Heather had never heard of Westhangar Hall.

'We don't claim to be a Stately Home,' Mrs Franklin had informed her on the phone, 'but rather what you might call a comfortable Gentleman's Residence, which has been in my husband's family for over 200 years.' Again, that slight catch in her voice and short pause before continuing, 'and it was his dearest wish to leave all the history, all the papers and stories of his ancestors in good order for our descendants just in case...in case they were not inclined to do so themselves.'

Just so. Heather's mother would have agreed whole-heartedly, having spent years of her own life visiting libraries, graveyards and Record Offices in search of their family history, resulting in an hilarious, near - scandalous memoir, which, privately, her children had regarded as largely the product of her over-fertile imagination. She'd been proud of the fact that it was owing to her influence that after their grandparents' deaths, when Heather, Craig and their mother had moved to a neat, small house in Hertfordshire, Heather had taken a combined History and Archaeology degree at London University. She'd been less than impressed, however, when she'd followed that by a year-long course in Practical Horticulture at an Agricultural College, which she'd regarded as a complete waste of time.

'Think of all those years you spent helping Gran,' she'd reproved her daughter, 'you must know more than enough about gardening already.' But Heather had been determined, her absent father had stumped up the money and she'd always been grateful for the experience.

As she and Frog coasted slowly through the village, she was suddenly seized with the desire to re-live her childhood and mount the Zig-Zag. She had plenty of time... why not? She parked behind the pub near the start of the footpath and began the steep, upward climb, through the beech-trees she remembered so well.

I wish Craig were here with me, she thought, catching her breath and stopping suddenly on one of the corners, suddenly overwhelmed with sadness as her thoughts flew to her adventurous brother, always the joyful, constant companion of her childhood, killed in a climbing accident on holiday in the Canadian Rockies more than four years ago. If only I'd been with him, she thought as she'd thought so often since that terrible time, I'd have been able to save him, warned him of the danger of that falling rock, persuaded him to try a safer route. 'Died doing what he loved best,' was how the local Hertfordshire paper had put it, but what comfort was that? He wouldn't have wanted to die at such a young age, surely, whether he loved what he was doing or not?

She remained a moment, listening to the insistent, repetitive note of an exuberant song-thrush in the branches above her head, then smiled as she heard the staccato call of an unseen, faraway cuckoo, the first she had heard that year – a good omen. She sighed, more cheerful now, before setting off again, determined to reach the top without stopping again for breath. She arrived more quickly that she had expected, quite suddenly emerging from the surrounding, graceful trees with their silvery trunks and waving fresh green canopy, into daylight and bright blue sky. The Wishing Stone was still there, and she turned round to take in the view of the Hampshire countryside in all its Spring glory spread out before her.

See, Selborne spreads her boldest beauties round, Heather remembered from her schooldays, *The vary'd valley, and the mountain ground, Wildly majestic...*Well, she'd always thought, not *exactly* mountainous and she wouldn't have described it as majestic, but unthreatening, gentle, but none the worse for that.

Not a soul around, just herself and the rustling beech trees, *'the most lovely of all forest trees'* as the Reverend Gilbert White had put it... and far below her the village rooftops, rosy-red and the Wakes, his house, a museum to his memory now, standing in its large garden with field upon field rising behind. She savoured the prospect of the next few months surrounded by all this beauty and utter peace and leaned against the stone, warm from the early Spring sunshine, listening to birdsong all around as the beech-leaves rustled softly in the April breeze.

I must bring Sally up here one day, she mused, thinking affectionately of her daughter, picturing the way her red-gold hair would wave in the wind and hearing, in her imagination, her peals of ringing laughter. Would she bring herself to join her mother in the childish fun of circling the stone and making a wish, she wondered, half-laughing as she looked cautiously round to make sure nobody was looking?

I will, she decided. Why not? She began to pace around the stone, trying not to catch her feet in the long grass until the three circuits were done, then stopped, unable to think of a single wish. No good wishing for Craig – or for Sally really, enjoying her busy life as a Primary School teacher in the historic town of St Albans.

'Should've gone into computers,' Heather's mother had commented when she'd heard of her granddaughter's choice of career, in the same way that she had criticised Heather's interest in horticulture. 'Much better paid,' she'd added with assurance, with which Heather had secretly agreed, though, considering that her mother hadn't the faintest idea how computers worked, or did, it was a wonder to her that she had even suggested it. Over the years, however, Heather, Craig and then Sally, had got used to ignoring her more caustic remarks. They were – mostly – kindly meant. And with her earthy sense of humour, loud laugh and huge capacity for enjoying herself, she hadn't been such a difficult mother and grandmother, after all.

So, in the end she simply wished that her new job would be as rewarding as she hoped, then turned to contemplate the view on the other side of the Hangar, over springing fronds of young bracken and tangled brambles, towards the Common... and found herself staring straight into the face of a previously unseen man standing like a statue not ten yards away.

Automatically she jumped, her hand pressed against her mouth, her heart racing. He and she stared hard at each other for a few seconds, then his mouth moved silently, and he waved his hand in a kind of apology. Even amid her fright she noticed that his was a sad but interesting face, weather-beaten to the colour of cinnamon – but deeply lined and, it seemed to Heather, nervous, troubled. His eyes, however, were so blue they could rival the summer sky and his mop of rich brown hair, lightly streaked with grey, blew across his forehead like that of a tousled schoolboy.

As he seemed disinclined to speak, Heather calmly asked him if it was possible to see Westhangar Hall from this lofty viewpoint. At this enquiry he jerked out of his temporary torpor and nodded vigorously, pointing down the path up which he must have arrived. He uttered a few almost inaudible grunts, twisting his face into grotesque shapes as he tried to reply. Show no surprise, Heather ordered herself, act as if there's nothing out of the ordinary and she nodded, looking in the direction he was pointing, where a row of chimney pots and the ridge of a long grey-tiled roof, a couple of hundred yards away were just visible between the waving branches of the beech-trees.

'It looks an interesting place,' she said, and the suntanned man nodded again, twisting his lips to try to smile and pointing at his own chest. Heather smiled back, reminded of the shell-shocked ex-soldiers she remembered seeing, aided by crutches, callipers or sticks, ambling distractedly along the streets of Manchester when she was a child in the 1940s. Her father had instructed her and Craig never to make fun of these damaged men and to smile at them if possible.

'Well...must fetch Frog now...my old car,' Heather explained after a few minutes, 'got to go all the way back down the Zig-Zag. And thanks for pointing out Westhangar Hall – I'm on my way there now. Starting a new job today.' She started off down the slope with a wave, determined not to look back and carry on as if she met such unusual people every day of her life – but she could sense that he stood there still, watching her until she was out of sight.

The vision of him nodding and pointing at himself stayed with her all the way down the hill and she sat for a moment in Frog before setting on her way. Was he, perhaps, trying to tell her that *he* lived at the Hall...or merely that he knew it well? She shrugged her shoulders, dismissing the incident as just one of those strange things that crop up from time to time and put it out of her mind. She would probably never see him again.

It was still too early to arrive at Westhangar Hall. The widow was expecting her at five o'clock and it was not yet four. Looking at the map she noticed that at the far end of the Hangar, the woodland thinned, and another footpath led upwards to a spot from where she might get a clearer view of the house and its surroundings and perhaps even a glimpse of the gardens. She followed the winding road through the village past old thatched, half-timbered cottages then turned into an even narrower side road which ended in a rough track with space for two or three cars to park or turn at the end by a dilapidated footpath sign.

Exploring new territory – how she relished it! She had always been a mischievous, disobedient and adventurous child, a risk-taker, never able to resist venturing down new pathways, opening shut gates or climbing onto the tops of walls. 'I just want to see what's on the other side' she would explain crossly to her mother or grandmother as she was being hauled down again. 'Miss Nosy' Gran had called her as she was growing up, 'and that will get you into trouble one day.' Her mother, genuinely perturbed by her daughter's spirited behaviour had made a cardboard sign with the word PRIVATE in large letters written on it and propped it up where Heather could not fail to see it, warning her in the most severe terms that she must *never* venture past such a notice. She might be tossed by a bull or bitten by dogs, even shot at by an over-zealous gamekeeper, or the police would be sure to catch her and send her to a reform-school. Heather had promptly taken the notice and pinned it onto her bedroom door, leading to an explosive row and no sweets for a week... but later, listening at the kitchen door she'd been cheered to hear Gran and Mum laughing heartily at her naughtiness. And Craig had slipped a few packets of chewing-gum under her bedroom door so that she could enjoy them in bed out of sight of Mum and Gran.

She smiled to herself at the memory and started up the path, excited to experience that flutter of anticipation she had so often felt as a child. What *would* be round the next corner? Not just the next bend of the footpath, apparently little-used and overgrown in places, but of the next phase of her life?

Heather was right about the footpath as, after winding through hazel-thickets, brambles and elder-trees, creamy with blossom, it straightened, revealing almost the entire length of the Georgian mansion, about forty yards below, built of muted grey stone and roofed in large tiles atop a row of evenly spaced and pedimented windows. The walls, as far as Heather could see were half covered in wisteria, just coming into shy leaf, budding roses and the bare branches of a climbing vine – Virginia creeper, she guessed. Across a rather unkempt courtyard stood a fine brick-built row of stables, two each side of a central coach-house with tall, green-painted doors and topped by an elegant clock-tower. The clock, she noticed with a wry smile, stood at exactly ten-to-three and the hands did not move for the whole time she looked at it. Was this by reason of a happy accident or by design?

'And will there be honey still for tea?' she misquoted under her breath, wondering if the stables still housed horses. As if to answer her, the heads of two beautiful beasts, a grey and a chestnut appeared from two of the stable doors, lightly blowing through their nostrils with well-bred impatience, alerted by the approach of footsteps and soft calling. A slender, grey-haired woman, armed with two buckets, emerged from a yet invisible part of the house and crossed the courtyard slowly and with care. Her slight limp left Heather in no doubt that this was the unhappy widow, Gwendoline Franklin, owner of the house.

Heather froze, embarrassed by the idea that she might be seen spying on her future employer even though her common-sense told her that the thick lattice of waving branches would be keeping her well-concealed. She watched silently as each horse was offered food from the buckets, munching noisily. Their owner then rested her head briefly on the forehead of the grey and seemed to heave a long, sad sigh. Then, with a pat on each nose, she made her way back towards the house, stooping to pull half-heartedly at a weed or two as she went.

Her mood more sober now, Heather remained where she was, letting her gaze stray over as much of the grounds as she could see from her vantage-point: undulating lawns edged with box, a few classical statues that had seen better days, several curving flowerbeds filled with tulips and flowering shrubs too far away for accurate identification and drifts of fading daffodils. Beyond the formal lawns she could make out a high brick wall, smothered in unruly clematis – needs a good pruning, she thought – pink, purple, white and blue, which only half-succeeded in concealing an arched, brick gateway in the centre. On each side of the wall the garden itself melted seamlessly into meadow and long grass, studded with buttercups, celandines and daisies.

'Just... wonderful,' mouthed Heather, heaving a sigh of pure pleasure and anticipation at the prospect of living here, even if only for a year or two... when the slightest of sounds from a few yards to her right alerted her to the unwelcome knowledge that she was not, as she had imagined, quite alone in these enveloping, hanging woods.

Instinctively she remained standing stock-still – then turned her head infinitely slowly, noiselessly, peering through the tangled undergrowth, although her heart was beating so strongly that she imagined it must be heard by anyone nearby. Perhaps... perhaps it was only a deer... or a dog... or...Then, just as she had decided it was nothing to be alarmed by and had begun to turn away, she did spot something that stopped her in her tracks and filled her with far more fear than any animal, tame or wild, could have done.

Almost concealed in the green understory of the beech trees, a mere twenty yards from her, she gradually made out the form of quite a young man, a khaki shirt worn casually over camouflage trousers – his head a mass of dark brown curls which waved to and fro in the breeze. Although her view kept being obscured by branches and leaves, she could see that he was engrossed in dealing with something on the ground, invisible to her. The next moment she was distracted by a movement beyond the trees below and she watched as Mrs Franklin came into view, about to cross the courtyard once more. At the same moment, the young man stood up, pulling hard on some sort of string beside his feet. There came a click and for a moment Heather saw the gleam of polished wood and shiny metal as he raised his arms, aiming directly at the widow standing before the stables... with a crossbow!

For a moment she froze, hardly believing what she was seeing – then, as the boy hesitated for a moment, she reacted automatically, starting towards him in a sudden panic.

'Stop!' she shouted, her voice cracking, 'stop... this minute!' The startled youth jerked round towards her, accidentally releasing the catch and trying to drop the weapon at the same time, but not before the slim steel bolt had landed harmlessly in a patch of damp earth well short of his intended target.

For a moment there was utter silence. Mrs Franklin, in confusion, looked up into the tangle of woodland above her, her hand shielding her eyes, searching for the source of the noise, as Heather retreated as far back among the trees as possible. The young man seemed frozen with shock and as the widow moved slowly out of sight, perhaps thinking she had merely heard children playing in the woods, Heather, her heart in her mouth, dared to approach him cautiously as he stared stupidly down at the crossbow lying in the undergrowth below.

'No!' she barked, as he bent to retrieve it, 'leave it! Just... leave it! What the hell do you think you were playing at?' As she got closer, she saw that he was trembling violently, biting his lip, his breath coming in short, horrified gasps. He slumped down gradually, his head resting against the trunk of a tree, eyes closed, his arms drooping, his cheeks deathly pale. Although tempted to turn and steal away, Heather forced herself instead to approach him with cautious steps, just in time to hear him whisper, as if to himself, 'My God! I nearly killed my... my m...,' before sinking down onto the ground in an attitude of utter despair.

He looked older now that Heather could take a closer look at him, twenty-two perhaps, twenty-three... and obviously in great distress. With a swift look at her watch but reluctant to leave him, she lowered herself onto the leafy ground beside him, raising him back into a sitting position and remained quietly seated beside him, her arm around his shaking shoulders, giving him time to recover.

Chapter Two

'Dear Craig,' she wrote a few hours later, 'you won't believe this but on the first day of my new job, I've already met a man with no voice, a potential assassin, a grieving widow, oh, and a rather jolly stable-lass...and I've only been here three hours!'

Heather looked at what she had written, secure in the knowledge that no-one but herself would ever read her words. She had discovered, two or three years ago, that writing to her lost brother was a safe way to relieve her feelings, face her fears, help her solve problems and plan her next course of action. She paused for a moment, more serious now, holding the thick book in protective hands.

Jerome had bought her this five-year, lockable diary the year before he died, when he was seriously unwell, but it had been several years before she could bring herself to deface its pristine pages by writing in it. She'd come across it one day, pushed into a bookshelf between a biography of Thomas Hardy and a volume of Wordsworth's poetry, and found, to her quiet surprise that she was no longer overwhelmed with sadness at the sight of it, but rather comforted to be reminded of Jerome's loving generosity, his kindness and concern for her and little Sally. She'd decided there and then that she would only use it in extreme circumstances when she needed a shoulder to cry on or the advice of a clear-sighted, sensible friend – and this was just such an occasion.

She closed the diary and locked it with the little brass key she always kept in her purse. In truth, though outwardly calm, her thoughts had been in turmoil ever since she had reluctantly parted company with the tousle-haired, disturbed young man she had met in the woods. She was still not convinced that she had done the right thing by not reporting him to the police. Yet...what could she accuse him of? What had he actually done?

She had prevented him from committing a pre-meditated murder and – this was where her doubt and dilemma lay – had extracted a solemn promise from him not to attempt to carry out his intention ever, *ever* again in return for her silence. For a young man to try to kill his own mother she knew there had to be deep-seated reasons behind such an appalling plan. What *could* that inoffensive, elderly lady *possibly* have done to force him into such action?

As she'd sat quietly beside the young man in the woods, the only words she could understand, jerked out in fits and starts as he slowly regained control over his distress sounded like, 'she's ruined my whole life...my own mother ... Why didn't she tell me before? She should have told me... for God's sake, they should have *told* me – now I don't know who I am... or what to do,' staring at Heather in a frantic attempt to convince her of the justification for his intention. Heather had not tried to question him, judging that, one day after the first trauma was over, he might see fit to explain what crime, in his eyes, his widowed mother – and possibly his father also – had committed.

When she'd quietly explained to him that she was going to be living alongside him and his mother for a year or so, his eyes had filled with renewed terror. This was the moment when, worried that he might do himself some mischief, she had reassured him that she would not betray him.

'Because I don't believe for one moment you *would* actually have shot her,' she'd said slowly, 'I saw you hesitate...but, you must understand... I *had* to stop you. Whatever your mother has done it couldn't have been as serious as murder. If you *had* killed her that would have meant, not only her death, but the end of your freedom for years and years if not for the rest of your life.'

She had persuaded him to walk slowly with her back to the car, carrying the crossbow awkwardly, guiltily, but he refused her offer to drive him to the house. She'd cheered him a little by asking if he would be able to pretend, when she was introduced to him, that they had never met. She'd watched him stumble off along the lane as she turned Frog round, sympathy in her mind yet with a lurking dread that perhaps she had just made a terrible mistake. What if he did try again – and succeed – how would she feel then?

As she'd turned Frog into the curving pebble drive, stopping in front of the porte-cochère at the front of the house she was met, not by Mrs Franklin but by a well-built, rosy-cheeked woman with a loud, confident voice who, after directing her to turn and park in the courtyard she had seen from the woods, (the Tradesmen's Entrance, she thought wryly; now I know my place!) introduced herself as Kathie.

'And you must be Mrs La Fontaine,' she replied, shaking Heather briskly by the hand.

'That's right. But I'm called Heather, not quite such a mouthful.' Kathie gave a relieved laugh and began helping heave her suitcase and bags out of the boot.

'Love the car,' she said enviously, 'don't see many of those around these days.' This remark, genuinely offered, made Heather feel much better about Frog and she warmed to Kathie immediately.

'I'm supposed to be in charge of the horses,' she continued, 'came here three years ago when Mr Franklin had his first heart-attack. Only supposed to stay six months but he never regained his full health. Gwen – Mrs Franklin – and I got on very well, she needed a helping hand, I needed somewhere to live...and so I just stayed. I'm a sort of maid-of-all-work now, I suppose.' She gave another burst of laughter which Heather found very reassuring. Kathie looked and sounded 'a good sort.'

To her surprise, she was escorted, not into the house but across the courtyard, where Kathie unlocked a small door set into one of the large green doors of the coach-house.

'You're in the coach-house flat,' Kathie explained, hanging the key on a rusty nail as they mounted a narrow wooden flight of stairs, 'you'll have peace and quiet for your work in here, just the horses below for company. It's where Mr Franklin kept all the family papers, accounts, old wills, log-books, photo-albums and God knows what which he'd been trying to put into some sort of order before he died.' She paused briefly at the top of the stairs, turning round to face Heather, a wry smile on her face. 'Personally, I think he worked in here to keep out of Gwen's way, she wasn't much interested in his family history, and he wasn't keen on all her bridge parties and W.I. sewing bees.' Heather nodded, smiling sympathetically.

'He was a really nice man,' Kathie continued, 'good tempered but quiet with a wonderful sense of humour. It might take Gwen a long time to get over it. I mean, we all knew he was very unwell – but, that final heart attack happened so suddenly...'

She left the remainder of the sentence hanging in the air and heaved a regretful sigh. 'But she'll be really glad you're here,' she added, dumping Heather's belongings onto the floor of a large, high-ceilinged room, lined with bookcases and shelves and filled with chests-of-drawers, trunks and cardboard boxes. It was also equipped, Heather was relieved to see, with a wide desk and swivel chair, typewriter, telephone, a small television and a collection of writing-materials essential to her work.

She liked the room instantly – the smell of old books and papers, nothing too tidy, nothing too new, just a comfortable armchair, one or two other wooden ones, a medley of woollen rugs on the floor and a large window that looked directly into the yard and across to the house.

'Bedroom and little shower through here,' Kathie continued, 'not the most modern arrangements in the world but ...' giving Heather an appraising glance, 'I'm sure you won't mind. If you want a bit more luxury any time, you can always come across and use my bathroom. And here,' she opened another small door, 'your kitchenette – though you'll be having most of your meals with me and Mrs Franklin when she feels well enough. Luckily, she has an excellent cook-housekeeper as I'm no great shakes on the domestic side. But it's Elsie's day off today.'

'Oh, it's all lovely,' Heather said, delighted at the prospect of having her own space, privacy, the chance to organise her working day just as she chose.

'Gwen was planning for you to have supper in the Hall this evening, but she's overtired and asked me to fix something. Will toasted cheese and a bowl of soup be enough to keep you alive until tomorrow morning? Might even be able to rustle up a bit of cake.' The question, Heather surmised, was rhetorical. 'I'll come over and fetch you when it's ready, you may get lost trying to find my rooms – and don't bother to change, not when it's just us. Adrian will go to the pub, I expect.'

'Adrian?' enquired Heather, remembering in time that she was not supposed to have met any young man that day and mentally planning where she was going to put all her belongings – the bedroom was quite small.

'Gwen's son,' Kathie replied, darting a quick glance in Heather's direction – and paused, her hand on the door handle.

'I'd better tell you now,' she said, her voice low, confidential, 'as you're sure to sense an awkward atmosphere in the house. There was an almighty row a few days ago, shouting, crying, banging doors...never heard anything like it. They thought I was out exercising Champion, the grey, but I was trying to finish writing in a birthday-card to catch the last post and could hardly believe what I was hearing...it was *awful*.'

She paused for a moment and Heather read real distress in her eyes.

'So bad for Gwen so soon after the shock of Mr Franklin's death – I was really, *really* worried. Adrian stormed out and went missing for three days – God only knows where he went. Gwen's been breathless and weepy ever since and Adrian's been sullen and silent since he came back, won't meet my eyes or speak a civil word.' She sighed. 'It's so unlike him, normally you couldn't wish for a more cheerful, considerate character.'

Heather stared into her half-opened suitcase to hide the sudden guilty flush that had risen to her cheeks. 'You've no idea what sparked it off, I suppose?' she murmured, rummaging for her washing things and make-up bag, disappointed to see Kathie shake her head.

'It all blew up when he came back from Brazil recently – he'd been staying on a cattle-ranch studying livestock management in preparation for the day when he takes over the estate here, I suppose. He's twenty-three now, still young for such responsibility but he'll have help from neighbours and friends. Mr Franklin was very well respected, can't imagine any of his farming colleagues refusing to help the son of an old friend. We've an estate-manager looking after things at the moment, just until everything settles down and Adrian feels confident enough to take the reins properly.' She sighed again, looking uncertain and depressed. 'Anyway...I'll fill you in with what I know when you come over for supper. Seven o'clock?'

Kathie clumped down the wooden stairs and Heather heard her fill the horses' water-troughs from a tap in the wall, pat their noses and slap their necks, before crossing the yard into the main house.

Heather sat quietly in the armchair for a moment, thinking back to her recent encounter with the distraught young man, consumed with agitation and curiosity. Whatever had happened recently between mother and son – as Heather knew but Kathie did not – had been evidence of far more serious import than even a family argument. She got up and ran her eyes over the bookcases and boxes stacked beside the desk – could there be something amongst all these piles of papers, files and ring-binders that might give her a clue?

She gave herself a reproving shake, frowning. Whatever it was, it was really none of her business. She was being employed to straighten out the muddle of the family's past, not speculate about its present or future problems. But she couldn't help just wondering.

'That nose,' she could hear her grandmother's warning voice from the past, 'will get you into trouble one of these days.' She half-laughed as she chased her thoughts away and set to the serious business of opening cupboards, arranging her possessions and making herself at home.

An old cabin-trunk at the bottom of the wardrobe, stuck over with overseas labels filled much of the space she'd have liked for her shoes and her own bags, but she managed to stow away most things without too much trouble. She would ask Mrs Franklin if the trunk could be moved sometime to give her a little more room, but it was not important – any time would do.

In the meantime, she'd have supper with Kathie and the chance to learn a little more about this unhappy family. Tomorrow she'd set to work.

'So,' asked Heather later, as she scooped up the last of her soup, 'when do you think I'll be meeting Mrs Franklin? There are things I should ask her before I start meddling with her husband's papers, find out if I'm supposed to work fixed hours, all that sort of thing. I haven't got a written contract so I'm rather in the dark.'

'I expect she'll be feeling stronger tomorrow – this row with Adrian has really set her recovery back. Mr Franklin's death was so sudden, even though he'd had heart-trouble for years, that she could have done with Adrian's support at the time. But he was in South America, communication was very difficult, and it was some weeks before he arrived home – missed the funeral, everything. Then there was such a hoo-ha when nobody could find the will! He'd left the usual copy with his solicitor, but it must have been mis-filed and the copy he kept here was in the safe – still is, I suppose – and Gwen was so stressed, she couldn't remember the combination to open it and none of us – the staff, I mean – knew it. No wonder the poor woman went into a collapse!'

'Oh, dear,' said Heather, biting her lip, 'what a chapter of accidents. No wonder everything and everybody was in turmoil.'

Kathie nodded, then leaned across the table, dropping her voice, 'The thing is,' she said, 'I think Adrian might have resented having to come home at all, he was having a whale of a time out on the ranch, freedom, adventure, responsibility. Gwen's brother did what he could but he's... 'She paused a moment, 'well, you'll understand when you meet him. He doesn't mix easily with people, quite a loner...must have been a lovely man once but...'

She paused again and Heather did not pursue the subject. She'd find out all she wished to know soon enough.

'Got the energy for a stroll before bedtime?' Kathie asked when they'd finished their toasted cheese and coffee – she seemed to have forgotten about the cake – glancing out of the window where the sky was still blue, and the surrounding trees swayed gently in the breeze. 'Show you round the grounds?' Again, a rhetorical question as Kathie had already leapt up and was heading for her door. 'I'll call the dogs; they love a run in the evening. Gwen usually takes them out but today... you OK with dogs?'

Heather nodded with enthusiasm. She still missed Lucy, the old black Labrador, bought for Sally as a puppy to help console her after Jerome's death when she was ten, but which had died itself three years ago.

Accompanied by two energetic spaniels, Dizzy and Dotty, their golden ears flapping wildly, Kathie led Heather back across the yard and behind the stables, waving a cheerful hand at the horses, optimistically poking their noses over their doors.

'Do you ride?' she asked hopefully. Heather, prepared for the question, had to admit that her equine experience amounted to little more than pony-rides at village-fetes or on the beach when she was a child. Kathie gave her a broad grin.

'We'll soon get you up and trotting. Since Adrian went to Brazil it was up to Gwen and occasionally her brother, Stewart, to keep them exercised but recently it's been all down to me. I do hope she recovers quickly. Although I love this place to bits, I have to admit it's all getting a bit much without Mr Franklin at the helm.'

Heather stole a glance at her companion as they emerged into an old apple-orchard where a few bursts of blossom were springing from the ends of the branches, noticing that, despite her hearty demeanour, there were worry lines around Kathie's eyes and she wore a slight, permanent frown.

'Doesn't anybody else help you with all this?' she asked, at which Kathie wrinkled her nose, giving Heather a sideways, sardonic look.

'The cook-general, Elsie, does a bit of cleaning here and there – she's Wonder Woman in a pinny,' she replied, 'and her sister Doris comes for the whole day on Saturdays for a 'blitz' as she calls it. She'll only do your rooms if you need her to. Mr Franklin didn't really like anyone in his domain in case they disturbed his precious papers.' Heather smiled in silent sympathy.

'And there are two part-time gardeners, brothers Bob and Harry, who cut grass, trim hedges, tidy the borders and other odd jobs from time to time – but spend a hell of a lot of time gossiping, smoking and sneaking down to the pub. They think I don't know but I do. Can't sack them, not my place and Gwen likes having a couple of strong blokes around who'll deal with wasps' nests, unblock drains, have bonfires, all that sort of thing. So, they stay on, no trouble to me.'

Once out of the orchard, the two dogs sped away across a field towards a patch of woodland a hundred yards away and the two women sat on a creaking wooden bench to wait for them to come back.

'They always do,' Kathie reassured Heather as they disappeared from sight, 'just hope they don't murder too many baby rabbits in the meantime. I know they're a terrible pest once they get into the vegetable gardens, but you can't deny they're the cutest little creatures.'

Heather nodded, looking out over the woodland towards Newton Valence, where acres of farmland, wheat, barley and field beans, well grown already, stretched out before them. Groups of cattle, their copper-coloured coats shining in the early evening sunshine grazed in two or three further fields, their tails swishing against the flies. Kathie gestured towards the horizon with an almost proprietary air.

'All Franklin land,' she murmured, 'almost as far as you can see, prime arable and pasture. They used to grow hops on some of it not so long ago. Hop-pickers used at arrive every Autumn, East-Enders mainly, whole families together, on their annual holiday. They'd sleep in huts or tents and you'd hear them singing and smell their campfires well into the night. That was before I came to work here, of course, just what Gwen and Elsie have told me.'

Heather cast her mind back to those days when she, Craig and their mother had lived with their grandmother and would cycle into Alton on Tuesdays, market day, pat the cows and sheep through the metal barriers and laugh at the geese, ducks and hens, cackling and squawking as they were rounded up for sale. Sometimes their rides had taken them past those hop-fields, and they'd stop and watch men balanced on tall frames erecting the hop-poles and strings precisely spaced for the vines, field after field of them. Alton could boast five breweries in the 1950s and the yeasty smell of malt and barley could be detected for miles around if the wind were in the right direction. Well... it was 1984 now and things were different.

'So, who farms all the land?' Heather asked, hoping that that was not yet one more of Kathie's many duties.

'All leased to neighbouring farmers now,' Kathie replied, getting up from the bench and calling the dogs, who came rushing back, their coats full of cleavers and dried grass. 'It's their rent that keeps this place going as well as half-a-dozen rented cottages in and around Selborne. Elsie and Doris live in one of them, rent-free. Gwen won't be short of a bob or two, never fear, Mr Franklin will have left everything in good order. He was forever carrying out repairs to the tenants' houses but was a stickler for them paying their rent on time. Yes... he was a good landlord. He'll be so much missed – by me, his friends and colleagues, by everyone in the village, the church. Just hope this wretched business between Adrian and his Mum doesn't throw a spanner in the works – there'd be plenty of takers for this place if it ever came on the market.'

Heather was silent as her thoughts flashed back to that extraordinary encounter with Adrian earlier in the day. Then, as the two women crossed a large, formal lawn edged with yew and wide borders, Heather noticed that they were drawing near to the brick wall she had spotted from the Hangar earlier.

'That's surely not the boundary of the garden, is it?' she enquired, as it looked to her as if the wall continued round a corner and was overhung in places by low branches.

Kathie glanced around them cautiously before replying. 'That's graced with the name of the Walled Garden,' she said, dropping her voice, 'it used to be beautifully kept with greenhouses up against the walls, where they grew peaches, oranges, apricots, melons, orchids...all sorts. There was even a pineapple-pit, apparently, although it hadn't been used for years. Gwen showed me a few photographs when I first came to work here. It was Mr Franklin's pride and joy but after his first heart-attack, three years ago, he had to give it up, Nature took over in a big way, the greenhouses fell into disrepair and all the plants died. He couldn't – or wouldn't – enter it again and no-one goes in there now, at least,' she paused, frowning, 'not often. Gwen's brother wanders about in there from time to time but doesn't do any tidying up. He... he's a strange man.'

She glanced at Heather again as if wondering how much she should be telling her about the family when she'd only just arrived. 'It's a sad, sad story. If you come across him, just act naturally, he's harmless. Won't bite you. It's a shame about the garden though. I did have a quick look inside when I was looking for one of the dogs but it's an absolute jungle. You wouldn't believe how quickly all those years of Mr Franklin's devoted work could be obliterated.'

She paused a moment close to the wall. 'There is a gap here between these two wooden panels where you can peep in – if you really want to.'

Heather peered in as best she could, only to discover that Kathie's description had been right, weeds and tangled undergrowth as far as could see, and she shook her head in dismay. What a mess...but wouldn't I like to get my hands on it, she mused as she and Kathie wandered slowly back to the courtyard. On the way they passed a large hen coop, home to five white and two brown hens as well as a splendidly haughty cockerel strutting possessively beside his harem, glancing suspiciously at the two women observing him.

'We call him Cock o' the North,' Kathie informed her, 'liable to wake up in the wee small hours and has been known to escape at times and jump up and down outside the back door, hoping for crumbs.'

Heather bade her new friend goodnight and made her way up the staircase to her own little world above the stables. Then, after a quick shower, pleased to see that it worked well and the water was hot, and arming herself with a mug of hot chocolate and a couple of digestive biscuits, she leaned back against her pillows, drew out the 5-year diary, and continued her letter to Craig.

'Well, what a day – WHAT A DAY!! I thought I was coming here to make sense of this family's past history – but I've a feeling that I might find its present situation a whole lot more intriguing. *I do hope so!!!*'

Feeling her head nodding before she could add more, she put her hands behind her head, listening to the night sounds, the wind in the trees, rooks settling down in the highest branches, then the quavering call of a tawny owl and answering 'ker-week' of its mate that brought tears of nostalgia to her eyes. She gazed up at the small Velux window set into the sloping ceiling above her head at the first pale stars studding the darkening sky, mulling over the extraordinary events of the day. Her heart pounded as she recalled how she had, possibly, prevented a murder and remembered the utter misery of that poor young man heaving with sobs as he came to terms with what he had – almost – done.

'They should have told me!' Adrian had gasped out as they sat together beneath that old beech tree, *they should have told me!'* What *could* his parents possibly have kept from their curly-headed son to drive him to such drastic action?

Chapter Three

Heather awoke early the next morning to the sound of horses' hooves clattering across the courtyard and peeped out of her curtains just in time to see Kathie on the chestnut mare – Conker – trotting down the drive towards the lane. It was too early for breakfast, so she made herself a mug of tea and began casting her eyes over the contents of the shelves and bookcases, opening the desk drawers, hoping to find out how far Mr Franklin had got with his research. I hope he left a helpful list, she hummed to herself but, glancing around the stacks of newspapers, notebooks and heaps of letters pushed under the desk her heart sank as, if he had, it was not going to be easy to find.

I wish I had Jerome's calm, unworried attitude to life, she mused, sadly. Even as his illness had progressed, leaving him weaker and more prone to infection with every month that passed, he had rarely lost hope and never his temper with either her or little Sally. Leukemia in adults was such a cruel disease, the treatment so protracted and uncomfortable that she'd often wondered who suffered most, he or she, unable to do more than hold his hand, read to him, play his favourite records and tapes and try, without frightening her, to keep Sally from upsetting him with her boisterous noise and childish high spirits.

The most difficult decision she had had to make as it became clear that his life's end was approaching, was how much to prepare Sally for the inevitable. The little girl knew her friends' daddies didn't spend all their time lying in bed or on the sofa or going into hospital on a regular basis. Yet how could one prepare a nine-year-old for the death of one of the most important people in her life?

'Daddy's very ill and we mustn't play too loudly,' Heather had often heard her instruct her friends on the occasions when she had let her have a few little girls round to play in the garden.

'What's the matter with your daddy?' she'd heard one child ask when Jerome had made a rare appearance, using crutches to reach a garden seat from where he could watch them turning somersaults and play chasing games.

'He's got funny blood,' Sally had replied airily, 'and he needs to rest so that it will get better.' Heather had sighed ruefully to hear her own explanation repeated in such a matter-of-fact way. It had been far harder to explain to her mother, a couple of years after their marriage that Jerome was not expected to live many years.

'Can't think what possessed you to marry a man in such poor health,' her mother had chided her for years after Jerome had died. She was not the most tactful of mothers as she would often go on to say, with an accusing look at her daughter, 'well, of course I know you *had* to...but really...!'

'Mum, I didn't *have* to marry him, I could have managed on my own. But I wanted to,' she'd tried to explain several times at which her mother would sniff with disappointment and disdain.

'And *I'd* wanted to see you walk up the aisle with all our family and friends, my only daughter, in spite of your funny foreign name. Can't think why you couldn't have found a nice English boyfriend,' she would continue to mutter under her breath, then walking away before Heather could reply.

Yes...it must have been hard for her mother, who loved nothing better than to boast of the achievements of her son and daughter to hear - after the event - that Heather had married whilst working abroad and that she must expect news of a grandchild a little sooner than was quite respectable. It always amused Heather to hear her mother talk about her marriage to her friends, explaining that Jerome had a particularly important job with the British Council in Athens and couldn't be spared for leave to get married in England but that they had had a very grand wedding at the English Church, glossing over the actual date of the occasion.

Well... in spite of his 'funny' name and his ill-health, her mother had, in time, come to appreciate Jerome's gentle good manners and deferential attitude towards his mother-in-law and had to agree that he was a wonderful father to Sally. And she, of course, was the most talented and beautiful granddaughter she would have wished for.

And now... time to stop reminiscing, Heather told herself sharply and prepared herself mentally for the next challenge, that of meeting Adrian's mother and perhaps Adrian himself without giving her the slightest suspicion that she and the young man had met before in the most harrowing of circumstances.

'Stay calm,' she told herself firmly as she trod down the wooden stairs, gritting her teeth and clenching her hands as she crossed the courtyard and entered the main house.

'Well, Craig – I've bearded the dragon in her den – and she's really not such a dragon after all, certainly not one that deserves to be slain with a crossbow – but then I'm not Adrian and am none the wiser about the rift between him and his Mum either. Curiouser and curiouser...'

Later that day Heather, seated at the desk – she hardly liked to call it *her* desk yet – surrounded by boxes and notebooks of many shapes and sizes, put away the diary and went to the window, fascinated to see the house martins dip and dive across the courtyard like flashes of blue lightning, their shiny backs lit by the sun. Gilbert White, for all his careful observation, had been bothered for years by the conundrum of where they and swallows and swifts went in winter, she remembered, almost sure they flew to warmer climes but never quite able to prove it. She wondered if he'd ever visited Westhangar Hall during his long curacy and tenancy of the Wakes. His parochial duties were rarely mentioned in the *Natural History of Selborne* as he seemed far more interested in studying the habits of birds, bees, worms, trees, wildflowers, his tortoise and other flora and fauna, noting all his observations meticulously down in his notebooks.

Heather's first impression of Mrs Franklin – or Gwen, as she was immediately invited to call her – was of a woman who must have been remarkably handsome in her youth. Even now, at the age of sixty or so she was, with her fine bone-structure, blue eyes like Stewart's and wavy, iron-grey hair, very well-looking. Taller than average, though stooping slightly, and elegantly slender she struck Heather as being a woman of firm opinions and good sense, her emotions well under control in spite of the recent death of her husband and the row (not mentioned) with her son.

Once she had ascertained that Heather had everything she needed for her work, they had discussed her terms of employment which were both generous and flexible.

'Just carry on at your own pace,' she'd said, 'and take time off when it suits you. You used to live near here, I understand, so perhaps you still have friends you'd like to visit or to visit you? How well do you know Selborne? Have you been up the Zig-Zag yet?'

As Gwen had raised the subject herself, Heather admitted that she had, only yesterday, for old times' sake. 'And,' she'd added cautiously, 'I think I may have met your brother at the top, although I'm not entirely sure if it was him.'

'Ah, yes – Stewart,' Gwen replied, turning her head away as she spoke, 'Stewart, my little brother...you will come across him from time to time, he's...he's...well, he suffered a terrible tragedy about five years ago.' She stopped and swallowed before continuing. 'We all did but it was far, far worse for him.' She fell silent, obviously not wanting to pursue the subject just then and Heather saw tears in her eyes.

'I'm sorry I mentioned him,' she said quietly, 'but it would have seemed curious if I did not and he...he then mentioned he had met me.'

'Of course – I'm glad you did,' Gwen had nodded, 'and there's no need to be scared if he tries to speak to you. The village children chatter away to him even though he can't answer properly, apart from nodding, shaking his head...and grunting....and he does love the company of children, poor darling.' Her expression turned to sadness once more and Heather, although bursting with questions, waited while Gwen composed herself, turning to Heather with the ghost of a smile on her face.

'There is hope, great hope, that he'll recover his full power of speech one day,' she confided, 'it may come back quite suddenly and unexpectedly, there'll be some trigger...' Her voice tailed off again and she'd risen, steadying herself with her stick and Heather rose too.

'Now,' Gwen continued, 'I expect you'd like to see over the house and meet Elsie, my cook-housekeeper. She'll be cooking for you as well, so be sure to let her know of any food allergies, likes or dislikes you may have.'

She led the way through a series of large, square rooms with intricately patterned plaster ceilings and carved wooden panelling, comfortably rather than ostentatiously furnished, with large marble fireplaces in every room. One led into the Library and Heather breathed in, enjoying the smell of old leather-bound books and the sight of gold-tooled lettering on their spines and the rows of portraits of ancestors, adding an air of dignity and solemnity to the room. The formal dining-room was adorned with similar plaster ceilings, the highly polished table set as if expecting dinner guests. Glass-fronted cupboards against the walls held more sets of porcelain, vases, dinner and tea services and a large collection of snuffboxes and delicately painted miniatures. Raising her head from these charming items, Heather was less delighted to see an array of stuffed trophy heads of kudu, impala, sable and even a moth-eaten rhinoceros, alongside the fearsome weapons with which they had – presumably – been dispatched by bygone members of the Franklin family, ranged on hooks along the wall. These included the crossbow that she had come uncomfortably close to yesterday afternoon and, momentarily, her blood ran cold. She must have let her gaze rest just a little too long on it as Gwen gave one of her deep sighs.

'Wretched thing,' she remarked, 'a silent killer, I hate it. My son used to take it down every now and again to shoot at trees or rabbits on the Hangar even though he knew how much I disliked him doing it. I was always expecting a visit from the police with the news that he had accidentally killed a child or someone's beloved dog or shot the bolt through his own foot. My husband kept telling me not to worry, boys will be boys – but mothers always worry.'

Heather nodded in whole-hearted agreement.

'Luckily,' Gwen continued, 'he seems to have grown out of that habit at last and it's remained untouched on the wall where it belongs.'

Heather nodded again, swallowing hard, hoping that Gwen would never have to know just how close she had come to being a victim of that unpleasant weapon. She followed her through more corridors, storerooms, pantries, flower-rooms and finally back to the large, stone-flagged kitchen, with two ranges, two sinks and draining boards, numerous cupboards and open shelves filled with shining copper jelly-moulds, saucepans, dishes and jugs of immense size.

'Never used now, of course,' remarked Gwen, 'But they've always been there, and...' Her voice tailed off as a well-rounded, cheerful-looking young woman bustled in from another door, carrying a mop and a bucket of water.

'Ah...here's my treasure...Elsie dear, come and meet Mrs La Fontaine.' Elsie smiled and put down the pail and mop with a clatter and proffered her hand, wiping it first down the side of her apron, glancing up shyly at the new arrival. There was a sudden pause as each gazed at the other – then Heather broke the silence, shaking Elsie's hand warmly.

'Surely...don't I know you, Elsie? Didn't you come sometimes with your mother to my grandmother's house in your school holidays and help with the dusting?'

Elsie flushed and smiled again, showing a mouth full of very white, rather crooked teeth.

'Yes, Mrs La...Laf...Miss Heather you was then, wasn't you?' She turned to Gwen, picking up her bucket, 'Didn't do much 'elpin! Played in the garden more like and got in the gardener's way.' She turned towards Heather again. 'I remember you all so well, your Gran and your Mum – passed now, I suppose. Mine too.'

'Sadly, yes,' Heather replied and rushed on quickly before Elsie could remember to mention Craig, 'but it's so good to see you again. I didn't think there would be anyone in the area who would remember me. We must have a chat one day.'

As she turned to go back to the stables, Heather suddenly remembered the cabin trunk in her wardrobe and asked Gwen if she knew anything about it.

'Ah, yes...I'd forgotten all about that wretched thing. It belonged to one of my husband's ancestors who went out to Australia, in the 1840s or 50s, I believe, to try to make his fortune. He and his wife spent a few years out there, prospecting for gold but as far as we know they didn't find more than a few fragments, just enough to buy their passage home. The trunk belonged to the wife, probably full of her old dresses, pots and pans and things – never been opened as far as I know – but quite how or why it landed up here I've no idea. If it's seriously in your way, my dear, we'll get the gardeners to remove it.'

'Absolutely no rush,' returned Heather, 'I wouldn't mind a peek inside if we can find a key that fits – even old clothes and household goods could throw light on their lifestyle in Australia. And there might be a diary or something of interest in there. And if there is, I'll let you know.'

It had been a strange experience to meet Elsie again and be reminded so vividly of her former life; but sobering to realize that of her family of four who'd lived together, she was the only one left alive. And yet – apart from Craig's early death – it was hardly surprising considering that she was now forty-four and that both Gran and her mother had lived into their seventies. Her father too had reached his late sixties before dying abroad, cared for by his young Filipina second wife. She felt comforted to have heard Elsie speak of them and to realize they were not entirely forgotten.

Heather began her work by making an inventory of everything on the shelves, giving each category a title and number, then entering them into a notebook with space beside them to be filled in with the date when she had read them and made a fair copy on the typewriter. When she'd asked Gwen if such a list already existed – for surely Mr Franklin would have had some method of keeping track of his work she'd merely looked anxious and waved her arm helplessly.

'I hardly ever came in here,' she'd admitted, 'I had my own responsibilities, here – and in the village. You may find something in the desk.' She'd looked so distressed at her inability to be more help that Heather had reassured her that she'd prefer to make her own list anyway. That would give her the chance to inspect everything and decide what was important and what could be safely ignored.

In the meantime, Heather settled into her new life, leafing through old recipe-books, lists of items of furniture bought for the Hall, details of cattle-sales, crop-yields, the coming and going and fluctuating rents of the various tenants of the estate cottages as well as boxes of old letters sent back home by far-flung members of the family. They would have to wait, however, until she had sorted out the family trees and sheafs of fascinating old maps and plans of the estate and village, newspaper cuttings of notable events in the area, some of which Heather herself could dimly remember from her childhood.

She was intrigued by a pile of old photo-albums – no recent ones, she noticed, presuming that they were somewhere else in the Hall – dated, thank goodness, and showing alterations and additions to the building, family weddings from the 19th-century, babies in frilly bonnets, boys in sailor suits. There were views of old Selborne too before the advent of the motor car, showing little girls in pinafores and small boys in short trousers, boots and caps, playing with hoops in the road, empty of all traffic apart from a horse-drawn baker's cart or coal-wagon and always, it seemed, a dog curled-up asleep in the sun. Another world, she sighed, wondering if any of those children were forebears of Mr Franklin's present tenants – but they were untitled. Perhaps one day they could stage an exhibition and invite the village inhabitants to try and identify them.

Heather did wonder from time to time where Adrian had gone, but as neither Kathie nor Gwen seemed anxious, she gradually ceased to worry, and her routine fell into a most pleasant pattern. Breakfast with Gwen, followed by a brisk walk round the grounds, just in time to say 'Good Morning' to Bob and Harry as they arrived and to Kathie as she returned from exercising Champion or Conker, then back to sorting, listing and typing up faded records of long-past village events, before sharing a sandwich lunch with Kathie in the garden or kitchen. While Kathie exercised the other horse, Heather took to strolling down the village, exploring lanes and footpaths new to her, crossing stiles into fields or small woods, pleased to be greeted by so many of the village people in a most welcoming way.

She found the village bookshop just where she remembered it, full of books about Gilbert White, old editions and new, but none so old as the copy she had inherited from Gran which had belonged to *her* father, the pages yellowing, yet each delicate engraving, depicted by a man with the delightful name of P.H. Delamotte, protected with thin tissue paper. I'd like to marry a man called Delamotte, Heather had declared to Craig when she was about eleven, but he'd only laughed and asked why on earth she'd want to marry a man with a French name, when she was an English girl.

She had no answer to that – then. But she *had* married a man – several years later – with a French name and she'd sometimes wondered whether it was his name, so musical and unusual, which seemed to suggest Romance and Mystery, which had encouraged her to accept his increasingly urgent pleas for her hand. In her heart, however, she knew there were very different reasons why she had married Jerome. These were reasons that not even her mother had guessed, accepting Jerome as her son-in-law and Sally's father without a shadow of a doubt.

Should I have told her, Heather sometimes wondered, let my mother know how much I owed that gentle man who had pleaded with her to let him save her reputation, her child's legitimacy and provide her with love and support at least for those years he had left to live? She'd struggled hard with her conscience at the time. Was it right to marry a man out of gratitude for the sake of a child, yet unborn? In the early 1960s conceiving a child out of wedlock was still regarded as a disgrace to be concealed if humanly possible. As the years went by and Jerome's health had worsened, any feelings of guilt disappeared, however, as she realized just how much she had come to love and rely on him as he did on her and how much she dreaded losing him.

It was only after his death that she fully realized the extent of his regard for her and Sally, leaving them so well provided for that she had no need to work if she did not wish to. 'That man spoiled you,' her mother had grumbled every now and again but never refused the extra comforts that Heather was able to supply for her. But there had always remained the lingering guilt at having kept such an important secret from her.

It had been far easier than she had anticipated to tell Sally, some years after Jerome's death, that the man she had always called 'Daddy' wasn't genetically her father at all.

'It was in a mad moment,' Heather had explained to her daughter when she considered she was old enough to understand that adults could act in impulsive, irresponsible ways just as children could. 'But believe me, Sally, you were conceived in a rush of passion and laughter and, although having a baby wasn't in my plan – I *had* no plan – I could never have imagined such a happy result.' Heather had often wondered whether it was the exhilarating, buoyant circumstances of Sally's conception that had given her daughter her carefree, forgiving and kind-hearted disposition.

Once Sally had got over the shock and had time to digest the news, naturally she had wanted to know her real father's name, where her mother had met him, why she did not marry him...questions that Heather had expected but was ashamed to admit that she had no simple answers to give her.

'But at least tell me what he looked like,' Sally had persisted, at which Heather had smiled and taking her daughter by the shoulders had replied, 'exactly like you, my darling...exactly like you. And I will explain it all to you in a letter one day,' reluctant to admit to Sally's face that, not only had she absolutely no idea where he lived or whether he'd been married, but that she never knew her father's real name.

'I only ever heard him called 'Skip,' was all she could tell her and had been suddenly and unexpectedly overwhelmed with a rush of such guilt about the fact that she hadn't been able to discover more about him, that she had rushed from the room. I should have done! I *could* have done, she had repeated to herself countless times during her marriage to Jerome. But, by the time she was certain that 'something had happened' Skip had been far away in the Middle East with his team of young gymnasts. To her credit dear Sally had made no scene, but merely given her mother an almighty hug the next time she had seen her.

Chapter Four

Adrian's absence was soon explained by Gwen volunteering the information that he had business in London to do with details about the estate in the wake of Mr Franklin's death. Though anxious to see him again, Heather became more and more absorbed by the photo-albums and the history of Westhangar Hall. There were so many questions she wanted to ask, tantalising hints of so many stories that Mr Franklin must have known but, unless he'd left a Memoir somewhere, they would have to remain mysteries. She had come across a diary, a bit like her own, buried under a pile of old magazines, but it was locked and although she optimistically tried her key, it wouldn't fit, and she was reluctant to force it. It would turn up somewhere, eventually.

In the meantime, her curiosity was rewarded, partly at least, when she opened another album and there – wonder of wonders! – she was confronted with a series of large black-and-white photos of what could only be early pictures of the Walled Garden. As she stared at them, she felt an almost painful surge of excitement throb through her. 'Been without a man for far too long,' she muttered to herself, amazed that she could be so aroused by pictures of that hidden world she had so far failed to penetrate.

Long borders crammed with roses, lilies, lupins, blocks and patterns of tulips and crocuses, unfashionable nowadays, bushes of lilac and mock-orange, hydrangeas, wooden archways dripping with honeysuckle and clematis; stone fountains standing in ponds filled with water lilies and bulrushes; wide, mown grass paths edged with paving-slabs to facilitate mowing which Heather had seen and admired at the Agricultural College in her student days and vowed that, given the chance, she would copy such a practical idea. Some photographs were of the interior of the Walled Garden, glasshouses, pergolas, espalier fruit trees alongside the walls. An entire quarter of the plot had been given over to vegetables, potato rows, marrow plants, beans climbing up bamboo frames, onions, leeks, spinach, cabbages, with a further area netted to house soft-fruit, raspberries, blackcurrants, gooseberries and strawberries nestled in long rows of straw. Tears of envy and frustration came to Heather's eyes as she gazed at picture after picture and thought of the neglected tangle of brambles, nettles and docks that time and neglect had allowed it to become.

What am I doing, closeted in this stable, surrounded by old documents, their contents forgotten for decades and, most likely, of little interest to future generations of Franklins when I could be out there, hacking back the overgrown shrubs, clearing the head-high weeds, uncovering those fine borders, re-creating those grass paths and vegetable plots? Aware that her mind was wandering into dreamland, she shut the albums, placing them as high as possible on a shelf and vowed not to open them again until she had made a good deal more sense of Franklin family history, which, owing to an old paperback book she'd found stuffed behind a cupboard, proved to be more than just interesting, but possibly of historical value as well.

How long she sat, absorbed by this new discovery, she could not tell. She was merely vaguely aware of hearing Kathie trotting out, then later catching sight of Gwen, stick in hand, heading towards the woodland with Dizzy and Dotty. It was as she was gazing at the engraving of a fine, three masted sailing ship, battling through icebergs and massive, threatening waves, that she heard a frantic cheeping and fluttering somewhere up in the ceiling rafters.

'Stupid sparrow,' she said aloud, reaching up to it in vain and trying to shoo it towards the open door. It was a fledgling, one of this year's brood, no doubt, which had taken a wrong turning on its way back to the nest and had no notion of how to escape.

What could she do? She couldn't leave the poor thing to batter itself senseless but there was no way she could reach it on her own. Both Kathie and Gwen were out, the gardeners had gone home, and Stewart was nowhere to be seen. Then she had a sudden thought. Elsie! She should still be here, would surely know where to find a stepladder and could hold it while Heather climbed up to rescue the little beggar...if it would allow itself to be caught.

Ten minutes later, Heather was teetering about on the top step of the ladder, while Elsie squeaked in terror at the bottom, supposedly keeping it steady. The bird fluttered here and there distractedly...they moved the steps here and there in pursuit... the bird flew the other way, its cheeps growing louder and more frantic than ever. Heather uttered more swear-words than she realised she knew, reducing Elsie, less frightened now, to helpless giggles as the bird continued to elude Heather's grasp. At last, the exhausted little creature dropped to the floor and Elsie scooped it up and sent it flying through the door.

'And stay out, you varmint,' she shouted, entering into the spirit of the occasion, 'you come back, and we'll wring your neck!' then clapped her hand to her mouth, relieved when Heather dismounted the steps and they both roared with laughter together.

'I shall keep that door shut in future,' Heather gasped, 'at least until the youngsters have all fled the nest,' and flopped down into the armchair, fanning her hot face with her hand. 'And I think this calls for a cup of coffee if you've got time to spare, Elsie.'

While she bustled about in the kitchenette, Elsie took the opportunity to glance around the room, a place she had only rarely entered, the last time being to give it a good clean a day or two before Heather's arrival.

'Don't envy you havin' to sort through all this lot,' she remarked as Heather entered the study, bearing the two mugs, then gave a little gasp of recognition as her eye fell upon Heather's 5-year diary.

'That...that looks just like Mr Franklin's diary,' she uttered in cautious surprise, 'surely he didn't leave...' She shot a conspiratorial glance at Heather as she took a step towards it, 'kept all 'is secrets in there, 'e did,' then giggled nervously as if aware she might have spoken out of turn.

'Secrets? Really?' said Heather, her interest instantly aroused, 'but I'm afraid it isn't his, it's mine. I've always kept a diary since I was a kid.'

'Oh, sorry, Miss Heather, didn't mean to intrude – but it did look just like, with a little lock an' all,' then as she stepped a little closer, 'ah, now I see...yours is blue and Mr Franklin's 'ad a black cover. I could never keep a diary myself, began each January the first and gave up by about the third. Nothing interestin' to put in it, I suppose, same old routine every day.' She laughed as Heather helped her fold up the stepladder and guided her down the stairs.

'I don't suppose,' said Heather, once they were safely down to earth again, 'you know where he kept the key? Might help with my research, you see.' And satisfy my curiosity, she said to herself.

'Well, I only come in here once or twice,' Elsie replied, 'Mr F. didn't like to be disturbed and the only time I did interrupt him was when I thought I'd see 'im go out and I nipped up here to borrow a drop o' milk, we'd run out in the kitchen. I was going to put it back,' she declared earnestly to Heather, who waved her confession away as if it were a mosquito, 'and when 'e saw me 'e was writing in his diary, same as you, Miss, but he looked thunders, snapped the diary shut and tried to shove it under a pile of papers. He didn't think I'd noticed but I did – I notices everything, Miss Heather, bad habit of mine.'

'A very good habit, I'd say,' rejoined Heather, 'and could be a useful one too, Elsie. And thanks so much for helping me catch that little blighter, I'll know where to come if any bats get trapped in here.' And she watched as Elsie, shuddering, crossed the courtyard into the house.

Secrets...what a temptation! Now she knew what she must be looking for as she sorted through Mr Franklin's papers. Probably only some financial dealings that he didn't want Gwen to know about...but...maybe not. Entirely innocent elderly gentlemen should surely have no reason to try to hide their entries in a diary when surprised by the unexpected arrival of the cook-housekeeper- should they?

Secrets...Heather sighed. Leaving the desk, she stepped over to the window and gazed out at the grey stone house and the beech-trees beyond, their leaves already beginning to lose that fresh light green of early spring, although it was only May. Everybody had secrets, past indiscretions to hide, however insignificant they might seem to other people. But some could have secrets serious enough to weigh on their minds for years, blighting their entire lives. Her mind went back to that promise she had made to Sally, to explain the circumstances of her conception, her birth and willing acceptance by Jerome as his own cherished child. There had been no actual need for her ever to have confessed – if that was the right word – and yet... there had always been the nagging doubt and fear that Sally would somehow find out what she had not been able to discover and blame her bitterly for not telling her the truth as far as she knew it.

She had promised Sally she would tell her, truthfully, of her origins in a letter, something she could keep and refer to in the future should it ever become important. It had taken her at least a year to settle to the job by which time Sally was acquiring and discarding boyfriends in alarming succession, emboldened by 'the pill' to indulge in the kind of carefree, guilt-free behaviour denied to her mother and her generation and even if precautions failed, there were enough young women prepared to embark on motherhood alone to render it almost acceptable. Looking back Heather had often wondered whether she would have preferred to be a young woman in the 'eighties rather than the 'sixties. There would have been more freedom, less worry and less guilt. But...as she wrote in her letter to her daughter, the very fact of there being danger only made it more exciting, more daring, more outrageous – and therefore more desirable.

By Christmas 1960, Heather had just finished her course at the Agricultural College and had to decide what to do with her life. Few options had been suggested at school other than teaching, nursing or the Civil Service. When she had mentioned that she would quite like to be an archaeologist, this suggestion had been met with pitying looks as 'most unsuitable for a girl', with 'all that climbing up ladders and digging in holes.' Even her idea of becoming a landscape-gardener was deemed to be 'unladylike', ridiculous when she finally got her way with her disapproving mother and been enrolled at the college of her choice and found it full of young women with the same aspirations as herself. In the event, after graduating with her diploma, she *had* found it difficult to find a job as it was still the fit young men, who were unlikely to fuss about their hair or make-up who were offered the best jobs.

Disillusioned, at the age of twenty-one, she had been offered a temporary job by a friend of her mother, looking after the three children of a wealthy businessman, whose Greek wife was an aspiring artist and whose nanny/governess had just left to get married This was not what Heather's education and aspirations had prepared her for but the job was in Greece, might last two years and the couple were wealthy enough to live in style with a comfortable town house in Athens, a flat in Pimlico and a holiday villa on the island of Crete. Apart from the youngest, a little boy of two, the two elder children, twin girls of six were ready to start at the British School and the household was well supplied with maids, cooks and gardeners.

Greece! And Crete! What an opportunity! Perfect climate; temples, statues, Greek theatres; lush vegetation, flowers, vineyards, olive groves; to say nothing of bronzed, clean-limbed, modern young Greek heroes on every side! Even if the children had turned out to be little monsters with two heads, she would still have jumped at such an opportunity. In fact, when she had met them at her interview in London, they had been shyly polite, and the little boy had even slipped his chubby hand into hers to lead her into their nursery and proudly show her the (rather unstable) bridge he had just built with wooden bricks.

She had not needed more than a day to accept the post. Her real career, if she ever got around to choosing one, could wait a couple of years. She'd flown with the family to Athens the following Spring, armed with a trunkful of summery clothes, swimsuits, new camera, books on Greek history, Greek myths, Mediterranean flora and fauna, sunhats and a lace-trimmed, white parasol her father had insisted on presenting to her when she'd visited him to bid farewell.

'Mustn't risk ruining your peaches and cream complexion,' he'd said jokingly, before giving her some practical advice on how to ward off the advances of lusty young men looking for innocent young girls to woo, love and leave – pregnant!

'Oh, Dad,' she'd said, 'I'll be far too busy looking after three little children to have time for any flirting.' But she'd remembered the suddenly sober, wistful look on his face as she'd kissed him goodbye – and remembered it again, nearly two years later, as she surrendered, in an ecstasy of intoxication and happiness, to the strong, insistent embraces of that irresistible man she had met, who'd loved – briefly! – and all unknowingly, left her...with Sally.

He had been the leader of a small athletics team which had travelled from their base in the south of England to Athens for a few weeks to take part in a series of displays to entertain the Diplomatic and Consular staff of various Embassies in the Near East. The boys under his leadership had been recent recruits into the Services, hardly more than children but 'Skip' as they called him, was older, nearer thirty, lean, fit and *almost* handsome, with dark, wavy auburn hair, teasing brown eyes and eyebrows slightly bleached by the sun. Heather, nearing the end of her two-year stint with the family she had grown so fond of, had made good friends with several of the British Council staff in Athens, helping in their Library on her day off, where she had met and fallen – very nearly – in love with Jerome, the serious-minded, sweet-natured Head Librarian. To their dismay, he had been obliged to return to the UK for a family gathering at Christmas and was not expected back until halfway through January. Although disappointed not to have his company over the festive season, Heather had cheered up when invited by one of the secretaries to attend the gymnastics display (and party afterwards) and to stay overnight with her in her flat.

The display had taken place in the early evening in one of the Consular staff's garden, the weather warm enough for the audience to sit outdoors beside the swimming-pool, illuminated by coloured flares. First, they were served with an anonymous alcoholic beverage and almond biscuits before the troupe of young men marched in, clad in immaculate white trousers and navy-blue T-shirts, criss-crossing the lawn, then cartwheeling round the perimeter of the pool, missing each other by fractions of an inch, their whirling limbs lit by the flares and reflected in the dark water. Then, to gasps from the audience, they had appeared to run and jump across the surface of the water itself, defying gravity and landing, unbelievably, almost dry-shod on the other side. It was only on their return, as the audience craned their necks in disbelief that the faint shadows of transparent planks, set just below the surface of the water, revealed how the trick was done.

Back-flips right around the garden came next, one lad after another in rapid succession, followed by a human pyramid, each diminishing row standing on the shoulders of the one below with the smallest and most agile boy standing triumphantly on the top, arms outstretched. Next the team stood close together in line, their heads bent, as one by one the boys leapt from a small trampoline, turning somersaults right over the line, landing on the other side to take his place on the end until all ten of them had successfully completed their headlong leap.

'Your turn now, Skip,' came the chorus of young voices and the whole team pushed and pulled their leader into position, as he feigned enormous reluctance. The audience joined in the catcalling and cheering, most of them – including Heather – wondering if it was really a good idea for this larger, taller, no doubt heavier man, to risk landing on top of one of his slender team. To everybody's relief, he completed his leap successfully, then, removing the trampoline and placing the team members further apart, he took a run and leapfrogged over them, one at a time. As the audience clapped and called for more, Skip quietly surveyed the audience, then asked for volunteers to take the places of the team, who had squatted down under a group of eucalyptus trees to rest and watch the fun.

Inevitably there were embarrassed shuffles amongst the audience, all trying to avoid meeting Skip's eye, who, no doubt used to such reluctance, stepped over to Heather, sitting in the front row and grasped her hand, leaving her no choice but to stand up and take her place at the start of the line. Gradually, a few more people were persuaded to join her, giggling nervously, until there were enough 'volunteers' to make a wide circle instead of a mere line, sixteen of them in all.

Heather braced herself anxiously as she heard the thump of Skip's feet as he leapt over each of them in turn, landing safely on the grass each time. Once round the ring, he turned and began the same routine in the other direction, cheered on by the rest of the audience. The volunteer just behind Heather, however, must have thought his part was over as, just as Skip was about to leap, he straightened up and left the ring, leaving

Skip so much off-balance that he cannoned into Heather, knocking her to the ground. As she lay there, shocked and winded, she could hear the combined concerned 'aaahhh' of the audience, mingled with the abject apologies of Skip, who most gallantly pulled her skirt back over her legs before pulling her upright again.

'Absolutely not your fault,' he reassured her, looking round in vain for the real culprit (who was nowhere to be seen) and, with a steadying arm round her shoulders, he guided her back to her seat. As their eyes met, she liked what she saw, the sparkle of fun in those brown eyes, the slightly cleft chin, the springy, thick hair and frown of concern as he settled her in her chair.

'Are you staying for the party?' he asked, and at her nod, the frown disappeared to be replaced with a broad smile. 'I'll see you there then,' he assured her before gathering his team, rather subdued now, and marching them off to the other side of the Compound.

'Lucky you,' remarked her secretary friend, poking her in the ribs, 'think we'd all got our eyes on that bit of cheesecake.'

Heather giggled at the old-fashioned expression, shaking her head as she fumbled for her jacket in the dusk – but, as they made their way across to the Sports Hall where the party was to be held, she couldn't help just glancing about her, trying to spot his whereabouts.

As they entered the Hall, an eightsome reel was in boisterous progress, and they had to skirt carefully around the sets to find seats. Immediately, a slim Greek waiter appeared with glasses of *retsina* and trays of honey cakes and they sat, drinking – too much – laughing and eating happily until the dancers dispersed and claimed their seats once more, fanning their faces and mopping their brows.

'Take your partners...for *Strip the Willow*,' called the MC, ignoring the feigned moans and groans from the crowd, 'Come on, you know you love it,' he urged and, as she looked round, hoping not to be left out, Heather felt her hand taken as she was led to the top set by no less than Skip.

As she whirled and twirled first him, then the next man in the row, she began to wish she hadn't indulged quite so heavily in the wine, which was beginning to have a delicious, but dangerous effect on her balance and Skip had to check her once or twice before she could continue with the dance. As she felt the strength of his supporting arm around her waist, she thought briefly of her father's advice again. 'Never get so drunk that you don't know what you're doing,' he'd told her solemnly before he'd thrown back his head, laughing heartily, 'unless, of course, you know exactly what you're doing and don't want to stop!' before adding, with a squeeze of her arm, 'just joking!'

'*I did know what I was doing,*' Heather had written in her letter to Sally, '*and I didn't want to stop. I knew I was behaving badly, flirting, catching his glance whenever I could, giving him all the signs that I was interested, not at all what well-brought-up girls should do. Then, when he suggested going out into the garden, to 'look at the stars' I knew exactly what he meant. He was just so attractive, Sally, so urgent but so attentive, finding a secluded place under a tree, making sure I was comfortable and then...well, I won't go into details, (must keep some secrets to myself!), but we were both so fired up with excitement that taking precautions wasn't even mentioned. In any case, as all women do, I'd made a swift mental calculation and knew – or thought I knew – that I was past the usual most fertile time, so I didn't worry in the least.*'

Madness, I suppose, she'd thought two or three weeks later when she first began to suspect that 'something' must have happened. But Skip's team had departed the morning after their display in Athens to repeat the same routine in Beirut, Jerome had returned as ardent as ever and Heather's time with the family was approaching its end. The twins were due to start at their English boarding-school late in January, and the little boy would be approaching five years old, school age and Heather's services were no longer required. She had regrets, of course. It would be the end of an era, an unforgettable two years in a beautiful, exciting country. But it had been the beginning of something far more rewarding and precious, something permanent, an anchor to her life; another life even more important than her own.

Chapter Five

At the end of May, the staff of Westhangar Hall joined almost the entire village of Selborne as they celebrated their Annual Fair with stalls hung with bunting set up along the main street, as the school children, dressed in white, danced around a maypole erected on the Plestor. A long procession of villagers, arrayed in colourful skirts and shirts with garlands of flowers round their necks and on their hats, and waving bunches of spring flowers, followed a tall man dressed in sober clothing, a circular black hat on his head, carried aloft in a carved wooden chair. This was borne by four burly men and Heather recognized two of them as Bob and Harry, the gardeners from Westhangar Hall.

'The Reverend's dressed as Gilbert White,' explained Elsie to Heather, almost jumping up and down in her excitement, 'He were a Reverend too, but he were small and the Reverend Garland's really tall! But 'oo cares, 'e looks a treat, don't 'e?' nudging Heather as the vicar passed by, waving graciously from his perch as he went by.

'Certainly does,' agreed Heather, her gaze following him as he went on his way, dispensing good-will and even a few blown kisses to the crowd, 'and a good sport as well,' she thought as one or two of the younger women dared to throw some of their flowers up to him. During tea in the village-hall, 'Gilbert White' made the rounds of each table, shaking hands with anyone he didn't already know, exchanging a word or two with everyone else and offering to fetch tea for anyone who doubted their ability to work their way from the tea-hatch to their table. Heather noticed that he paid special attention to a large, loud lady, wearing an old-fashioned navy coat-and-skirt and navy straw hat.

'Bishop's sister!' Kathie whispered in reverential tones, then added 'important!' while making a less than polite face at Elsie, and leaning across to Heather, 'she's an awful old bag really – but Chris the Christian thinks the world of her.'

During their stroll back to Westhangar, bearing beribboned bags of fudge, biscuits, one or two balloons and a tin of cakes for tea, to save Elsie the trouble, as 'Gilbert White' had insisted, Heather gathered that their vicar took his pastoral duties very seriously and would probably be arriving at the Hall someday to make Heather's proper acquaintance. 'Don't mind if he does,' she thought idly, noticing that there were still a few bluebells blooming in the hedgerows along with wild garlic and bright, white stitchwort and wondered if wild orchids still grew in Selborne as they had when she was a child.

After two or three weeks of wet weather, June began to live up to its reputation, 'bustin' out all over' and Heather began to fret at the amount of time she was spending indoors, poring over Mr Franklin's archives. From the stable windows she could catch glimpses of the barley-fields changing from fresh green to pale gold, shimmering temptingly in waves as the breeze blew across them and one morning soon after breakfast, she felt a deep urge to revisit her childhood home only a few miles away. 'And poor Frog must be feeling neglected,' she murmured to herself, 'he needs a bit of excitement,' and began to gather up her papers, intending to call on Gwen to let her know she would be away for an hour or two.

Before she was halfway down the stairs however, she was forestalled by Elsie, red-faced and out of breath with traces of tears on her cheeks.

'Oh, Miss Heather,' she gasped, 'there's been such a scene! Mr Adrian arrived home early this morning in such a rage, banging the table and shouting fit to bust! And Mrs Franklin's took so bad, I don't like the look of her at all and Kathie's out with one of the horses...and I don't know what to do!'

They hurried down the stairs, Heather's mind working overtime as she tried to recall all the first aid she'd ever known, expecting to find Gwen collapsed on the floor, foaming at the mouth, clutching at her heart or possibly all three. As they entered the dining-room, they heard the front door crash shut as Adrian made his exit and beheld Gwen sitting, grey-faced and sobbing, gazing at a sheaf of papers on the table.

'She'll be all right,' Heather reassured Elsie, 'fetch her a drop of brandy – just a drop, mind. I think she's had a shock. We may have to phone the doctor, find the number, just in case,' and was relieved to see Elsie, calmer now that she had jobs to do, bustling off in the direction of the hall. Gwen looked up at Heather, her expression distraught.

'My poor Adrian,' she gasped, 'not fair...not his fault...all mine... I'd hoped so much...' and, using the edge of the table to heave herself up, she headed, stumbling, for the door leaving the papers behind her in her confusion. In the briefest of seconds before she returned for them, Heather was just able to see at the top of the first page, the words 'The Last Will and Testament of John Lawrence Franklin' and the date, 5 March 1981 – just over three years ago. Wasn't that just about the time he'd suffered his first, serious heart-attack?

'I'm so afraid Adrian will do something stupid,' Gwen muttered distractedly, 'he was hoping...hoping so much that his...his father would change his mind.' She looked up at Heather with a kind of wildness in her eyes as if debating the wisdom of sharing her family troubles with someone she'd had only known for a few weeks. 'We may have to sell...we *will* have to sell!' she repeated, biting her lip, then, as Elsie came in bearing a tiny glass and the telephone-book, she recovered herself, shaking her head, an anguished expression on her face, 'please, forget I said that...I don't know anything yet. But please, would you look for Adrian? When he's upset, he...he often heads straight for the Hangar.'

'Of course,' Heather replied, happy to do anything that would take her outside on this lovely June morning, 'I'll do my best.' And leaving Gwen to the tender mercies of Elsie and the restorative effects of the brandy, she hastened back to the stables to put on strong shoes before heading out towards the woods. Before she reached the steep climb onto the Hangar, she spotted Kathie on Champion trotting back towards the Hall and just had time to give her a brief resume of the morning's happenings, cheered by Kathie's 'Leave Gwen to me, I'll sort her out,' before setting out on her search for the distressed young man.

As she wound her way through the trees, looking in every direction, Heather pondered over what she had just seen – and heard – wishing she could have had longer to look at the will. Had Mr Franklin, in a fit of madness, left the whole estate to a several-times removed cousin or a Home for Distressed Donkeys? From what she had gathered from Kathie and from Gwen herself, he didn't sound the kind of man who was given to spite, deceit or sudden rushes of blood to the head. But 'Where there's a will there's a relative,' she remembered her Gran and mother chanting in unison every time they heard of a disappointed widow, whose apparently loving husband had left all his money to his secret mistress or the Salvation Army in revenge for some perceived misdemeanour of his wife's twenty years before. But to disinherit his own son? For that's what it sounded like from Gwen's reaction. Even if Adrian was a bit wild, surely his father could have put safeguards in place to prevent him squandering the profits of the farms and cottages and the value of the estate, built up by his ancestors over the last two hundred years?

But this was all pure speculation. Perhaps there was something in the legal, formal language of the will that Gwen had misunderstood. And she, Heather, was supposed to be searching for the boy. Where on earth could he have got to?

On second thoughts she decided to try the village first before the Hangar, realising that there were too many opportunities up there for Adrian to hide. She raced back to the courtyard to collect Frog, parking him in the pub carpark before she scouted up and down the village street, hoping to catch a glimpse of him flying round a corner or down a footpath into the fields. She paused outside the Wakes, the house where Gilbert White had spent almost his entire life, wondering if he might have slipped into the garden, but the gate was shut and bolted. She stood a while, pondering...what would *she* have done if she'd been distracted and upset? Struck by a thought, she approached the Plestor, first looking behind the huge yew-tree, then she wondered about the church in case he'd wanted somewhere quiet and peaceful to calm down. The door was on the latch, and she slipped inside as quietly as possible, looking warily to left and right, then by some instinct, ventured into the side aisle where she knew the Gilbert White Memorial window was situated.

She sighed with relief. There was Adrian, seated cross-legged on the stone floor like a small boy, looking up at the window, a handkerchief pressed against his face, his whole body convulsed with silent sobs. Heather stood quietly for a moment, just observing him, uncertain of his reaction if disturbed. But he must have sensed her presence as he turned his head round sharply, both fists raised as if to ward off any approach, dropping them again when he saw that she was not his mother. Fetching a hassock from the nearest pew, Heather sat down beside him, saying nothing, but just studied the window for the hoopoe as she and Craig used to do. She breathed hard and gently touched Adrian's arm, pointing at the orange bird, its crest upraised.

'My brother and I used to come in here and look at that bird...many years ago,' she murmured, her voice almost too low to be audible, 'and we'd sit here...side by side...just like this. I'll tell you about him one day...he died, you see, far too young ... before he'd hardly had time to live.'

Adrian gave her a sharp glance and murmured a few sympathetic words and they sat in silence for a few minutes.

Then Heather, although unsure of the wisdom of bringing up the subject of his antagonism towards his mother, decided to tackle the subject head on.

'Look,' she said, keeping her gaze fixed on the stained-glass window, 'I don't know what the problem is between you and your mother, and I don't want you to think I'm prying into your private affairs – but we're all, Kathie, Elsie and I, really worried about you and Gwen. But all I will say is that whatever *is* the trouble, there are always solutions to every problem, even if we may not like them very much.'

Adrian turned his head away, drawing in a deep, shuddering sigh.

'Not to this one,' he quavered at last, 'no solution ... no hope...the harm was done years ago...and,' he gulped and blew his nose, but managed to carry on, 'it can't ever, *ever* be put right.' He looked up at Heather with imploring eyes. 'I can't tell you...I can't...not now...it's too awful...'

Heather returned his gaze, astonished again, as she had been all those weeks ago when she first encountered him on the Hangar, at the deep blue of his eyes and his abundant curly brown hair and felt quite a tug at her heart. Must get Sally to meet him one day, she thought, before mentally slapping herself on the wrist...there I go again, she thought, building castles in the air, but...what a pair they would make!

'If I'd had a son,' she remarked idly as she and Adrian rose from their uncomfortable seats on the floor, 'I'd have liked him to look just like you...but I wouldn't swap my darling daughter for all the tea in China.'

'China?' Adrian queried, looking bemused. Heather realised he had probably never heard the expression before and chuckled as they left the church and emerged into the sunshine.

'Just an expression we used to use when I was young...well, younger than I am now,' she added, realising that Adrian probably regarded her as almost an old fogey. 'Did you know I used to go to school not far from here, near Alton?'

He shook his head – and his curls! Heather was pleased to see that the strained look of worry was beginning to leave his face and there was even the ghost of a smile. They stood for a moment beside the huge yew tree and Heather sighed. 'My brother and I used to hide our bikes here when we ran up to the top of the Hangar – up the Zig-Zag.'

To her astonishment, she felt Adrian slip his hand into hers and give it a comforting squeeze.

'One day,' he murmured, 'I'll run up the Zig-Zag with you – and I'll be your brother!'

'Oh, Adrian!' Heather stopped in her tracks, just looking at him, catching her breath – then, regaining her composure, she added, 'that's the loveliest thing you could possibly have said.'

They were both silent as they made their way across the Plestor and over the road towards the carpark. Just as they reached the pavement, they saw a figure emerge from the footpath that led up to the Hangar, dash across the road and in through the church gate, clutching a bunch of roses that Heather recognised from the garden at Westhangar Hall. She stopped to gaze after him before turning to Adrian, a questioning look in her eyes.

'Wasn't that your Uncle Stewart?' she asked, 'going somewhere in a hurry?'

Adrian glanced behind him, as Stewart disappeared into the far corner of the churchyard.

'Oh yes,' he answered, 'he's off to put flowers on his wife and kids' graves. He comes in here regularly. Mum says he's morbid and should get a grip. It's been five years now, after all.'

Heather, momentarily taken by surprise, paused a moment before getting into the car with Adrian beside her. 'Hm...'was all she said as her mind returned to that day when Gwen had explained – partly – why Stewart had lost the power of speech through shock. She'd have to come back one day on her own and see the grave for herself – it might help to fill in another piece of the jigsaw that was the recent history of this unfortunate family.

'Want me to come in with you?' she asked Adrian as they got out of the car in the courtyard and Adrian headed for the door. 'Be sure to let your Mum know that you are safe and well...she does worry about you, you know,' but all he did was give a curt nod and disappear indoors.

Heather looked at her watch – a bit too late to go off in Frog this morning and she didn't feel like immersing herself in past history after the emotions that her meeting with Adrian had stirred up. What *had* happened between Adrian's parents to create such hatred and feelings of revenge in their son's heart? None of her business – and yet, living in their house, delving into their past, seeing the distress, not once but twice, in Adrian's face; having witnessed his attempt to murder, or, at the very least, to maim his mother; then having heard Gwen's outburst earlier that day, she felt that it was becoming more and more her business. And now Stewart, still unable to come to terms with the loss of his wife and children...well, that at least was understandable, however it had happened. Although there were still mysterious gaps in her knowledge of the Franklin family, she was beginning to realise that all of them were suffering from the deepest of deep wounds.

She made a mental note to ask Gwen if Sally could come and spend part of her summer holidays with her. Then they could go to visit their old home together, that would be more fun than treading the paths of their past alone and Sally might remember things that she had forgotten. As she stood uncertainly at the bottom of the stairs to the study, she heard Kathie's urgent call and turned to see her striding purposefully into one of the stables to fetch a couple of leading ropes and, more mysteriously, a mallet!

'Got a spare minute?' she called. Another rhetorical question – Kathie was good at those. 'Damned horses have knocked down the fence in the paddock and they're having a high old time gorging themselves on fresh grass. We'll have two cases of bloat on our hands if I can't mend it quickly.'

Without stopping to enquire what she meant, Heather hurried to Kathie's side and, rather to her consternation, had one of the halters thrust in her direction. As she held it awkwardly, Kathie was already half-running towards the field where Champion and Conker spent the summer months. There she saw the two horses, chestnut and grey, grazing contentedly on a patch of fresh grass and wondered what all the fuss was about.

'I'll grab Champion and you get Conker,' Kathie called, ''we've got to get them off this grass a.s.a.p.' Swallowing hard to cover her nerves, Heather watched out of the corner of her eye as Kathie approached Champion from the side, calling softly while the horse continued to munch noisily away, a rim of white foam along his lips. Taking him by surprise, Kathie slipped the halter over his head and tightened it, then encouraged him with a few hearty slaps on his backside to be dragged away. As quickly as possible, not wanting to be seen as utterly useless, Heather crept up on Conker, who unfortunately saw her coming and began to career away across the field.

'Steer her towards the fence – or what's left of it,' shouted Kathie, 'she'll have to stop then.'

Heather ran up behind Conker, trying to keep clear of her heels and flapped her arms in an effort to divert her into a new direction. 'Git on with yer!' she heard herself yell, hardly realising where the sound had come from and, to her utter amazement, Conker turned towards the ragged fence and stopped abruptly, thinking she couldn't go any further. Quick as a flash Heather slipped the rope over Conker's head as the horse gazed at the fence, no doubt wondering whether she could jump it. Also, to her amazement, as she led her towards Kathie and Champion, she came quite tamely with her, merely swishing her long chestnut tail in mild frustration at having to leave the luscious treat she had been enjoying.

'Well done,' said Kathie, 'can see you've done that before,' and taking hold of both halters, she handed them to Heather before picking up the mallet and heading towards the fence.

'Never in my life,' replied Heather, alarmed at being in charge of not one, but two hefty beasts who would undoubtedly discover, before too long, that they were in the hands of a quaking amateur. Whether Kathie heard or not she could not be sure as she was putting all her efforts into hammering the fallen fence posts back into position and didn't turn to face Heather again until she had finished the job to her satisfaction.

'Well done, then,' was all she said abruptly as she took the two ropes off the horses and sent them cantering back across the field.

'Have to be careful when they get the taste of fresh grass,' she explained as the two women walked towards the stables, 'their stomachs can fill with gas and, if not treated, it can prove fatal.'

'Just like in *Far from the Madding Crowd,*' murmured Heather, 'I always hated that bit where Gabriel Oak has to stick a spike in the sheep's side – but it did save its life.'

'Really?' uttered Kathie, looking blank and Heather realised that, quite possibly, Kathie had never heard of Thomas Hardy or his Wessex novels. Perhaps she'd lend her the book one day. But Kathie was continuing.

'We do move the fences gradually so that they can eat a little at a time, then later in the summer when the grass has lost its first potency, they'll have the run of the whole field. Now, what's the news on that dratted Adrian?'

Over a restorative mug of strong coffee in Kathie's rooms, Heather recounted her successful search for Adrian, reassuring Kathie that he was now calmer and unlikely to do himself any harm. As she finished her coffee and rose to go back to check that Elsie was coping satisfactorily with Gwen, she paused a moment and asked the question she had been anxious to have answered ever since her first encounter with Stewart by the Wishing Stone on the day of her arrival in April.

'When Adrian and I were in the churchyard,' she ventured, 'we saw Stewart. Adrian told me that he was on his way to put flowers on his wife and children's grave – but it didn't seem appropriate then to ask him to explain, so I wondered...'

'Hasn't Gwen told you what happened to them?' Kathie asked in astonishment, rinsing out the two mugs and turning to face Heather, 'I thought she must have done by now. You ought to know, it explains so much about that poor man.' She put the two mugs on hooks beside the sink and looking at her watch, considered for a moment.

'Come up here after lunch,' she suggested, 'I've too much to get through this morning but I'll fill you in then.' She sighed, shaking her head, the frown between her eyes deepening with concern. 'This family has had more than its fair share of bad luck in the last few years, and I was hoping that, with Adrian growing up and getting more responsible, that they could put all that behind them. But with Mr Franklin's sudden death...' She left the sentence unfinished, and Heather left her to go in search of Elsie, mulling over the troubling events of the morning as she went.

Chapter Six

A few hours later, Heather and Kathie sat on Kathie's sofa, watching footage of the miner's strike on her television as the rain poured down outside. 'Yes...' Kathie uttered at last, sighing as she spoke, 'poor, wretched Stewart. Gwen told me about him not long after I came to work here, just after Mr Franklin had been taken ill. Stewart and his family lived in one of the estate houses just along the main street, not far from the church. He hasn't been back to it since, can't face seeing all the children's toys and Jennifer's clothes and all that. Gwen did persuade him to let her and Elsie clear the fridge and freezer and do a little tidy-up in the kitchen. But he was adamant he wanted it left as it was, said he'd do it one day.' She sighed deeply. 'But that day never came, and I doubt if it ever will. He and Jennifer used to sing in the choir, and she taught in the Sunday School. Apparently, he has – or rather had – a very good baritone voice, even performed solo occasionally. He was a church warden too and had a good job at an estate-agents in Farnham.'

They both fell silent for a few moments. 'Will the horses be all right?' Heather asked anxiously, listening in some consternation to the drumming of raindrops on Kathie's attic roof, reassured when her friend explained that there was a wooden shelter in one corner of the field to which Champion and Conker could retreat in wet or cold weather.

'A bit ramshackle, but better than nothing,' she said, 'might try and get one of the gardeners to do some repair work one of these days. Now if Stewart could only pull himself together that's something he could do instead of wandering around the village like a lost soul. There's so much he could do; help with the horses; tidy up the walled garden; keep those paddock fences in order; go into Alton to fetch things for Gwen. No-one should remain in mourning for years on end – can't be healthy. He does take the dogs out from time to time but that's about it. Of course, I've only known him for about three years, so I never met his wife or family. I'm told he was a totally different character before the accident.'

When Mrs Thatcher appeared on the screen to give her scathing opinion of the damage Arthur Scargill and the strikers were doing to the economy, by mutual agreement Kathie switched off and they both stared into space for a moment or two, while Kathie collected her thoughts. After a moment or two she went to pull the curtains across the window to shut out the noise of the rain lashing against the glass before continuing her narrative.

'Every summer they'd drive down to Cornwall for a fortnight by the sea – somewhere near Woolacombe, I believe, never been there myself but I'm told the beaches are superb. They'd always go down in two cars, Jenny and the three children in the Ford Cortina, while Stewart followed on with all the camping gear, tents, sleeping bags, cooking equipment, boxes of food, even the kid's bikes stuffed into his Landrover ... must have been so exciting for those children, getting closer and closer to the sea.

Well, that summer, five years ago, they set off, Jenny leading the way as usual, then, about ten minutes later Stewart remembered he'd left the camping lanterns and torches behind, so he flashed his headlights to warn Jenny and found somewhere to turn round to go back for them. Jenny pulled into a layby behind a tradesman's truck to wait for him as they liked to travel together in case either of them had a puncture or something. If only she hadn't...'

Kathie paused, glancing briefly at Heather, who mentally braced herself for the story she knew she was going to hear.

'Well, he was a bit longer than he'd expected to be, couldn't remember exactly where the lanterns were so it was a good half-hour before he approached the place where Jenny had parked. Before then he'd been passed by two speeding police cars and an ambulance and must have had that horrible sinking feeling, suspecting, but not knowing, that something dreadful might have happened along the road ahead. As he got closer, he could see flashing lights, the traffic was slowing and he was waved on by police who were guiding all the cars around the site of a lorry that had crashed into the back of a parked car, which in turn had been crushed under the back wheels of a vehicle in front.'

Heather put her head in her hands, as an icy chill washed through her, hardly bearing to hear what followed.

'Stewart knew it could only be Jenny's car – you can imagine how ghastly he felt at that moment! While he could still speak – it was delayed shock that robbed him of his speech a few days later – he told Gwen that he kept hoping that Jenny and the children had somehow got out and that he'd see them all waiting for him by the side of the road. It wasn't easy to pull in – the police kept trying to wave him on – so in the end he simply stopped as near to the scene as he could and frantically raced back down the road.'

'My God...that poor man,' Heather murmured, looking away from Kathie as she noticed tears beginning to roll down her cheeks. 'I suppose...there was no hope...?'

'They stood no chance,' Kathie replied as soon as she had regained control over her voice, 'the car was practically embedded underneath the truck. Ambulance men and police were shining torches underneath the two vehicles and trying to listen for any signs of life but there was nothing...just the smell of petrol, Stewart said and the sound of cars swishing by. Once he'd managed to tell the police who he was, they were kindness itself, he said, a policewoman led him a little way away and sat him on the grass verge while the men did their best to retrieve the bodies as quickly as possible. Gwen said

Stewart told her that his sharpest memory was of one of the police screaming to onlookers – who always mysteriously appear from nowhere – to put out their cigarettes and get the hell away.'

'I'm afraid it's human nature,' Heather said soberly, 'we simply can't resist gazing at an accident, thankful it's not we who are involved.' Done it myself many times, she admitted to herself with shame.

'Thankfully, the next hour or two passed Stewart by in a sort of blur...he refused point-blank to move until he was absolutely sure there was no chance that even one member of his family had survived. As you can imagine, the next few days must have been a nightmare for everybody concerned. Mr Franklin and Gwen had to help Stewart with every detail of the police enquiry, the press, both local and national who swooped down like vultures, picking over every personal detail of the tragedy, trying to get interviews with witnesses, the lorry-driver's family – he had died too in the crash – photographers who were not above trespassing in the garden here to try and catch a glimpse of Stewart. The funeral, here in Selborne, had to be cut short as Stewart broke down in such a state as each coffin was carried into the church, that Chris – the vicar - simply couldn't conduct a proper service, nobody could hear the organ and half the congregation were in tears too, as they all knew Jenny and the children. Eventually everyone was ushered outside as soon and with as much dignity as possible into the churchyard, but the interment was just as traumatic as he howled as each coffin was lowered into the ground. He was, literally, demented with grief. Gwen said she was thankful that Adrian was away helping at a scout camp in Yorkshire and didn't have to witness the worst of his uncle's breakdown.'

The two women fell silent once more, each busy with their own sombre thoughts until Kathie roused herself to speak again.

'It must have been unimaginably awful. Poor Stewart. He kept blaming himself, over and over, for forgetting to pack the damned torches and things. "We could have bought new ones...when we got there..." he kept sobbing to Mr Franklin and Gwen...and, of course, they could! But how could he have foreseen that the lorry driver would have a blackout just as he tried to steer into a space in the lay-by. The police reckoned he was dead even before he hit Jenny's car. The awful thing was, that at the inquest they discovered that he had suffered blackouts before but never told anyone, not his boss, not even his wife. Afraid of losing his job, I suppose.'

'Doctors should be able to report people like that,' said Heather, frowning distractedly, biting her lip, 'I know this is hindsight...but four, five, lives could have been saved and another one saved from a lifetime of guilt and misery if he'd just dropped a word in the right quarters.'

'The doctor was called as a witness,' Kathie answered, thoughtfully, 'and he was adamant that he had insisted most strongly on the lorry driver's giving up driving forthwith and this was corroborated by his producing his notes of the consultation and the fact that he had booked an appointment for him to see a specialist at Winchester Hospital just a week after the accident – but he didn't inform the police. Exceedingly difficult dilemma for doctors – they can't risk losing the trust of their patients.'

'My God,' said Heather, her head in her hands, 'it makes you never want to set foot in a car again, doesn't it?' She had had a sudden terrifying flashback to when the lorry carrying pallets had just missed her on her way to Selborne all those weeks before and for a moment felt shaky and faint.

'Well,' said Kathie, in a matter-of-fact tone of voice, getting up and fetching her biscuit tin from her cupboard, offering Heather a Bourbon. 'I never could pass my test. Tried five times so I thought I'd stick to horses...and my bike. Might possibly kill myself but unlikely to kill anyone else. That reminds me,' she continued, fixing Heather with a determined stare, 'when am I going to get you up on Conker now that you've made friends with her? It's a wonderful way to see the countryside, and you can look into other people's gardens over the hedge. It's an education to see what people hang on their washing-lines!'

They both laughed, relieving the tension and Heather promised to give it some serious thought. Always a good thing to acquire another skill and after all, Conker had behaved very well once she had managed to catch her. Yes...why not?

Next morning it was still raining. Gwen seemed subdued but not unduly upset at breakfast and, after a word with Elsie, Heather was relieved to hear that the tot of brandy yesterday had had the desired effect and, after a second one, she had recovered quickly. Adrian had returned home in a bad mood, 'like he's lost sixpence and found a farthing' as Elsie described it and had merely grabbed a sandwich, 'doorstep, more like' and kept to his room all day then left the house early in the morning without even a cup of tea.

Once back in the study, Heather began to leaf through the pile of old newspapers she had briefly glimpsed some weeks before, to see if Mr Franklin had kept the report of the accident which Kathie had described so vividly yesterday. After about ten minutes she found several accounts, some of the accident, others of the coroner's report and, after reassuring herself that it was family history and quite justifiable research, she spent the next half-hour immersed in the tragic details, gazing at the photographs of those three young children, their faces alight with life and curiosity, then at the crumpled remains of the car wedged underneath the truck. There was also one of the lorry-driver, hugely overweight, standing proudly beside his lorry, smiling cheerfully, on the day he'd started work in it when it was shiny and new. There was another photograph too, of the family at Christmas, dated 1978, wearing paper hats and waving crackers about, then... Heather caught her breath as she came across one of Stewart on his own of the same date, smiling broadly, his tanned skin and blue eyes glowing out of the picture, and she felt tears pricking at the back of her eyes once more.

He was quite a stunner when he was younger, she thought, with more resemblance to Gwen then than he had now, and rather more hair without a trace of grey, looking full of energy and purpose. She thought back to that first sight she had had of him, suddenly appearing before her at the top of the Zig-Zag, inarticulate, apologetic, nervous. He'd looked nearer to twenty years older than in the photograph rather than a mere five.

She really wanted to go back to the churchyard and see his family's graves, but the rain persisted, so she contented herself with studying the dog-eared paperback she had come across the other day. It was, she was amused to see, an account of the voyage of the sailing ships *Erebus* and *Terror* which had set off in May 1845 to try to find the north-west passage through the Arctic which would provide a link between the Atlantic and Pacific oceans, an expedition that ended in disaster with the deaths of both crews after getting trapped in ice about half-way across. Most died on the ships themselves and the few survivors had tried to walk to safety but, suffering from botulism, scurvy and lead poisoning, they were too sick and weak to make the journey and died on the way.

This ill-fated expedition had been led by none other than Sir John Franklin and, despite its failure, he and his crews had been celebrated as heroes and fine examples of English daring, tenacity and endurance. Had Mr John Franklin of Westhangar Hall been hoping to prove a connection, possibly even direct descent, from his adventurous but unfortunate namesake?

From studying the pages of his family's descent she'd found in the study, Heather thought such a possibility unlikely. But everyone hankers after a famous ancestor and perhaps he'd been trying to find a link that previous genealogists had overlooked. Maybe his father or grandfather had speculated in his hearing when he was a boy that, 'we might, you know, be descended from that brave Sir John Franklin of the 1845 expedition to the Arctic,' and the idea might have lodged in his mind. She made a mental note to visit the Public Library in Alton one day to consult their encyclopedias.

Would sensitive Adrian have been impressed with the idea of a famous navigator and explorer as an ancestor? Gwen had obviously been only marginally interested in her husband's investigations, having made no effort to assist him with his research during his lifetime and, after his death, had been more than eager to hand his unfinished work over to a stranger. Had she, perhaps, felt some guilt for her lack of interest but duty bound to his memory to try to complete his work? It occurred to Heather that there had been something unnaturally cold in Gwen's indifferent attitude to her husband.

It hardly mattered. What mattered to Heather was the chance that had brought her to Selborne and to this unlucky family whose lives were proving to be every bit as tragic and fascinating as the unfortunate Sir John Franklin, whether he were a true ancestor or not.

She stood up and stretched her arms, then, glancing out of the window, she noticed that the rain had stopped, and a weak sun was breaking through the clouds. Why not pop down to the churchyard now while the story of Stewart's family tragedy was still fresh in her mind?

Kathie trotted by on Conker as Heather left the courtyard and called down to her as she passed.

'Your turn tomorrow – I've looked out a hard hat and some boots. What are you, size six?'

'Five, actually – but I've got some thick socks, might be all right. Hope the rain holds off.'

She felt a surge of excitement and apprehension pass through her as she strode off down the drive and into the road. Suppose she fell off? Suppose Conker bolted? Oh, shut up, she reproved herself, Kathie will take good care of you. And it would be interesting if the two of them could go riding together with the chance to explore more of the nearby countryside without having to get into the car. Thinking of Frog sitting neglected in the courtyard revived Heather's desire to drive to her home village soon and see what changes there might have been. But not today.

She crossed the Plestor, reminded of Adrian's spontaneous suggestion that he should act as a substitute for Craig one day and 'run' up the Zig-Zag with her. My running days might be over, she thought ruefully...but it was such a sweet thought.

'Oh, damn!' she said out loud as she crossed the wet grass, then felt guilty as she glanced up at the church. 'Sorry, God.' She'd meant to bring some flowers...but perhaps the ones Stewart had brought with him would still be fresh.

She'd seen him emerge from a corner of the churchyard yesterday out of a group of young birch trees and headed that way, dodging small gravestones as she went, some very old, the lettering covered in lichen, the stones themselves green with moss and ivy. She'd always had an attraction to graveyards, finding the dedications, especially the earlier ones, so fulsome in their praise of the dear departed, who had apparently all led utterly blameless lives that she had often wondered what they had really been like...swindlers? Liars? Wife-beaters? She had even been moved to write a poem on the subject which she had submitted for publication in her local Parish magazine in Hertfordshire. The editor had returned it, deeming it 'inappropriate and unseemly' which had made her laugh out loud. After all, she'd thought, whoever used words like 'unseemly' nowadays?

She reached the corner, wishing she'd thought to bring something to kneel on, soberly amused to realize that even atheistic amateur historians or family history enthusiasts like herself were forced to adopt an attitude of devotion in a churchyard if they wished to check a date or name to aid their research. Doing the best she could with a corner of her anorak she peered at the inscription, swallowing hard as she shared in Stewart's grief.

CHAPTER SIX

HALLIDAY

Sacred to the Memory of
My beloved Wife Jennifer, aged 35 and
My Adored Children,
Piers Stewart (aged 7)
Laura Jennifer (aged 5)
Thomas Adrian (aged 2)
Passed away together 10 April 1979.
God rest them and keep them in his care
Until we meet again

The inscription was bordered with carved flowers and leaves. Oh, dear. Stewart was quite obviously a believer. As tears welled up, she realized that she had no handkerchief and was forced to wipe her eyes and nose on her sleeve. Three things forgotten...flowers, a kneeler and her hanky.

She rose awkwardly and turned to go, catching sight of a figure coming slowly towards her across the grass. Dark suit and dog-collar... and, she noticed, tall, good-looking rather than strictly handsome and with a head of abundant silvery hair. Last time she'd seen him he was wearing a curate's black hat with attached curly grey wig, but she recognized him immediately as 'Chris, the Christian' as Kathie had called him. He hesitated as he approached and realized she was a stranger, then, noticing her tear-stained face, he nodded towards the tombstone.

'Did you know the family?' he asked gently, with a sympathetic smile. Heather hesitated a moment.

'Not the whole family,' she returned, 'I've only been living here for a few weeks. But...I know the father, Stewart ...as much as anyone can know him after such a traumatic event. I'm staying at Westhangar Hall, helping Mrs Franklin sort out her husband's family history papers...Heather La Fontaine.'

She held out her hand and the vicar grasped it firmly, smiling again and staring into her eyes with curiosity and concern. His were chestnut brown and that slightly over-long hair grew strongly back from his forehead in deep waves. Lucky Selborne!

'Of course – I saw you briefly at the May Fair,' he uttered slowly, looking suddenly solemn. 'Y...yes,' he said again and paused as if wondering just how much she knew of the Franklin family's circumstances. Then, clearing his throat, he ventured to speak again.

'I knew Mr Franklin very well, a loyal supporter of the church. He's buried here, alongside several of his ancestors, as I expect you know.' He waved towards the opposite corner of the churchyard from the Hallidays' graves. 'And I know Gwen and Adrian, of course, Miss Parker too, she often gives me a wave as she goes by on her horse.'

'Oh, you mean Kathie,' Heather said, smiling mischievously, 'she's threatening to put me up on the mare, Conker, tomorrow. Haven't ridden since I was about eleven, so wish me luck.'

'I can do better than that,' he replied quite seriously, and gave her another long look. 'I shall pray for you.'

He sounded so sincere that Heather suppressed the laugh that lurked just short of her throat and turned it into a slightly embarrassed 'thanks' instead, before turning towards the Plestor once more. That's one seriously attractive vicar, she thought – and he didn't say, 'haven't seen you in my congregation yet' as many men or women of the cloth might have. She strolled home slowly, her head full of the most surprising, rather troubling thoughts. She'd write to Craig this evening, she decided, and see if that would help to calm her down. And, if Gwen were going, as she went most Sundays, she might even go with her to church one day.

Chapter Seven

'Dear Craig,' Heather wrote later from her study. She had just spent two hours straining to read a cross-written letter from a certain Alicia Franklin, dated 1852, from Victoria, Australia, with the aid of a magnifying glass and no small measure of guesswork. Fascinating stuff, worthy of an article in the National Geographic Magazine, she thought, as it described the wild successes, abject failures and the almost intolerable conditions she and her husband's colleagues had to endure as they strove to make their fortunes during the Australian Gold Rush. Alicia explained that they were booked on the next ship home and would be hoping to stay at Westhangar Hall with their cousins for a few weeks before finding a home of their own. She also hoped most fervently that her letter would arrive safely in Selborne as no less than three ships carrying mail had recently been lost in storms, along with their entire crews, passengers and tons of goods (including boxes of gold nuggets) destined for the markets of London Town. Half of the last page had defeated Heather as the ink had faded to pale cream; very annoying, as she'd have to wait until she could find some way of getting it enhanced, at the Library perhaps or else she'd look for a specialist printer's workshop. How brave those early colonists were, she thought, to take such risks…but what sort of conditions in England had forced them into such a dangerous course of action?

Heather wondered if Mr Franklin had ever bothered to read it or if perhaps her eyes were the first to see it after one hundred and thirty-odd years; crossed writing required good eyesight and much patience. She could see in her mind's eye

Alicia, sitting bolt upright on an uncomfortable chair, longing for home, scratching away on the few sheets of paper she could spare, then turning the pages around and writing at right angles, confident that the recipient would know what to do. The first reader would have been a great-great grandparent of the recently-deceased Mr Franklin, she thought, and then, quite possibly – me! She made a neat, typed copy with only a few gaps where the notepaper had been creased and the words erased and made a mental note to ask Gwen if she knew anything about it. Was Alicia Franklin buried here in the village amongst her ancestors, she wondered and made another mental note to go and check the names again on the Franklin graves, then carried on writing to Craig.

'Some time since I wrote – you'll think I'm neglecting you. First of all, I'd better tell you that I think I'm falling in love with this pretty village, even lovelier than I remember it and such interesting people. I'm indulging in a little matchmaking too – just like Emma Woodhouse though I hope I won't keep making her mistakes! I'm hoping to see Kathie hook up with Stewart, once he's recovered his power of speech, then... Adrian with Sally! They would make a splendid pair.'

She paused, allowing her imagination to run riot, as she usually did, then hearing a clatter in the courtyard, she left her desk and looked down to see Kathie, holding Champion, and Gwen deep in conversation before Gwen got into her own car and drove slowly out of the drive.

Should she be driving ... with her uncertain health? She called to Kathie, standing uncertainly beside the horse and waved before racing down the stairs to join her in the courtyard.

'Will she be OK?' she asked with a worried frown and Kathie sighed and frowned uncertainly before answering.

'She's off to the solicitors again – it's only in Alton, not far. And of course, Gwen won't tell me what the doctor has said about her driving. She's been sneaking off somewhere in the evenings recently, but I don't worry too much now that it's still daylight– and she does seem stronger now, hardly ever needs her stick. She's as stubborn as Adrian in her way.'

'Want a cup of tea?' Heather asked, 'I'm nearly cross-eyed after reading a cross-written letter, must have a rest.'

'In the garden would be good,' Kathie called, her face brightening at the prospect, 'I'm just about to take Conker back to the paddock. You'll find me on the seat beside the Walled Garden. Two sugars.'

Minutes later the two women were sitting side by side, mugs of tea in hand with Heather's biscuit tin between them, and Dizzy and Dotty, tongues hanging out in anticipation, one each side of the seat. Once she had finished explaining what a cross-written letter was, Heather bit into another custard cream, tossing a few pieces to the dogs and tentatively broached the subject she'd been longing to bring up ever since her distressing encounter with Adrian on the Hangar all those weeks ago.

'I'm trying really hard not to be nosy,' she began with a half-laugh, looking Kathie directly in the face. 'My gran used to tell me my nose would lead me into trouble – but I'd give my back teeth to know what on earth is troubling this strange family. I haven't found anything in the archives – yet – to suggest any nefarious goings on in the past, nothing to explain why Adrian has taken so vehemently against his mother.'

'That's not to say there isn't a good reason,' Kathie returned thoughtfully, avoiding Heather's eyes and gazing into the distance. 'Adrian was such a cheerful, carefree character before he went to Brazil, cheeky yes, but never unpleasant. It's got to have something to do with Mr Franklin's will, Gwen's been in such a state ever since they found it. I don't know if she confides in Elsie – don't know if she confides in anyone particularly. Although...' she stopped a moment and considered. 'Chris – Chris the Christian – was kindness itself when Mr Franklin died, called several times in the weeks following the funeral, helped her track down Adrian eventually. I expect she trusts him – he's a good sort, Chris – but if she told him any family secrets it wouldn't be right for him to divulge them. Hey, Heather, you're blushing! I take it you've met him.'

'Oh, quite by chance,' returned Heather, looking away, 'earlier today when I went to have a look at the Halliday graves. And I saw him at the May Fair, heavily disguised. But I must say...I was impressed.'

They both laughed, a little self-consciously. 'Well,' said Kathie, 'the field is yours. I like him a lot - who doesn't? - but he's just not my type and, anyway, I'd be the most God-awful vicar's wife on the planet.'

Heather shook her head ruefully. 'Oh, I think my romancing days are over,' she said, 'middle age will be upon with me soon. And anyway, no good falling for someone who's already married.'

'Married!' exclaimed Kathie, giving Heather's arm a knowing nudge, 'no! He's not married...not now.'

'But I saw his wedding-ring!' countered Heather, at which Kathie gave her another nudge and a shout of laughter.

'You were looking, you mean,' she said, 'No – he wears that to ward off any too familiar advances from certain female members of his congregation. He *was* married – in his former parish, somewhere near Newcastle. Apparently, she ran off with one of the bellringers.'

This unexpected revelation reduced them both to giggles – but then Kathie's expression became serious.

'I think there would have been a divorce – not a good idea for a vicar – but his wife and her bellringer went off on holiday, cruising in the Caribbean, in the early seventies, I think and the ferry they were on sank – can't remember all the grisly details except that some of the poor passengers might have been eaten by sharks.'

'Oh, God!' said Heather, clapping her hand across her mouth, 'I wish I hadn't laughed now,' but Kathie gave her a sly look, muttering 'serve 'em right, I reckon,' then they were both silenced as Elsie appeared, dusting off her hands and they made room for her on the seat between them.

On hearing that Gwen had gone out in the car, she looked concerned. 'We'll just have to keep our fingers crossed that she gets back safely. She was off to the solicitors again, I suppose.'

'Elsie, do you know what's behind all this family trouble?' asked Kathie bravely, 'We're both concerned about Gwen, and we'd do anything we could to help. We hate seeing her so troubled and Adrian behaving erratically – so out of character.'

Elsie pressed her lips together and looked away, her forehead creased with a worried frown. Then she turned as if she had suddenly made her mind up about something.

'Well,' she said at last, 'since you ask...there is summat I must tell you, summat what's been botherin' me ever since Mr Franklin's funeral. I've only told Doris...and she says not to gossip...but...well, I feels I must tell...'

Heather and Kathie gave her their full attention while Elsie rolled her hands together, obviously in an agony of indecision.

'Well,' she began again, sighing, 'It may be nothin' but I come back with Gwen after the funeral to ask 'er if she'd like me to stay the night – keep 'er company-like. She said no, she'd be all right, so I got my coat an' things and went out the door. A few minutes later I remembered I'd left my 'ouse keys on the kitchen table so I crept back in, ever so quiet-like to fetch 'em. I 'eard a funny noise from the dining room, a bit squeaky and I wondered if she were weeping... upset. I peeped in through a crack in the door and couldn't believe my eyes! She were dancing! And sort of singin'! Wavin' her arms about and waltzin' round the table! I didn't know what to think!'

'Well!' uttered Kathie when they had all recovered their senses, 'sounds as if she was thankful to see the back of him! What an extraordinary thing! He seemed such a likeable man! You never really know people, do you, particularly married ones? Very good at putting on a show, especially people in their position. Well, I'm damned! What's going on in your mind, Heather?'

Heather, equally stunned, had found her attention distracted by the memory of one of Thomas Hardy's poems that she'd read at school, which had made her both laugh and cry. It was about a widow, 'a lonely manor-lady' who'd been spotted in a mirror by carol-singers who'd come to console her after the death of her husband, doing exactly that.

'*We saw her airily dancing,*' she remembered and was just about to relate this co-incidence to Kathie and Elsie when Kathie pointed across the lawn to where Stewart was ambling along in a distracted fashion. The dogs raced towards him, and he stopped to ruffle their ears, then seeing the three of them seated companionably on the garden bench he gave a brief wave, then stumbled on his way.

'Now there's someone who could solve the mystery for us,' Kathie murmured, 'both mysteries, possibly – but especially the most recent one. Gwen must have shared her problems with her brother – but...who knows when he'll get back to normal and be able to communicate properly again?'

They all fell silent. Then, at the sound of Gwen's car arriving in the courtyard, after breathing sighs of relief, they rose with one accord and began to make their way back towards the house.

'Conker tomorrow,' Kathie reminded Heather, 'shan't let you off the hook. After lunch – in the paddock?'

'It's a deal,' she replied, and gathering up the mugs and biscuit tin, she began to wend her way back towards the stables, her mind whirling with speculation brought on by Elsie's surprising and disturbing revelation.

Next afternoon, arrayed in hard hat, boots and an old hacking jacket lent by Gwen, Heather and Conker took their first tentative steps together around the paddock, led by Kathie, who called up instructions to her pupil from time to time, 'keep your hands together,' 'squeeze your knees together – and stop laughing! – keep your heels down and your head up,' followed by 'you're doing fine. Just keep going as you are and if Conker stops give her a gentle kick with both heels.' Thus, they made their way three times around the field with Heather breathing in the delicious smell of crushed grass, buttercups and horse, even brave enough occasionally to glance around her at the surrounding fields, the crops well-grown now. Kathie instructed her how to indicate to the horse a change of direction, pulling on first one rein then the other. 'Not too hard...just feel the bit... Conker'll know what you mean. Now we'll try a trot.'

She gave Conker a sudden slap on the rump, and the little mare instantly changed pace jerking Heather up and down uncomfortably as Kathie ran alongside. This was decidedly *not* much fun.

'Hang on now,' Kathie called, after a few painful minutes 'you're going to go a bit faster. Don't worry, cantering's easier, just sit tight and enjoy the ride. We'll come back to trotting later.'

Oh, please don't, thought Heather, as Conker glided into an easy pace, covering the ground smoothly, as Heather clung gamely onto the reins, her legs clutching Conker's slippery sides. I like this, she thought, and managed to remain upright for several circuits of the paddock, then had to grasp hard onto the pommel as the horse slowed to a trot again, sending her off-balance and nearly onto the grass. Kathie grabbed her just in time as she slid off, her legs trembling, breathing hard as she let go of the reins.

'That was very well done, apart from the ungainly end. Enjoy it?' Heather's broad smile was all the reply she could give at that moment, so she nodded enthusiastically and patted Conker's velvety chestnut nose.

'Can't wait to have another go,' she replied, dusting the grass off her trousers, 'I'd forgotten how wonderful it feels to be that high up on a living, moving creature.'

Kathie showed Heather how to remove the saddle and bridle. 'Always in that order and never let go of the reins until you're ready to take off the bridle,' she instructed her, 'you need to stay connected until the horse is free to go.'

Her legs still shaking, Heather gave Conker a farewell pat, before they left the paddock.

'And shut the gate properly,' came the next instruction, 'they're smart beasts, they always know if you've just pushed it to and will nudge it to get back to that fresh grass again.'

Well, I've learned a lot today, thought Heather as she made her way back up the wooden staircase. And I don't mean just about horses. Now...I'm going to have a thorough search for that key to the cabin trunk and see if I can learn any more about Alicia. I'll bet she was glad to get back to the peace and tranquillity of Selborne, after that tough, dangerous life in the goldfields.

She had no luck finding the key. I'll have to ask Gwen, she thought, or Elsie perhaps, she or her sister Doris might have come across a bunch of rusty keys while cleaning. She glanced outside to see the sky blazing with late afternoon sunshine, sapphire blue and cloudless, far too lovely to spend any more time hunched over old documents or searching for elusive keys. Flinging on a light jacket she walked through the courtyard into the garden, revelling in her solitude – Bob and Harry had left for home – listening to the rooks settling down in the trees, the far-off drone of tractors at work and the twitter of baby house-martins anxious for their late afternoon fill of insects to sustain them during the night.

As she walked across the lawns, heading for the orchard, she wondered again about the problems concerning the Franklin family. *We may have to sell*, she remembered Gwen crying out in her distress – but surely that could never be the case after two hundred years of Franklin ownership and occupation? Even if Mr Franklin had regarded his son as too immature or reckless to inherit such a valuable property, surely it would have been left to Gwen for her lifetime? And again, her husband, ignorant at the time of his heart-trouble, would have confidently expected Adrian to be in his early forties by the time he took over. Time enough, surely, for the young man to have outgrown his youthful rebellious stage.

As she left the orchard, the apple trees laden with ripening fruit, some already dropping onto the grass ('the June drop' she remembered) and attracting too many wasps for Heather's comfort, she arrived close beside the Walled Garden and paused. Why not walk right round behind it, just 'to see what was on the other side?' The going was difficult, the grass long and tough, with brambles snaking their way underneath ready to trip her up with almost every step, but she persevered. No-one's been this way for a while, she decided, her heartbeat speeding up at the prospect of discovering new territory. She followed the wall around, pushing heavy curtains of ivy aside and was excited to come across another wooden door, the panels rotting and unstable but – to her joy – unpadlocked. It gave way to her gentle push, only by a few inches but she was sure she could ease it more fully open without making it collapse.

But...should she? Kathie might have come in this way when Dizzy or Dotty got in once but that was some time ago and she had intimated that she regarded it as Stewart's territory, even though he didn't look after it. But...Heather reasoned to herself...she hadn't been specifically *forbidden* to go in and she only wanted to take a look around, keen to see what horticultural treasures might be lurking there. She'd only stay for five minutes.

She tentatively gave the door a harder push or two until she was able to shove her way past the unruly growth on the other side. Hurray! She was in at last although she couldn't see much past a tangle of entwined branches, and she carefully pushed the rotting door closed again before venturing any further.

How she wished she had some strong loppers with her as she tried to hack a spyhole through the obstacle of an out-of-control espalier fruit tree right in front of her. With a mighty effort, she parted two of the nearest branches, and by bracing her elbow against the gap she was just able to widen it enough to crawl through sideways.

That was better. At least she could see, now that she was past the espaliers. She carefully followed the outlines of an overgrown brick pathway that led through an abundance of thistles, teasels, old sunflowers, dead hollyhocks, lupins, even some delphiniums which still showed a few signs of vivid blue and some spikes of bright orange *mombretia,* lighting up the dreary remains of so much decay and dereliction.

'All is not lost,' she breathed, as, interspersed with the neglected, dead and dying plants were several healthier looking shrubs, philadelphus, jasmine, viburnum, a few bedraggled acers and several well-grown and interesting trees; all in need of serious trimming but the mere fact that they were there made her heart jump with delight. Peering through the mass of decay, she could distinguish birch, ornamental cherry, rowan, hawthorn and...she stopped in delighted surprise in front of a sturdy tree bearing dull green, five-sided leaves and unusual green and lemon-yellow fluted flowers bursting out of the ends of some of the branches. Heather had never seen one before but knew exactly what it was ... *Liriodendron tulipa,* the tulip tree, one of the loveliest trees imaginable.

As she stayed gazing at it, she became aware of the sound of footsteps on the pathway behind her and swung round, clutching at a low hanging branch, suddenly guilty at the idea of being challenged by someone, Gwen perhaps, who might be seriously annoyed to find her strolling around without permission. But, to her relief – but also not a little concern – she made out the figure of Stewart carefully picking his way towards her. Show no fear, she told herself, greet him with a smile. As he approached, she slipped her hand underneath one of the flowers growing a little way up the branch and held it out towards him, speaking directly to him, inviting him to inspect it carefully.

'I've always wanted to see a tulip tree,' she exclaimed, 'look how much like garden tulips the flowers are and such a delicate colour. You're so lucky to have one growing here in your garden.'

Stewart simply stood there, blinking with surprise, and, stepping closer, he inspected the flower in Heather's hand, nodding in agreement as he did so. Then, to her surprise he gently took her elbow and guided her through a wilderness of tall buddleia stems, their mauve flower spikes towering over both their heads and stopped before another handsome tree, its deep green, sycamore-shaped leaves already tinged with red and yellow although autumn was still many weeks away. This one she had seen and admired for the few years she had been married to Jerome as they had planted one in their garden to celebrate their marriage. She had cherished it through all the twelve years of her widowhood, while it had grown high and broad and was a delight to the eyes at all seasons but especially in September and October when the leaves turned into a living furnace of crimson, ochre, deep purple, lemon and pink, a wonder to behold.

'*Liquidamber*,' she almost whispered, turning towards Stewart, her expression suddenly serious. 'Sweet gum. My late husband's and my favourite of all trees and with the loveliest of names. I hope my daughter's looking after it well while I'm away.'

She fell silent for a moment as she sensed that Stewart was struggling to speak, his mouth working hard as he tried to force the words out.

'Jen...Jen...thistry...this...tree,' he managed at last, clutching at one of the leaves that was already changing colour. With swift understanding, Heather took his hand and squeezed it comfortingly.

'Your wife's favourite tree too?' she asked tentatively, rewarded by his clear response of 'yes...yes...Jen...Jen,' before he lapsed again into silence.

They stood together quietly for a while, each busy with their own melancholy shared thoughts.

He spoke to me, Heather marvelled to herself, he spoke... not too clearly...but enough. He will recover, I'm sure of it... he will...given time.

'Could I come in here sometimes please, Stewart?' she asked after a minute or two, a little apprehensively. 'I believe

Mr Franklin loved this part of the garden and now you love it too...I'm glad. I've seen some black-and-white photographs of this garden from years ago, must have been magic in the Spring and Summer. Would you mind very much if I came in from time to time?'

To give him time to digest her bold request, she told him about her year at college, studying horticulture. 'One of the best things I ever did,' she assured him, 'it taught me so much about design and choice of plants, the different types of soil, which plants prefer sunlight or shade, and I can see, even with all these dead and dying plants that this must have been a magnificent sight. And could be again,' she bravely added, hoping that she was not pushing her luck before she had won his confidence. Because what she wanted, above all else, was to pitch her energy and expertise into clearing away the debris, seeing what could be saved, expose the original layout of the garden and breathe new life into it before it became totally unmanageable.

She stared round what she could see of the garden, avoiding Stewart's eye, nervous about what she might see in them. Resentment? Sadness? Eagerness? Perhaps that was too much to hope as, after a minute or two, he made his way to the opposite side of the garden, gesturing to her to follow him, weaving his way along what must have been the central path until they reached the gate which she had glimpsed from the Hangar all those weeks ago. He took out a large key and undid the padlock, ushering her in front of him as he turned and carefully relocked the gate. Heather hesitated, wondering whether to apologise for her intrusion...until she noticed that he was summoning up the strength to speak again and she bent nearer to catch his words.

'One... day,' he said, almost clearly, 'one... day, come, come,' and as she departed, she could have sworn that she saw the hint of a shy smile on his weather- beaten face.

He didn't say no! He didn't fly into a temper or burst into tears. He didn't do anything at all to put me off, she thought.

And he spoke to me – just a few but real meaningful words. As she climbed her staircase, she felt a wave of cautious optimism course through her. Perhaps, one day, when she'd completed her work on Mr Franklin's papers, perhaps…she might?

She didn't have long to dream, however, as, as soon as she'd changed into something more suited to indoors, her phone rang. It was Elsie, breathless with excitement or distress, it was hard to tell which.

'Sorry, Miss Heather, I know you've only just come in. Gwen wants us all to come into 'er kitchen and hear something important she's got to say. Oh, dear…!' She was catching her breath with every word she said, 'It must be something serious as she's asked the vicar to come as well. I'm sure it's going to be bad news. I hope it doesn't mean we're all going to get the sack!'

Chapter Eight

Heather hastily changed her outdoor jacket for a smart woollen cardigan, flung on a pair of leather shoes, then raked a comb through her hair. As she glanced at herself in the mirror, she was surprised to notice how flushed she looked, her cheeks healthily rosy and her eyes unusually bright. Was this the result of her success in coaxing Stewart, however briefly, out of his melancholy silence? Her excitement at penetrating the inner recesses of the Walled Garden? Or – she frowned at herself in annoyance – could it, possibly, be the prospect of seeing Chris the Christian again?

Don't be ridiculous, she admonished herself as she raced down the stairs. If Elsie's fears are realised, I'll be on my way home to Hertfordshire in a week or two, my work barely begun, and my dreams shattered. As she paused for a moment at the bottom to regain her composure, two things happened to cause her consternation. There came a sudden hard shower of rain sweeping across the courtyard, threatening to leave her soaked if she tried to race across to the door. Simultaneously, she saw a large grey Volvo turn into the yard and out jumped the man himself. On seeing her hesitating by the stables, he leaned into the back seat and brought out an immense striped umbrella and tip-toed across the wet tarmac towards her.

'I imagine you're invited too,' he remarked as he held the umbrella expertly above them both with one hand, holding her elbow with the other as they crossed the yard, dodging puddles as they went. As Heather smiled her agreement, she glanced up at her saviour, catching his glance in return, which rested on her just a moment longer than was strictly necessary.

'Oh, God!' she thought, irreverently, 'my hair has gone crazy already, I must look a fright.'

As they entered the kitchen together, Heather happened to catch the eye of Kathie, who gave her a broad wink. Feigning a frown, Heather noticed that she and Chris would have to take the only two chairs left vacant, beside each other next to Kathie. To her annoyance, Heather felt herself blush as he courteously drew one back for her to be seated first and heard again in her head the words that had come so often from the lips of her mother, "Oh, I do so love a man with good manners!" then had the sudden awful thought that she had spoken the words aloud.

Of course I didn't, she reassured herself, then looked round the table to see who else had been summoned to hear Gwen's pronouncement. Stewart was there, still in his outdoor clothes and she flashed him a quick, conspiratorial smile, then there was Elsie, Doris her sister, Kathie, the vicar and herself. No Adrian...that did not bode well, she thought, then braced herself for what she was about to hear. Gwen looked nervously around the table, clearing her throat and licking her dry lips.

'I know you've all been aware of some ...some tension... between my son and myself recently,' she began tentatively, 'and, as you all know me well...yes, you too, Heather, even though you've only been here a few weeks...I've thought it only fair to explain the reason for his...his distress and his anger towards me...as it's possible that it may affect us all.'

As her spirits took a dive, Heather looked down at the table, remembering her first encounter with the desperate young man on the Hangar. And you, dear Gwen, don't know the half of it, she thought to herself, or how nearly you came to losing your life that day. Perhaps now at last she might be about to learn what it was that *they should have told me,* as he'd kept repeating between sobs on that fine Spring day in April.

'We all make mistakes,' Gwen almost whispered, avoiding all their glances, and Heather felt rather than saw the vicar's hands tighten as he too prepared to pay close attention to what she was saying, 'but I made a bad one once ...then made it worse by trying to keep it a secret from the person...the person who would be the worst affected by it...Adrian.'

Gwen paused a moment to collect her thoughts, then continued.

'My husband, dear John...' she caught her breath again, 'he agreed with me that the news should be kept from Adrian for as long as possible in the hope that some solution would present itself before he needed to know...but John died so prematurely and so suddenly...that there was no chance to tell him or, perhaps, to get things changed... find a legal loophole... anything.'

There was a longer pause this time as the silence round the table became almost tangible. Then the vicar gently cleared his throat and put out his hand to touch Gwen's shaking fingers. 'Are you sure...?' he began but she nodded vigorously and bravely began again.

'Yes,' she answered, her voice firmer now, 'it's important that you all should know. Not long after John and I were married, he had to go away for a few weeks and... a man I'd known before I met John and who had wanted me to marry him, turned up again and began to...well, to court me all over again. It sounds ridiculous now but...with John away...and with this other gentleman assuring me that he need never know... that we were both lonely and perhaps still a little in love. Well, with John likely to be away for about three months...we just sort of...dropped into an affair.'

No-one spoke – what was there to say? Stewart shuffled his feet, and the Reverend Garland clasped his hands even more tightly, while Heather tried hard not to catch anybody's eye. Gwen? That elegant 'lady of the manor' with the cut-glass voice and aristocratic bearing? But then...why not Gwen? As a young woman she must have been extremely attractive, fun-loving and tempting prey to a former admirer without the constant presence of her husband to protect her.

'We...we weren't as careful as we should have been,' continued Gwen, with a sight catch in her voice, 'over-confident...reckless even...so you can guess what happened.'

There was a long pause. Heather stole a quick glance at Gwen feeling a rush of warm sympathy with that elegant pillar of society, risking all for the chance of a thrilling, stolen few weeks of romance. She understood only too well what it was to have been reckless in her own younger days.

'I wouldn't believe what was happening to start with,' she murmured, 'in denial, I believe, is the term one uses nowadays. So, I just carried on, hoping that all would turn out well – but it soon became obvious that...there really was a child on the way...and it could never be passed off as John's.'

Heather felt her colour rise as she thought back to her own instinctive feelings of dread, fear and shame all those years ago when she'd realised that her own moment of madness had had the same predictable outcome. But she had not been married, hadn't cheated on anyone and she had had the great good fortune to have Jerome to turn to in her trouble, so eager, so desperate to marry her to save her from what, in the 1960s, would have been the greatest disgrace. I was lucky – so lucky – she mused, and even if I wasn't in love with Jerome at the beginning, I knew, I just knew it was the right thing to do...for all three of us. And it was. It must have been so different for Gwen.

Gwen's voice, resuming her story, jerked Heather out of her daydream and she paid attention once more.

'I can't tell you how dreadful the next few weeks of my life were,' Gwen continued, 'awful...awful! This other man would have married me, gladly. But, as soon as John found out, he was adamant that he wouldn't give me a divorce, too proud to admit to the world that his wife had betrayed his trust. My... my principles, if it can be said that I had any, would not allow me to even think about getting rid of the baby and John would not hear of it either.'

There was a subdued murmur of approval round the table as Gwen gathered herself together to continue the story.

'So, we made a pact between the three of us. John and I would bring the child up as if it were both of ours with no recriminations, it would have his name and we agreed never to refer to...to the real father again. The other man promised solemnly, in writing, never to try and contact Adrian or us again. And we always thought we'd have more children; Adrian would become part of a family of siblings and somehow his origins would become less important. But...that was not to be. I couldn't have any more children.'

She fell silent again and everyone around the table began to wonder if that was all she had to say...but, if so, why all the trouble, the passion and hatred between Adrian and Gwen when the boy knew he was loved and accepted by the man he always regarded as his father? As Gwen, visibly shaking, began to speak again, it soon became clear.

'What I didn't know...and what John never told me... although he might have done if he had lived longer...was that his pride in the Franklins ... the fact that his Franklin ancestors had owned Westhangar Hall for nigh on two hundred years meant that it had to be, to quote rather antiquated legalese, 'a child of his body' or his own blood relation, that could inherit the property, no-one else, not even the lad he'd brought up as his own for more than twenty years.'

Gwen held her head in her hands at this point, trying to control her breathing as all her listeners sat quietly, embarrassed and distressed in equal measure at this revelation. Elsie and Doris heaved with silent, sympathetic sighs, Kathie looked daggers as if to say 'Men!' in disgust, and Stewart took both of his sister's hands in his, chafing them to try and stroke the pain of her distress away.

Gwen raised her tear-stained face, and the little company gave her their full attention once more.

'The worst of it was,' she gulped out eventually, 'that until we found his will, which took weeks, as you know as some idiot boy on work experience had filed it under 'Farms', there was no way of knowing what his intentions were so my poor

Adrian, although mourning the death of his...of John... naturally thought he *was* his heir, had started to make plans to carry on his...John's work with the estate, full of ideas after his time in Brazil. All, all turned to dust and ashes in a moment.'

So that was it, thought Heather soberly. In his fury at his parents' deception and the destruction of his future, the thought of the humiliation he would suffer at the hands of his friends and villagers, once the truth was known, the young man's first, maddened thought was to visit revenge on his remaining parent and grasped at the first agent he could find to try to destroy her; the crossbow hanging on the wall. Thank God I was there to stop him, she thought, her face paling at the memory of his frantic sobs as he dropped the ghastly weapon onto the leafy ground. Thank goodness I arrived on the scene just in time... but only just in time...and quite by chance.

As everyone seemed struck temporarily dumb, Elsie rose from her chair with a loud scraping noise.

'Shall we all have a cuppa tea?' she asked brightly, 'I think we could all do with one. I'll go and put the kettle on,' and she trotted off to the range, fetching mugs, spoons, teapot, tea-cosy, milk-jug, sugar basin and tongs out of various drawers and putting them all on one huge tray.

'A mug all right for you, Reverend?' she asked the vicar, who gallantly took the tray from her, arranging the mugs in front of each person, fetching the milk-bottle which Elsie held out to him and filling the jug. When his back was turned, Kathie dug Heather in the ribs. 'Domesticated as well as holy,' she whispered, 'you're in luck!' Then, noticing Heather's still fraught expression, she looked at her with concern. 'Hey, you all right? You look as if you'd just seen Dracula on his way to bite your neck!'

Heather nodded, collecting herself, but didn't trust herself to speak. When her tea arrived, very milky and over-sweet, she stirred it idly, preoccupied, mulling over the news they had just heard from Gwen.

'It's a pity they ever found that rotten will,' said Kathie, decidedly, 'and a pity they couldn't have burnt it when they knew what it said...after all, who'd have known?'

'The solicitors, I'm afraid,' the vicar said sadly, 'they'd have found out eventually. And it would have been strictly against the law to destroy it. And,' he glanced round the table, 'morally wrong too.'

'Hm,' replied Kathie, with some disdain, sniffing impatiently, 'well, I don't think it's fair. If Mr Franklin brought Adrian up as his own child and never told him he wasn't, then he ought to be able to inherit. In my opinion,' she added, staring the vicar boldly in the face, 'that would be morally *right!*'

The vicar stared into his mug, while Heather hid a smile. Dear Kathie...she loved her forthrightness and her courage to express her opinions in front of a man of the cloth. Gwen too nodded, uncertainly, clutching and unclutching her hands.

'That was our biggest mistake, mine and John's. We should have told Adrian years ago so that he'd have grown up with the idea. As it was...it came as a terrible shock to him, but a shock to me too when I discovered what was in the will. I simply can't understand why John never told me his plan. He was as fair as his conscience allowed him to be – he left me and Adrian very generous allowances, but that's not the same as leaving him the estate. And, as an executor, together with the solicitor, I'm supposed to carry out his wishes, however unfair they might seem. But, as far as we know, he had no blood relations as an only child, no cousins...'

As Heather drained her mug, Heather caught sight of Stewart struggling to compose his features and force some words out, his mouth opening and closing, a deep frown of concern creasing his forehead.

'What do you think about this, Stewart?' she said, addressing him directly, 'do you know why Mr Franklin didn't tell Gwen what was in his will?'

They all fell silent, biting their lips as Stewart gradually found his voice, his eyes fixed on Heather. 'Angry,' he forced out at last, 'and...' the words came out singly but remarkably clearly, 'afraid ...Gwen... leave...with boy.' The effort to speak left Stewart visibly exhausted but at the spontaneous round of subdued applause, he caught his breath and his cheeks flushed with something like pride. The vicar leaned across and squeezed his hand.

'Well done, Stewart...well done,' he said before turning to Gwen. 'Did you know this, Gwen? Was he perhaps punishing you for what had happened years before? Couldn't quite find it in his heart to forgive?'

Both Gwen and Stewart nodded silently, while Kathie tossed her head in protest.

'Well, I still think it was jolly unfair,' she said, 'what's that in the Bible, Vicar, about "let he who is without sin cast the first stone?" Don't want to be rude or disrespectful, Gwen, but I'd bet my bottom dollar that your husband had a few flings in his time. But, of course,' she added, glancing round the table, 'it's always the woman who gets the blame and is left, literally, holding the baby.'

Although they all secretly wanted to laugh, nobody did. Heather, whose mind had been working overtime for the last few minutes, torn between memories of her own dilemma all those years ago and Gwen's present predicament, drummed her fingers on the table and prepared to speak.

'Surely,' she began, and all heads turned towards her, 'if the estate has been left to you for your lifetime, what's to stop you appointing Adrian as your equal partner...and then,' she paused and smiled as she added, 'like Jane Eyre, try to stay healthy for as long as possible and not die. That should give you both many years to work out what happens next and to see if there's some way the will can be re-interpreted.'

'Or find another solicitor,' added Kathie darkly, darting another challenging glance towards the vicar, who was gazing thoughtfully out of the window. Gwen raised her head and looked across at Stewart, while Elsie and Doris looked at each other, trying to work out what on earth Jane Eyre had to do with all this.

'There may be some mileage in that suggestion,' the vicar said quietly at last, turning to Gwen, 'Some sort of family agreement, something along those lines. No harm in asking Mr Grundy to look into it for you. I'm surprised he hasn't suggested it already, but then it's only recently that the will has been found. Perhaps,' he added, turning to Heather with a mischievous smile, 'it should be you sitting in a solicitor's office sorting out people's complicated and sometimes spiteful wills and finding ways to – not break– but just slightly adjust unfair rules to keep the living happy while the dead can rest calmly in their graves.'

'I've seen plenty of wills in my work researching family history,' returned Heather, 'and some of them make the most bizarre reading. I remember one old gentleman who stipulated that all his pets should be well cared for after his death, 'not forgetting the parrot' which made me wonder whether all his relations hated the bird so much that he was afraid they'd strangle it as soon as he was in his coffin.'

'And did they?' asked Doris, her eyes round with horror and excitement.

'No idea,' answered Heather, 'he died in 1859 and all his nearest and dearest must have died long ago too.'

'But perhaps the parrot's still alive,' Doris continued in all seriousness, then looked affronted when everyone else laughed. 'Well... might be,' she went on, defensively, 'they can live an awful long time, you know.'

'Go on,' Elsie ribbed her, 'you're thinking of elephants,' and to prevent the meeting descending into a sibling row about the longevity of parrots and elephants, the vicar rose and took Gwen on one side, no doubt to discuss her next appointment with the doughty Mr Grundy, solicitor, and that was the signal for them all to get up and leave.

'Want any help with these?' Heather heard Kathie say to Elsie, indicating the empty mugs on the table, then, at her thanks and refusal, she went over to Stewart as he levered himself out of his chair and shook his hand.

'If you want some entertainment, Stewart,' Kathie said, 'come and watch Heather have her next riding lesson on Conker – she's particularly good at sliding off sideways.'

Heather joined her at Stewart's side.

'If you do come and watch me,' she said, 'you must promise not to laugh.'

Stewart looked confused but not displeased to find himself suddenly the centre of attention and worked himself up to attempt an answer.

'Not...not... laugh,' he got out at last, shaking his head and Heather was aware that the vicar had turned round at this exchange and was looking at the three of them with puzzled delight. As the rain had stopped and they all went their separate ways he caught up with her just as she approached the stables.

'Did you know Kathie told me that Stewart has actually invited you in to see the Walled Garden?' he said. At Heather's cautious nod and admission that she had already, technically, broken in, he raised his eyebrows in surprise.

'That was his family's favourite playground,' he told her, 'his holy of holies if you like. John – Mr Franklin – knew he retreated there after the accident, re-living the happy times the children used to have playing hide-and-seek, all the things that children do and just left him to it. I think Stewart was supposed to keep the place in some sort of order, but John didn't insist – in spite of this family turmoil he's left behind him, he was actually a very generous, tactful man. Then, two years later he had his first heart-attack and couldn't have tackled the jungle it had become even if he'd wanted to. Whatever's it like in there now?'

Heather smiled ruefully, shaking her head.

'Well, jungle's the word, weeds head high...but there are some wonderful trees and plants in there, my fingers itch to clear the place out and put it back into some sort of order. I've found this photo-album from the early 1900s, you see, beautiful borders, statues, fountains, glasshouses...just glorious. None of my business, I know...but I'd give anything to see it restored to its former state. But,' she sighed, 'although Stewart didn't seem uneasy at my being there the other day, I think he was glad to see me go. But the thing is, Vicar...he spoke to me in there...just a few words, but perfectly understandable...and you heard him speak again in the kitchen ...I'm sure he will recover, slowly but surely.'

'Y-yes,' returned the vicar slowly, 'it's been five years now... time he came to terms with it...re-joined the human race. I see him in the churchyard every now and again, but he's never come inside since the day of the funeral. And please, please do call me Chris or I shall be forced to keep calling you Mrs La Fontaine.' Then, reverting to the subject of Stewart he added, 'How much time do you think a man like that needs? Isn't five years enough?'

He looked enquiringly at Heather as if she might count counselling the bereaved amongst her other accomplishments. Suddenly reminded, Heather grinned.

'Did you know that young Adrian does? Enter the church, I mean,' she remarked, 'though perhaps he'd rather you didn't know. He likes to sit on the floor and look at the Gilbert White memorial window, just as my brother and I used to do when we were children.'

There was a surprised silence for a moment as Chris regarded her with a quizzical expression. Heather spoke again, earnestly looking into his face.

'Adrian is a very dear, thoughtful boy,' she informed him, remembering the artless, innocent way he had offered to be a substitute brother and run up the Zig-Zag with her one day, 'sensitive too. I can understand how deeply the implication of his...of Mr Franklin's will must have affected him. He must love Westhangar just as much as John Franklin did. Poor lamb.'

They both stood in silence again. Then Chris spoke, his voice low, thoughtful, his eyes never leaving her face.

'We must have a talk one day,' he said at last, 'when we can find the time.' Then, with a light laugh, he added, 'as you seem to know more about some of my parishioners than I do! And...,' as he turned away towards his car, 'perhaps I could come and see you on Gwen's horse one of these days.'

Heather mounted the stairs to her haven above the horses' stalls, her mind in a whirl as she tried to process all the surprising events and emotions of the afternoon. She knew what her next task should be...to trawl through the old Franklin family trees to see if there *were* any blood relations who might be entitled to inherit. But supposing she found one, distantly related but with no connection with or knowledge of Westhangar Hall? That would be worse than finding no trace of anyone at all!

Fuelled by Elsie's tea, with her head in a whirl, she went straight to her diary, anxious to record all her thoughts and feelings whilst they were still fresh in her mind. For some reason, however, she found it hard to concentrate. As she tried to pin down the reason for the low-level bubble of excitement disturbing her thoughts, it was Chris's voice she kept hearing, their last conversation re-playing itself, unbidden, repeatedly.

'Well, Craig,' she wrote, scribbling fast as the biro seemed to have acquired a life of its own, 'I've a funny feeling Kathie might be right. Well-mannered (yes!); domesticated (possibly); holy (probably); sympathetic (certainly); handsome? (well, good-looking anyway) and I like his silvery hair. So, what do you think, Craig? Am I too old to fall in love?'

Chapter Nine

After the revelations and surprises of the last couple of weeks, July arrived, coinciding with a period of calm warm weather and few interruptions which gave Heather the chance to concentrate on trying to find any evidence that might connect John Franklin with his namesake, the celebrated Sir John Franklin of North-West Passage fame, but in vain. When relaying the disappointing news to Gwen over the breakfast table one morning, Heather was surprised to see an expression of exasperation pass over her face.

'I did try to tell John that he was wasting his time,' she almost snapped, 'but he seemed obsessed, so I just let it go. I suppose it was his father's naval background that excited his curiosity. He was a Chief Petty Officer, but I've forgotten on which ship – that and having the same name – but the amount of time he spent closeted in the study chasing rainbows, when I wanted to ask him something or go out together really, *really* annoyed me. And he could turn quite silent and stubborn if he was disturbed. And all for nothing...'

Heather was taken aback by the sudden venom in Gwen's voice and expression and her surprise must have shown in her face as Gwen almost immediately recollected herself and regarded the younger woman with interest and her voice grew softer. 'But tell me, Heather, are you making any progress with sorting out his papers? Any surprises or shocks? Any close relations who might want to march into Westhangar and claim it for his or her own?'

Heather wondered whether to disclose to her employer that, in fact, a great deal of her work apart from anything pertaining to the Walled Garden and the photograph albums was proving repetitive and, frankly, rather dull. But she was enjoying her life at Westhangar Hall so much that she had no desire to see it curtailed so, even if she had to feign enormous interest in her husband's unexceptional ancestors, she would gladly do it. And her recent discovery of Alicia's letter had made up for a good deal of plodding through old wills, covenants and codicils which, so far, had failed to throw up any connection with his hoped-for illustrious antecedent or any close blood relations, but there were still sheafs of old documents to go through.

'Did he ever mention a great-great aunt, a relative by marriage called Alicia Franklin?' Heather asked by way of a reply. 'She left a fascinating account of her life in Australia during the Gold Rush in the 1850s and I believe she's buried here in Selborne, though I haven't had the chance to check all the Franklin graves yet.'

'Was that the letter you were trying to decipher a week or two ago?' asked Kathie, reaching for another piece of toast and addressing Gwen, 'scribble, scribble, all crossed out – but this genius managed it.'

'Alicia,' Gwen repeated slowly, passing Kathie the marmalade, 'yes...yes, I believe I do remember him mentioning her once as I told him I thought the Gold Rush was in North America and he told me about this other one in Australia. I don't *think* he ever deciphered it. I have to admit, Heather, I found it hard to take much of an interest in his family, wrong of me, I know, but that's why I couldn't work up the enthusiasm to carry on with his research.'

Elsie appeared and lifted another pot of coffee off the hotplate, filling their cups before sitting down herself.

'Couldn't help overhearing, Miss Heather,' she said with a glance at Gwen, who nodded for her to carry on, 'but I've seen that grave, not easy to read the words as it's all overgrown with moss an' that. But it's such a pretty name...Alicia,' she let the name roll round her tongue. 'Alicia...now, why couldn't I have been christened Alicia instead of boring old Elsie?'

'Well, they're not that different,' remarked Heather, 'So Elsie – or Alicia – would you be able to show me where her grave is sometime, save me getting my trousers covered in mud?'

Elsie looked at Gwen enquiringly. Gwen frowned and considered carefully for a moment.

'Do you think it could wait until Saturday, Heather, when Doris comes? I was really hoping Elsie might be able to give the Berlin china on the dining-room table a wash today and there's a pile of ironing to be done, as well as my bedroom and bathroom. And tomorrow I thought it might be time for her to give a quick sweep and dust round your flat. What about you, Kathie, anything need doing in your rooms?'

'Not that you'd notice,' Kathie replied, 'I quite like a bit of dust, cobwebs and a few crumbs. Reminds me of home. By the way, was that Adrian I saw just now tearing off somewhere on his bike? He looked remarkably cheerful… and if I may say so Gwen, you're looking a whole lot better and brighter too.'

Gwen smiled, nodding, and, glancing at her, Heather was amazed to see how much the smile lit up her face. She must have been a real beauty in her younger days.

'We've asked Mr Grundy to look into the circumstances of the will again,' she said, glancing across at Heather, 'following up your suggestion. His business partner, a bright young woman, Miss Hibberd, is giving it the once over just to see if anything can be done, no promises mind but… So, yes, I'm feeling cautiously optimistic. Now, Elsie, if you want to go off with Heather on Saturday, you'd better get your skates on.'

As they rose from the table, Heather had to avoid looking at Elsie, hiding a smile of her own as she noticed a pronounced pout of irritation and annoyance cross her face.

'Slave driver,' Kathie mouthed to Heather as they entered the hall, 'what's got into the old girl? She's not usually so unhelpful. And Elsie works her socks off in that big house. Anyway, if you've got a spare hour this afternoon, how about another riding lesson?'

Over the next few days, they found time for a couple more lessons, still in the paddock with Heather mastering 'rising to the trot' and, biting her lips with determination, she found she could control Conker sufficiently well to go round the paddock at the walk, trot and a very brief canter, turn to the left and right and bring her to a controlled stop all on her own, leaving her glowing with satisfaction. Stewart came once, smiling broadly at her improving efforts and clapped her as she slithered off, a little more gracefully than before.

'Soon be able to come with me down the village or on the Common,' said Kathie, smiling broadly, 'you're a quick learner. It'll be a godsend to me not to have to exercise both horses separately. Next stop, the Horse of the Year Show at Olympia.'

As they unsaddled the horses after her third lesson, they heard a call from beyond the fence and Heather felt her heart give a jump as she saw Chris waving at them over the gate. He looked quite different from the last time she had seen him, sporting an open-necked shirt and a pair of well-worn jeans, a panama hat perched jauntily on his head.

'Must be having an afternoon off,' muttered Kathie as they strolled over to see what he wanted, 'looks almost human, doesn't he?'

'Have I missed all the fun?' he asked, grinning at the two perspiring women, before opening the gate for them and closing it carefully. Kathie gave him a scornful look.

'Heather's coming on a treat,' she informed him, 'we'll soon be trotting down together to the Vicarage to disturb your peace. She's a natural.'

'Well, let me know when you're coming,' he said, taking off his hat and fanning his face with it, 'and we'll have a cup of tea in the garden. I'm sure we could find us all some scones or something.'

We? For one dreadful moment, Heather thought he must have a live-in girlfriend – was that allowed for vicars? – and

Kathie couldn't resist a shout of laughter at her crestfallen expression.

'He only means Doris!' she said, 'Elsie's indispensable sister. She does for Chris twice a week, cleans in the Wakes Museum for another two, Dr Hawkins on Friday, then comes to Gwen on Saturdays. She has Sunday off – but even then, she goes to church with Elsie and Gwen.'

'Yes, my faithful few,' sighed Chris, 'all good voices too – just wish Stewart would come back, he had a very pleasant strong voice, helped drown out some of my more enthusiastic but off-key ones.'

'Busy woman, Doris,' remarked Heather, hoping her lack of devotion would not be brought up – then, after a moment's thought, she decided to bring it up herself, just so there could be no misunderstanding and glanced nervously at Chris.

'I have to admit,' she said, 'I do go to church occasionally, enjoy singing hymns, carols especially. I love looking round churches, their architecture, stained-glass windows, choral music, religious art. But...,' she paused for a moment, feeling both Kathie's and Chris's eyes resting on her...then, in a rush of courage, she carried on.

'But – I may as well tell you – I'm ninety-five percent atheist, simply can't bring myself to believe in things I can't see or touch.' Chris gave a slow smile and a low, reassuring laugh.

'Five percent is enough for me,' he assured her, smiling, 'and I wouldn't be surprised if that's the measure of belief of most of my parishioners, although they don't have the courage to tell me,' he added quietly glancing at her with an appraising look. They all fell silent for a moment as they walked together towards the house, where Chris waved his goodbyes.

'Well, that's scuppered your chances,' muttered Kathie crossly, frowning at Heather, 'What did you have to say that for? I mean, how can a vicar marry an atheist?'

'Who said anything about marrying?' retorted Heather, 'I've only just met the bloke. There must be a huge queue of frustrated widows and spinsters, all good Christian women panting to walk up the aisle with him. Now...here's Elsie, rushing about as usual. I wonder what she wants.'

Armed with a dustpan and brush, yellow duster and cleaning cloths Elsie spent a happy half-hour clattering round Heather's tiny flat, even standing on a chair to dust the top of the wardrobe – which, judging by the cascade of debris that landed on the floor hadn't been visited for months, if not years. As she clambered down to sweep it up, Elsie gave a cry of triumph, shaking the dust off a tiny, shiny object, which she handed carefully to Heather as if she had just discovered the Crown Jewels. To Heather, the discovery was equally valuable.

'Looks like the key to Mr Franklin's diary!' she cried, 'Elsie, you're a star! Shall we give it a go?'

She fetched the diary from underneath a pile of yellowing newspaper articles, fitted the key into the lock and tried to turn it. To her dismay it refused to budge whichever way she moved it.

'Bunged up with the dust of ages, I suppose,' she muttered crossly, reluctant to force it in case it broke inside the lock. Elsie, with her store of practical common sense, came to the rescue.

'Got a bit of oil or summing, Miss Heather?' she asked, and Heather went to look in the kitchen without much hope but emerged waving a bottle with a minute amount of olive oil lurking in the bottom.

'Perfect,' said Elsie. Turning it upside down and sticking her finger into the yellow liquid, she smeared it onto the key and round the lock.

'Try again,' she suggested, and Heather carefully inserted the slippery key into the hole, gave it a wiggle or two and was rewarded to hear it click and the diary fell open. She turned the pages eagerly, then, pressing her lips together with annoyance and disappointment, she looked at Elsie with a frown.

'Damn the thing!' she uttered loudly, 'you won't believe this! Look at it – it's in code! Well, some of it. I can read the first few pages but the rest...!' Elsie looked, turning over a page or two, shaking her head.

'Just like his great-great Aunt Alicia!' she exclaimed, 'making it as 'ard as possible for anyone else to read it. Think you can decipher it, Miss Heather?'

'If it's a simple substitution code, which I hope it is, there should be a key somewhere, a written one I mean, to help crack it. Of course, he probably knew it by heart...' She sighed impatiently, looking at Elsie with a frown.

'He must have had some dark secrets that he didn't want his wife or Adrian – or anyone – to know,' she murmured thoughtfully, shutting the little book again and carefully locking it. 'Thanks, Elsie, if it hadn't been for you, I doubt if it would ever have been found. Oh...and that reminds me.... I'm still hoping to find another key, a big one that'll fit Alicia's trunk. Amazing to think that it's been sitting there for well over a hundred years and nobody's thought to open it.'

'Don't suppose Mr Franklin or his father before 'im wanted to be bothered with a whole lot of ladies' underwear,' suggested Elsie mischievously, 'especially if it all needed washing! But I'll keep an eye out, Miss Heather, don't you worry,' and with that she gathered up her brushes and dusters and clattered down the staircase, chuckling as she went.

What words or phrases could Mr Franklin possibly have used to construct his code, she wondered over the next couple of weeks? People sometimes used favourite proverbs or a string of names. She tried various combinations of John, Gwen, Adrian, Stewart, even Champion and Conker, then tried Westhangar, Selborne, Gilbert White, Alton...all hopeless, nothing matched. She stared and stared at the tiny writing, hoping to discover a pattern, or series of repetitions that might give her 'ing' or 'the' or 'and' to give her a start...to no avail. She'd have to think, *hard*. I'll have an inspiration one day, she told herself and then it will all become clear.

Half an hour later, as Heather and Kathie were enjoying a cup of tea and trying to think of any likely phrases that might help to crack Mr Franklin's code, Elsie appeared again, bustling up the stairs as if the devil were after her.

'This a good time to come and see Alicia's grave?' she gasped. 'Gwen doesn't need me until 4 o'clock so I've got a bit of free time.'

'Why not?' agreed Heather, turning to Kathie, who shrugged her shoulders but could find no excuse not to accompany them.

'Even though mooching around a graveyard's not really my idea of a good time...but I'll come anyway, keep an eye on you both.'

Heather raced up her stairs to collect a notebook and caught up the others at the end of the drive. At the same time the postman's van drew up beside her and, winding down the window he waved a letter which she stuffed into her trouser pocket. From Sally, hurray! Probably her reply to the invitation Gwen had extended to her to come and stay with her mother during the summer. Although dying to rip it open and read it straightaway, she resisted the temptation and turned into the church gate with the others.

They trooped across the grassy churchyard, smiling and waving at a group of visitors being given the Gilbert White tour by one of the Wakes Museum staff and made their way towards a neglected, rather gloomy area, opposite Stewart's family's graves, shaded by small yew trees. The tombstones here were mostly askew, lichen-covered, with ivy creeping across the names but Elsie led them unhesitatingly towards one of the oldest and began to clear the long grass and moss away.

'There,' she announced, dusting off her hands, 'there's the lady 'erself. Can you read that, Miss Heather?'

Heather bent closer, screwing up her eyes, speaking slowly as she made out the badly eroded words. '*Alicia Rosemary Franklin, 8 February 1793 – 23 May 1853. Beloved wife of*

John. Home again where she belongs.' Goodness, she said, turning to Kathie, 'that's only a year after she sent that newsy, chatty letter home with all the news about the goldfields...I wonder how she died.'

'She were only sixty,' said Elsie thoughtfully, 'but same age as a lot of the other poor souls in 'ere.'

'No National Health, no vaccinations,' added Kathie, 'and perhaps the Australian climate had affected her health.'

'She did say in her letter that both she and her husband were feeling the strain of the heat and the hard work, even though their pitch was quite a productive one...and many other prospectors died out there without ever profiting from their labours. Then the long sea-voyage to get back home,' put in Heather, with a deep sigh, 'goodness... was it worth it? But at least she made it back to Selborne just in time to see her homeland once more. I wonder where her husband is buried, must be near here – so long as he made it back as well.'

'Same grave!' Elsie announced in triumph, after scraping more grass off the bottom of the stone, uncovering another, barely visible inscription. 'Oh, no!' she cried, clapping her hand to her mouth, 'look, Miss Heather!'

Again, Heather squatted down to read the words. '*John Frederick Franklin, devoted husband of the above, 12 June 1790–30 May 1853. Reunited in the arms of God our Saviour.*...Just one week later!' Kathie, her expression severe, sounded almost accusing as she gazed at the grave again.

'Well,' she announced, 'all I can say is that He didn't save them long enough to enjoy their hard-earned wealth, jolly unfair, I call it. I suppose their undeserving descendants got to spend it all on riotous living. I'm off back now, Heather. Gwen's cooking again tonight, isn't she? She must be feeling a lot better, that's three times this week.'

Heather nodded, hoping her relief at the thought of a decent supper – Kathie had been right to admit to being not much of a cook – did not show too much in her face and after scribbling down the inscription in her notebook, she and Elsie took their time over wandering back to the Hall, meeting the eager tourist group they had seen earlier, on their way to climb the Zig-Zag.

'Larvely village!' two or three of them exclaimed enthusiastically, 'aren't you lucky to live here! We visited Jane Austen's house this morning, you know, in Chawton, so charming...we even saw the little table where she wrote some of her books.'

Heather could not resist telling them that she had lived nearby when she was a girl. 'We often passed that cottage on our way into Alton,' she said smiling, 'and my ambition was to be a writer like her when I grew up...never was, though.'

'And I used to live in the same village,' chimed in Elsie, not to be outdone, 'We came to Selborne on a school trip once but the only thing I remember was that Gilbert White had a tortoise called Timothy, same as my brother.'

'I'd forgotten you and Doris had a brother,' Heather remarked as the group moved on, 'where is he now?'

'Doing rather well for 'isself, actually,' answered Elsie, her cheeks reddening with pride, 'got a job with a coach and removal company down in Alton soon as he left school. Did so well 'e moved on to a garage in Winchester, where they trained 'im up to be a proper mechanic-like. After five years he got 'is Public Service Vehicle Licence and 'e was such a promising lad that, after another few years 'e was took on as a partner. My Mum was so proud, it was embarrassing 'earing 'er talk. Married a lovely girl too, Betty, two little kiddies now. But, hey, Miss Heather, whatever 'appened to your lovely brother, right mischief 'e was, always teasing us girls.'

As they walked on, Heather told Elsie the sobering story of Craig, killed by falling rocks in the Rocky Mountains.

'Oh, dear,' sympathised Elsie, her hand to her mouth, 'can't believe it! I'm so, so sorry. So now you got no-one. No aunts, no uncles...'

Heather felt in her pocket and pulled out Sally's letter with a smile, waving it in the air.

'I've got the best person in the world,' she corrected Elsie, 'a lovely, clever, good-natured daughter, who thinks it's her mission in life to keep her old Mum happy. And...,' she paused a moment as she felt tears pricking her eyelids and blinked rapidly, 'and...if Gwen can agree on a date, she'll be coming to stay here for two or three weeks...quite soon. Can't wait!'

Gwen seemed remarkably animated when Heather broached the subject of Sally's visit at suppertime, only regretful that she wouldn't be there when she arrived.

'I'm off for a little holiday,' she informed Heather and Kathie coyly, her eyes shining with anticipation, 'such a long time since I've been able to get away. First, John needed a lot of nursing...then there was the funeral...then all the trouble about his will and trying to get in touch with Adrian. Doctor Hawkins has agreed it would do me good to have a change of scene. But now,' she beamed round at the two women, tucking into lasagne and vegetables from the garden, 'I've got you two, Stewart and Elsie and Doris to look after things here. I'll only be a phone call away if there's a crisis, so I can go away with a clear conscience. Adrian's coming with me for the first two or three days but then he'll be back here after that to keep an eye on things.'

Heather, whose heart had sunk when she heard that Adrian was going with his mother, cheered up at these words. Of course, there was absolutely no guarantee that Gwen's son and her daughter would take a fancy to each other ... but where was the harm in dreaming?

Kathie walked back to the stables with Heather, Dizzy and Dotty at her heels, on her way to take a last look at Champion and Conker in the paddock before bedtime.

'If you ask me,' she remarked confidentially, glancing back at the house to make sure she was not overheard, 'I wouldn't be surprised if our lady of the manor wasn't off to meet lover-boy. She had that sort of lustful gleam in her eye, and I've never seen her look so...so alive.'

Heather stopped at the foot of her stairs, gazing at Kathie with astonishment.

'Lover-boy?' she repeated, blinking in confusion, 'whoever can you mean?'

Kathie pursed her lips, narrowing her eyes.

'Well, Adrian's real father might still be alive and kicking somewhere...and she might still be holding a torch for him. Elsie overheard a conversation she was having on the phone a couple of days ago and told me she sounded almost girlishly excited, was all flushed up and looked quite guilty when she realised Elsie might have heard her. You never know...stranger things have happened. And even though she must be pushing sixty, she's still a remarkably handsome woman. Think about it,' she said as they parted company, 'it's a much more exciting prospect than those dusty old ancestors you've been digging up over the last few months. Could do with a bit of scandal to liven this place up a bit!'

She went off laughing, leaving Heather staring after her, her mouth half-open with amazement.

Chapter Ten

'Dear Craig,' Heather wrote a few evenings later, 'Really excited now as Sally's coming to stay with me for a couple of weeks while Gwen is away. Kathie thinks she's got a not-so-secret lover somewhere, Gwen I mean, but I'm not so sure. I'd be pleased to find out it's true, not too sure how happy the Franklins' marriage was... and if it really is Adrian's father, there might be a happy ending for all three of them. This doesn't solve the problem of who the estate will belong to after Gwen dies, but she's not yet sixty and this is the twentieth century, she must have years left before the inheritance becomes a serious issue.'

Not like the unfortunate Alicia and husband John, Heather mused, who must have had barely more than a few weeks to enjoy the return to their roots after three gruelling years in Australia. She would have to try and obtain a copy of their death-certificates to find out how they died, so close together in time. In the meantime, she had this infuriating code to crack so that she could uncover what secrets Mr Franklin was so determined to keep hidden.

She needed to find a phrase, a saying, a proverb perhaps, that contained every letter of the alphabet. As she tried lines from well-known nursery rhymes or first lines from famous books, even verses from hymns, she suddenly remembered something they had learned to chant at school about a fox and a hare when they were learning how to do joined up writing and needed to demonstrate that they could write all letters in legible, cursive script.

But...how did it go? Quick fox? Brown hare? Where did the 'z' come in? Lazy...that was it! Lazy ... not hare... dog, dog!...

and quick fox. She stood up and looked out of the window where Stewart was leaving the house carrying a suitcase, which he proceeded to place carefully in Gwen's car. Of course - tomorrow was the start of her holiday and she and Kathie would need to parade for an early breakfast so that she could give them her final instructions.

Lazy brown dog...no, that wasn't it. In a flash the entire sentence came to her, and she squeaked with success, dashing to her notebooks and writing it down before she could forget.

The quick brown fox jumps over the lazy dog! How could she possibly have forgotten, considering the number of times she must have written it out as a child, trying to get each letter perfectly formed and spaced, with downstrokes and upstrokes all the same length? Such practice was frowned on now, Sally had never had to do it, it was all free expression and scribbling words down quickly to keep the flow of inspiration coming! But now... she had something to work on and if that failed, she'd give up and Mr Franklin's secrets would have to remain, literally, a closed book.

She took the diary to bed with her that night and began by reading the first few pages, written in ordinary handwriting, as she sat propped up against her pillows. You couldn't call it thrilling but interesting in its way, the everyday events of a young man in charge of a thriving estate, crop-yields, milk-yields, how many fields needed cutting for silage, the number of eggs from the hens and ducks each day, the cost of barbed wire, creosote, fencing posts, mash and corn with just the occasional reminder to himself to 'telephone Mother' or 'Gwen coming over tomorrow, tidy up.' Must be when they were courting, Heather surmised, feeling a little self-conscious as she read snatches of their blossoming romance, then smiled as she read the words 'Tomorrow, I shall be a married man! Goodbye bachelorhood for ever!'

There were only a few scribbled notes about the wedding, '...it rained...the bridesmaids' dresses got wet and one of them was sick...,' and about the honeymoon in Majorca, 'gorgeous weather, wall to wall sunshine…hope Stewart's remembering to shut the henhouses every evening…' and so on until, a couple of weeks later came the joyful entry, 'carried my darling over the threshold today, the beginning of our life here together. I must be the luckiest man in the world.'

Heather sighed and pressed her lips together, leaning back on the pillows both saddened and amused at the optimism and joy of a young, wealthy couple starting out on married life in such splendid surroundings with their golden futures stretching out before them. They must have thought, as perhaps most newly married couples feel, "now that we're together how can anything go wrong?"

How and why did it go wrong? What could John Franklin have done to make his young, attractive wife fly back to the arms of a former admirer so soon after their marriage? Did he neglect her, too busy with the farms to pay attention to her needs? Was he violent? A drunk? Surely Gwen would have been aware of any such defects in his character well before their wedding. And from what he had written in his diary so far, he gave every impression of being the archetypical young man in love, Romeo to her Juliet.

After a few more pages of mundane reports of village affairs, meetings with his bank-manager and so on, she came to a page, about three months into their marriage where his writing grew less legible, written in a hurry or else as a result of excitement or distress.

'Been offered the chance of a few weeks away, too tempting and lucrative to pass up, just a pity I can't take Gwennie with me, she'd love the sun. Have to leave Stewart in charge.' Then followed a list of jobs to be done before his departure, clothes to be taken, which consisted mainly of sportswear and swimwear, train and ferry times and a short list of phone numbers and addresses. For the 'wish you were here' postcards, Heather surmised, then, turning to the next page she saw with a sinking of the heart that the following pages were in that dratted code.

I'll see now if I've guessed the right key, she thought, if I simply write down the alphabet and the equivalent letters beside it, it shouldn't be too onerous to decipher, just extremely time-consuming. With her eyes closing and the prospect of having to get up earlier than usual next day she locked the diary and put it away until she could find enough spare time to carry on the work.

She awoke next day to the patter of rain on the roof, so threw her anorak over her shoulders as she walked across the courtyard to join the others for breakfast. Gwen had already had hers, taken upstairs for her to her room by Elsie (who had come in early) but nevertheless darted here and there asking where things were, reminding them of things she wanted doing while she was away, looking at her watch in something of a state of agitated excitement. Elsie had volunteered to run Gwen to Alton station to catch the Waterloo train in her own car and, just as she was about to drive off, she leaned out of the window to say she'd forgotten to bring Gwen's breakfast tray downstairs and would Heather or Kathie mind doing it for her. As they all waved goodbye, Heather told Kathie she'd run up for it while Kathie got ready to take Champion out for his morning exercise and she'd do the washing up as well, no problem.

And it will give me the chance to see upstairs, Heather thought, that old desire just to see 'round the corner' or 'what was on the other side' assailing her again as she mounted the curving staircase, the walls dotted with ancestral portraits and old prints of Rome, Florence, Athens, Constantinople and Jerusalem, testimony to a former Franklin's Grand Tour. The landing was long, wide and softly carpeted with several heavy oak doors facing her. Boldly she opened one after another and through the third she glimpsed an unmade bed, heavy pink curtains half-drawn and a tumble of clothes on the floor as well as the breakfast tray balanced none too safely on a bedside table.

'What a mess – poor Elsie,' she thought and glanced at the coloured prints of Victorian ladies taking tea or standing at the harpsichord, simpering at the artist with faces of peaches and cream, swathed in lacy shawls and wide-brimmed hats tied down with flimsy scarves. How the other half used to live, she thought, then, as she turned to leave, she stood stock-still, transfixed by a modern portrait on the wall beside the door ... and almost dropped the tray and all its contents onto the floor.

Putting it down carefully on a nearby chair, she forced herself to face the portrait again, her heart racing and legs shaking as her mouth went dry. Young, virile, a humorous quirk to his mouth, chestnut hair waving off a wide forehead and...oh, yes... there it was as she feared...a cheeky cleft to his chin. The room suddenly darkened as she felt a wave of faintness sweep over her as she stared...and stared...into the face of Skip!

There could be no mistake. This was just as she remembered him, leaping over the naval cadets' backs by the swimming pool, swinging, setting and executing energetic reels- of -three in an Eightsome Reel, then puffing and panting as he regained his breath. And then...out into the moonlit garden, looking up at the stars as he laid her so carefully down on the grass, massaging her body with rough, brown hands until she writhed and moaned, pulling him down, kneading his back, forgetting everything as they moved together, sighing and laughing when it was over, longing, longing for it to happen all over again.

But...it never did. Skip went away with the cadets the very next morning on their tour around the Mediterranean while she returned to her job, disappointed beyond measure that she would never see him again. A few weeks later she found herself hastily married to Jerome and a few months later still she became mother to her precious daughter...Sally.

Oh God! Sally! Heather clutched at her head, overcome with sudden fear and horror. Gwen and probably Kathie, Elsie, Doris, Stewart and half the population of Selborne – but especially Gwen – couldn't fail to see the resemblance, it was plainly, devastatingly obvious. What, in Heaven's name could she do?

She tottered to the bed and sat on the edge, staring at Skip totally bereft of coherent thought. Should she stop Sally from coming? She'd be here in three days' time, far too late really to put her off – and how could she possibly explain why? Phone and tell her to dye her hair? That glorious red-gold hair? No. That would be sacrilege. Perhaps she should run away? That was a possibility...but could she bear to leave this place just as she was beginning to feel rooted to it? What...could...she... possibly...DO!

She made her way slowly and carefully down the stairs, washed up Gwen's cup, bowl and plate then reheated some coffee in the kitchen, drinking it down, hot, strong and sweet. Then, as the rain had stopped, she went out into the garden to try and calm down...to calm down and to think- *think*.

What would her father have suggested? She already knew the answer. 'Deal with it,' he'd have said, 'just...deal with it... if the problem won't go away, *do* something about it or it'll only get worse.'

Yes – but how? *How*? It was worse already and couldn't get any more so. She needed to get out and walk, think, if possible and try, try to make a plan. Leaving a note for Elsie and Kathie on the kitchen table she went back to the stables, changed into wellington-boots and made for the footpath onto the Hangar, squelching through wet dog's mercury and ivy, fending off rain-sodden branches with her arms until she reached a clear area from where she could stare down on Westhangar Hall and let the pent-up tears flow freely without fear of being seen or heard. Now she knew how Adrian must have felt when faced with a situation for which he was totally unprepared.

How could she have foreseen such a disaster? She'd always known that, somewhere in the world, there was a man who knew nothing about the daughter he had sired, and she had experienced surges of guilt on that account. But...why here?

And why now? How could she possibly have even guessed at such a remote possibility? Seeing that portrait had revived all those feelings of joy, regret, exhilaration and fear that had accompanied that unforgettable encounter more than twenty years ago and she realised that, perhaps hidden even from herself, she had harboured the idea that she might, one day, meet him again.

But now…he would never know that he had 'a child of his body'. How that archaic phrase stuck in her head! – and she would never be able to tell him – *never*. As her tears dried, she felt a great urge to visit the churchyard, just to look at the grave of John Franklin and tell him of the child he would never now know. Perhaps the question of what she should do next would, in some way, become clearer once she had shared her anguish with the person who had given her her daughter.

Feeling calmer now, she stumbled along the pathway that led to the Wishing Stone and made her way carefully down the slippery Zig-Zag. As she reached the bottom and approached the road, she saw the back view of Kathie on Champion trotting calmly along in the direction of the house and breathed a sigh of relief that she hadn't met her a few minutes earlier when she might have had to make cheerful conversation when all she wanted was a little quiet time and space to settle her whirling thoughts.

She stood for a moment before the stone memorial not far from that of his antecedents Alicia and his namesake John and read the words she had read many weeks before which, even then, had almost caused her to shed tears – and that was before she knew hardly anything about him.

Sacred to the memory of John Laurence Franklin
Who departed this life
4 February 1984, aged 59
Fondly remembered and
Always in our thoughts

What *was* she going to do? Telling Sally would be no problem, she'd think the whole situation a huge joke and she'd be thrilled to see the portrait of her father. Kathie would give one of her horse laughs and smack her on the back and accuse her of having known all along of her dalliance with Mr Franklin. Elsie and Doris – after their initial horrified shock – would see the funny side and would take a warm, sympathetic interest in Sally. Stewart – who could know what Stewart would make of it all? No – it was Gwen, poor Gwen who would have the greatest shock to discover that the husband, 'fondly remembered' and 'always in our thoughts' had been only too ready to forget his new bride in the heat of the moment and the warmth of a starry Mediterranean night ... and with this... this *person* she had so readily invited into her home and the bosom of her family!

And yet... as they had all heard during Gwen's tearful speech recently, explaining why Adrian was not her husband's heir, she had admitted to having a serious affair with 'lover boy' as Kathie liked to refer to him, whereas she and Skip had had the briefest of flings and she'd had no idea he was married. But I didn't make any effort to find out, she reminded herself sternly ... and to be honest, if I'd known, would it have made any difference? And if I'd known that, years later, my new job would bring me into close contact with his widow...would that have made a difference?

Most certainly. She'd have run a mile to avoid causing pain to Gwen...or anyone. But now, quite by chance, she had landed herself in the very middle of an unholy mess, deeply embroiled in the problems of this attractive but unfortunate family and simply had no idea how to extricate herself.

Unable to restrain her tears, she stumbled over to a seat a few yards away, took out her soggy handkerchief and putting her head in her hands tried to stifle her sobs, panic threatening to overwhelm her as, perhaps for the first time in her life, she felt helpless with absolutely no idea what she was going to do.

Aware, through her tears, of a shadow crossing her body, she looked up fearfully to see Chris standing in front of her and attempted to rise and escape, desperate to hide her distress. Putting his hands on her shoulders, he pushed her gently back than sat beside her, saying nothing, not even looking at her until she had searched her pockets for another handkerchief and made a better job of mopping her wet face.

'If there's anything you want to tell me – in confidence – I'm here,' he said softly as she cast her eyes down to the ground and sniffed hard before answering.

'I...I simply can't tell anyone...' she hiccupped, 'it's all too...too difficult...and complicated...and there's nothing I can do, *nothing*.'

Chris slipped a comforting arm around her shaking shoulders, holding her until her breath steadied and she dared to look him in the face again.

'It's not your daughter, is it?' he asked, sudden concern in his expression, 'she's not...not hurt...or anything?'

Heather almost managed a weak smile, shaking her head.

'No...she's not hurt...nothing like that...but...but it does concern her...and Gwen...and Adrian...and, oh! Everything! Everybody!'

Chris remained silent but, glancing at him, Heather noticed that his eyes were closed and his lips gently moving. When he opened his eyes again, Heather cleared her throat and managed to speak.

'You've been praying for me again, haven't you?' she murmured, and he smiled, taking her damp hand in his and giving it a little shake.

'Do you mind?' he replied, the beginnings of a slight smile on his lips and Heather turned her head away to hide the sudden confusion that had swept over her.

'Not at all,' she muttered in reply, 'I'm going to need all the help I can get...to get through...the next few days...weeks... months.'

Chris looked doubly concerned at the desperate tone of her voice, then, as if he hardly meant it, he spoke again.

'I'm not going to pry into your private troubles,' he said thoughtfully, 'but...I couldn't help noticing that you were looking at John Franklin's grave...as if...as if...' He paused, looking away from her, 'as if that had something to do with your distress.'

Heather sighed a shuddering sigh, then a surge of courage rose through her as she stared into the distance and, almost as if she were listening to another person, she heard herself speak.

'It has everything to do with it, Chris and you're going to be shocked, perhaps horrified by the reason ... but I must tell someone.'

'Tell away,' he said, shortly, 'that's what I'm here for.' But even he, who had heard every kind of story in his career as a clergyman, was unprepared for her next words, spoken low, hesitantly.

'I've only just discovered that I met Mr Franklin over twenty years ago when I was working abroad. I only knew him as Skip – Skipper – just the name naval cadets give their leaders or elders and never knew his real one or who he really was until...' She paused once more to look away and heave a deep, shuddering sigh. 'Until this morning when I saw a portrait of him in Gwen's bedroom. The terrible thing, Chris, is...I knew him for less than six hours as he and the lads he was with moved on the next day and I never saw him again. But... but months later – nine months later – I had my darling daughter Sally, who looks exactly like him, and, 'she heaved another sigh which turned into a sob, 'she's coming here to stay in three days' time.'

As she had predicted, Chris, for all his worldly wisdom and experience was genuinely taken aback by this admission and could find no words to reply for several minutes.

'Does she know?' he asked at last, 'does Sally know?'

'She knows that Jerome, my husband, who most gallantly married me to save me from disgrace as he called it – and it *was* a disgrace in the early sixties, not like now when almost anything goes – was not her real father and accepted it as she accepts most things, with complete equanimity. He was a wonderful father to her and husband to me. When I did finally tell her, in a letter, a few years after Jerome died, of her real origins, she just hugged me and said she didn't care how she was conceived, she was just grateful that she had been born at all. She loves life,' Heather murmured, her face softening as she thought of Sally's merry laugh and generous nature, 'but... how can I tell her about Mr Franklin? And how will she be able to face the people who knew him here in the village who will surely guess the truth?'

Chris rose from the bench and held out his hand to her and she followed him meekly towards the church gate.

'Don't do anything rash,' he said earnestly, 'do nothing for the moment. After all, who will really suffer once they know? Gwen possibly, for a while...Adrian? Probably not at all, he might even find it reassuring to discover that people he regards as almost middle-aged, were young once. And, Heather, my dear, there may be gossip for a month or two... yes, there certainly will and some old biddies will pretend to be shocked. In my experience however, I've found that people are far too concerned with their own affairs – and I mean that in both senses of the word – to worry about something that happened years ago. And,' he added mischievously, 'if your vicar isn't shocked, why should they be? If you like, I could drop a word in at Westhangar Hall next time I'm passing, just to prepare the ground a little – but not if you'd rather I didn't.'

Heather bit her lips as she gave this suggestion some thought, then nodded slowly.

'That would be very kind, Chris,' she murmured, glancing up at him gratefully, 'not sure I've got the guts to confront them all myself.'

'Go home now then,' he said briskly, 'and leave me to think of what you should do next. I'll be in touch.'

Heather left the churchyard feeling as if a tremendous load had been lifted from her shoulders and her heart. Why had she worried so much? Chris was right. Who would care two hoots about her past life if she could find the courage to face the world, her head held high? So long as Gwen...that was the sticking point. How would Gwen take the news that her husband's unknown, unacknowledged daughter was coming to stay here in Selborne in her house...in three days' time!

Chapter Eleven

Even though Chris's wise words were comforting and encouraging, Heather still needed time to calm her battered nerves before having to face anyone she knew. She approached Westhangar Hall nervously, relieved to see that Kathie and Conker were missing and there was no sign of Elsie or Stewart. She darted into the kitchen and amended the note she had left for them then went up to her study to fetch her car-keys.

'You'd better start first time,' she lectured Frog, realising that it had been some weeks since she had been driving and turned the key. Thankfully, it needed only a few gentle touches on the accelerator to set the engine throbbing nicely and she turned the car and slipped slowly down the drive, winding the window down the better to inhale the summer scents of meadowsweet and woodland as she approached the main road.

Now, she sighed...where should she go? Home! That was her first instinctive thought, even though it hadn't been her home for more than twenty years and she'd intended to wait until Sally was with her. She just needed the comforting sight of old familiar places, however, to settle the turmoil that still filled her brain, kept her heart thumping and her body trembling as she thought over the shocks she had sustained since seeing that portrait of Mr Franklin early that morning.

Must drive carefully, she lectured herself, keep your mind on the road. It was impossible, however, to block out the recurring image of Skip's face staring at her from Gwen's bedroom wall and the memory of Chris's reassuring hand on hers, the tone of his voice and the assurance that, somehow, he would help her through this emotional crisis. Half-way up the road she saw and heard the steam train, restored by enthusiasts, roaring and puffing past to her right beyond the fields, that train she had taken so often to get into the town.

Oh, I wish I were a child again, she moaned. Suddenly overcome with waves of sadness and nostalgia, she had to pull into a long lay-by formed when the road had been straightened some years before and let out a pent up-roar that became noisy, hiccupping sobs.

After a few minutes she felt more in control and carefully re-joined the main road, glancing from side to side as she passed old familiar sights. There was the place where she and her family used to see milk-churns awaiting collection by the milk lorry and her grandmother would regularly remark, 'cows been busy today, I see.' None there now. There was the bungalow where Elsie and Doris's parents used to live, very much altered and the site of a café they'd frequented occasionally, replaced now by three modern houses, with a board opposite proclaiming the proposed arrival of half-a-dozen new executive properties and she could not resist a deep sigh of regret that so many of her childhood memories had been erased.

This was where she had to turn right along the lane that led 'home' and as she passed more well-remembered houses, she felt her throat constrict with the threat of more tears. Memories came flooding back as she glanced at the fine flint house where her grandmother's rich old bachelor cousin, who owned the only Rolls Royce in the village used to live. His gardener would occasionally don a peaked cap and take Heather and the whole family for picnics, the traditional wicker hamper filled with sandwiches, cakes, pork pies, flasks of coffee and bottles of Tizer, deck- chairs and picnic-tables. Even though her mother and grandmother would bicker and argue for the whole journey, they were good memories and she missed them all so much.

All gone now. Even so, as Heather drove along the steep, curving lanes, she felt a comforting glow envelop her as she realised that at least she could still remember what it had been like in the 'forties and fifties', and she'd passed many of her memories on to Sally. Ah...here...she slowed Frog and pulled into a small lay-by the better to gaze at the large white house, framed by woodland, approached by a wide drive, where she had spent the greater part of the first twenty-two years of her life. The iron gates had gone as well as the flower beds each side of the drive that had been filled each year with tulips. Where there had once been a large lawn where first Craig, then she, had learnt to ride their bikes, there was an impressive circular pond, edged with bulrushes and irises surrounded by paving and a few concrete statues.

'At least they're not gnomes,' she murmured, wishing she could see round the side into the field where the poultry houses and duck-shed had been. How she'd loved feeding the hens when she was hardly more than a toddler, dipping her hand into the slippery corn, trying to throw it far enough away from those greedy pecking beaks and dipping the scoop into soft heaps of mash to mix with warm water for the baby chicks when they had any. Their twelve ducks used to run round and round their pen in line and her and Craig's favourite job had always been to open the nest-boxes and bring out their large blue-green eggs. As it was so soon after the war the government had decreed that most of the hen's eggs had to go to help feed Britain's hungry population. The duck eggs, however, had been spared.

Another time...another world! Heather laughed aloud as she remembered the Government rule that permitted them to keep double-yoked or cracked eggs for themselves and how she had once caught her mother surreptitiously knocking a few eggs against the feed bucket to increase their share.

'Well!' she had said defensively, 'we've looked after these little blighters since they were a day old, kept them warm, fed them, mucked out their old straw...why shouldn't we treat ourselves to two or three extras occasionally?'

In spite of the unpleasant rows that had broken out all too often and the toxic atmosphere that had surrounded the departure of her father from the family group, Heather had always been aware that it had been a privileged childhood. She and Craig were never cold, ill-fed or ill-clothed like some of the village children she used to see playing with clay marbles in the lane outside their cramped cottages, wearing cotton dresses or short trousers and dirty plimsolls in all weathers and seasons with occasionally a ragged cardigan, buttoned up wrong, dragged across their skinny bodies.

I wonder where they are now, she mused, hoping that they had all managed to get well-built, roomy council-houses when the new estates went up in the late 'fifties and 'sixties. But unemployment had been rife with so many ex-soldiers returning from the war and re-claiming their old jobs, putting countless women, often mothers of large families, out of work, so that even finding enough money for the rent would have been a struggle.

She drove on slowly, reluctant to arrive back in Selborne too soon, realising just how much explaining she was going to have to do to so many people and wondering what they would think of her. Would they all be as tolerant and forgiving as their vicar? Would she be able to remain in Selborne? At Westhangar Hall? Once they knew of her 'moment of madness' and her daughter's parentage? Until today she had been looking forward to Sally's visit with such joyful anticipation. Now there was nothing but fear and trepidation.

She pressed her lips firmly together as she drove down the road to Alton again and gave herself a stern lecture. Deal with it, she heard her father say in her mind, tell the truth and shame the devil! In the meantime, she must plan what she and Sally were going to do while they were together, and - she had almost forgotten! In a fortnight's time it would be her birthday...forty-five years old...only five years away from the dreaded big Five-O.

Heather was dumbfounded to find a reception committee waiting for her as she drove into the courtyard and parked Frog close to the back door. Out of the house came Elsie, Doris, Kathie, Stewart and – to her surprise – Chris! They were all wreathed in smiles and cheering! Elsie held a big bunch of sunflowers and cosmos, Stewart was clutching a single rose, Kathie waved a bunch of buttercups, dandelions and other assorted weeds ironically above her head, while Chris nursed a most beautiful pot-plant between his hands. She emerged cautiously from the car, looking round to see who might be behind her to explain this unexpected welcome when they all shouted 'hurray!' and rushed to escort her into Gwen's kitchen, the table laid for lunch.

'Here you are at last!' shrieked Kathie, giving her a playful push, 'you dark horse! Little Miss Butter wouldn't melt in my mouth, when all the time you'd been having it off with the Lord of the Manor.'

'That was years ago,' protested Heather, trying to gather all the flowers in her arms, while Elsie rootled in a cupboard to find a couple of vases, 'and I didn't know who he was at the time, or I'd never have set foot in this place.' Not knowing whether to laugh or cry, she turned to Chris, trying to keep a low profile in a corner, 'I suppose I have you to blame for letting the cat out of the bag!'

Kathie took her elbow and guided her towards a chair. 'You mustn't blame Chris,' she said, 'he was worried about what you might do once you'd found out who your daughter's father really was so ran all the way up here to check that you were all right.'

Chris stepped forward and took up the tale, blushing as he realised that, after all, she was safe and well.

'It was when I got here and found your car gone that I really began to worry,' he said, 'then Elsie came out and told me you'd left a note and when I read, "...it might be some time before I'm back," I had this sudden awful thought that you'd done a Laurence Oates, left the shelter of the tent and gone out into the snow, never to be seen again. If you hadn't come back by six o'clock, we were going to send out a search party.'

'What's the Reverend talkin' about?' asked Doris, turning to her sister, 'what snow? And who's Laurence Oates when 'es at 'ome?'

'Wasn't he the bloke who went with Captain Scott to try and find the South Pole?' chimed in Elsie, arranging hers and Stewart's flowers in one of the vases. 'And they all died. What shall I do with these things, Miss Heather?' she went on, holding the wilting weeds at arm's length and moving towards the door.

'Oh, don't throw them away,' Heather said, 'I'll put them in a jam jar somewhere and every time I look at them, I'll remember what Kathie thinks of me.'

After they finished feasting on cheese flan, salad and crusty rolls, Elsie proudly poured out coffee for everyone.

'Real coffee today – and the best china, I see,' remarked Chris, sipping from the delicate porcelain cup with his little finger raised in the air, 'we are honoured.' Kathie nudged Heather in the ribs.

'When the cat's away,' she muttered, then went to the sideboard and fetched herself a thick china mug. 'Don't trust myself with anything valuable and breakable, but I might just be able to manage a plate without dropping it on the floor.'

'Well,' said Elsie, defensively, 'Gwen insisted on me washing all this fancy stuff, so I thought to meself, you've washed it, why not use it?'

'Quite right too,' agreed Chris, 'what's the point of having beautiful things if you don't use them occasionally? But perhaps we'd better not tell Gwen. Now tell me, Elsie, how is it that you honour Heather with a 'Miss' when poor Kathie has to make do with plain 'Kathie'?'

'Ah...' replied Elsie, with a knowing look in her eye, 'me and Miss Heather goes back a long way...her Gran was quite the great lady in our village, always good for a tip at Christmas, the first to offer a raffle-prize for our Socials, always 'ad the carol singers in for mince-pies and sherry, didn't she, Miss Heather? *And* paid for a Christmas party for the kids in the village hall with a conjuror, and a great big cake made of ice-cream. I know because I went to some of 'em, so did you, didn't you, Dorry?'

Chris looked from one to the other with surprise.

'Elsie's Mum used to clean for us when I was growing up,' explained Heather 'and Elsie sometimes came along too in her school holidays, so that's how we know each other. By the way, Elsie, I passed your old house yesterday...I see the new people have added a smart conservatory.'

'Hm!' sniffed Elsie, 'you and I might call it that. When the people who bought it from us had been there a year or two, they invited me and Dorry to call in for a cuppa tea and the first thing they said was...' She stuck her nose in the air and affected a high-pitched 'posh' voice, "you must tell us what you think of our Orangery!" Well, I nearly did but then thought better of it! Orangery indeed, glorified green'ouse I'd call it!'

As they were all giggling at this, Heather noticed that Stewart was swallowing hard, trying his best to force words out of his mouth and she was suddenly reminded of the album of early photographs of the Walled Garden she'd seen in the study.

'Do you remember the greenhouses in the gardens here, Stewart?' she asked, addressing him directly, rewarded by seeing him nodding vigorously and clenching his fists with the effort to speak.

'All broke...broken...long ago...glass, glass,' and he pointed downwards as if to indicate shattered glass on the ground then lapsed into silence.

'Ah...,' said Heather, 'The first day I came here, Kathie showed me round the grounds, and I saw the remains of brick fireplaces just outside the walls – so the Orangery, if they had one, must have been on the other side with the heat of the fires keeping the trees and plants free of frost.'

Stewart nodded again, frowning and his lips twisting as he formed his next sentence.

'Come...come see...one day...come see...' He stumbled to a halt again.

'Oh, thank-you, Stewart, I'd love to,' Heather replied then she added tentatively, 'could Kathie come too?'

He nodded once more, 'Kathie...Kathie...come too,' he uttered, and it was then that Heather became aware of four pairs of eyes gazing at her in wonder. Kathie was the first to speak.

'Tomorrow afternoon,' she said to Stewart, 'Heather and I are going off together for a hack with the horses, then, after that...about half-past three?' she said and then, with one accord, they all got up and carried – with great care – the delicate china over to the sink.

'I'll do all that,' ordered Elsie, 'have to put towels in the sink and on the draining-board and do 'em one at a time, Dorry'll give me a hand.'

'And thank you all so much for...for being so understanding... and so kind,' Heather said as she headed for the door, 'you've all cheered me up so much. I seemed to have spent the whole day in tears before I saw all of you standing there.'

Feeling tears threatening again as she remembered the first dreadful hours of the day, she crossed the courtyard quickly... then remembered she had left the pot-plant behind. As she hesitated for a moment, she saw Chris approaching, pot in hand, a broad grin on his face.

'I'll bring this up for you,' he said, brooking no refusal and followed her up the staircase, waiting as she unlocked the door to let him in. She would have taken it from him, but he strode right inside, looking round at her neat piles of notes, books stacked upright on the shelves, her writing materials laid out in an orderly fashion alongside the typewriter and telephone.

'Goodness!' he said appreciatively, 'this used to be little more than a dump when Mr Franklin was here. Tidy room, tidy mind,' he added thoughtfully and put the plant down on one of the bookshelves. He looked at Heather with a strange expression in his eyes.

'I wanted to say,' he began, 'just...that I hadn't heard Stewart speak so much...or so clearly...since before that terrible accident. And, as far as I know, no-one has ever actually been *invited* to enter his family's favourite playground.' He stepped a little closer and put his hands on her shoulders, looking searchingly into her eyes. 'You seem to have the gift of encouraging people to confide in you – they trust you – and that's a wonderful gift.'

Heather shrugged, bit her lip and gazed past Chris out of the window, where the rooks were wheeling overhead, describing swooping circles in the sky.

'I'm glad you feel happier now,' he continued, 'I can imagine the shock you must have had when you saw that portrait. I'm sure I don't need to ask you – but I will – are you *absolutely sure* it was... your daughter's father...?' He paused and Heather sighed and nodded before answering, her voice low and a little shaky.

'You know that...that sudden... click of recognition?' she murmured, 'well, that, the hair, the expression in his eyes and the cleft in his chin...it was if my Sally was looking at me out of the picture just about to make me laugh with some silly joke of hers.'

She caught her breath suddenly, furious with herself as a wave of emotion swept over her again and she felt Chris's hands tighten on her shoulders.

'The thing that's really worrying me now,' she said, looking up at him, frowning slightly, 'is...Gwen. How will she take it? Will she believe that I didn't know anything about Westhangar Hall before I came here and that I never knew Sally's father's real name?'

Chris moved a little away from her, considering.

'I'll try and arrange to be here when she comes back from her holiday and prepare her. Anybody know when that'll be? Does anyone even know where she's gone?'

Heather shook her head. 'Even Elsie doesn't, and I don't think Stewart does either. But Adrian was going with her and is supposed to be back in a day or two so of course he will. Oh, God!' she remembered, clapping her hand to her head, 'that's another person I'll have to tell...Chris, what have I got myself into? I must have been living in a fool's paradise all these years, believing my past would never catch up with me... and now it has at the worst possible time.'

She sat down suddenly on the easy chair, running her fingers distractedly through her hair and Chris squatted down beside her and took both her hands in his, shaking them gently.

'Now listen,' he said, 'you've had quite enough worry and soul searching for one day. Forget Adrian for the moment. Think about your ride with Kathie tomorrow and your visit to the Walled Garden and I guarantee you'll feel a whole lot better. Personally, as far as young Adrian is concerned, I don't think he'll give a toss, just as none of us do. Now,' he said, getting to his feet again, 'I'd better be off, got a couple coming to prepare for their marriage – and I believe from what Doris has told me, they're pretty prepared already with a baby due in about four months. What can I possibly tell them that they don't know already?'

Heather smiled then and saw him to the door, watching his silvery head disappear down the steep stairs and he turned and smiled back. She fetched her transistor radio from the bedroom, returned to her chair and sighing with relief at the way the day had turned out she switched on some soothing classical music, flung herself onto her bed, shut her eyes and in less than five minutes she had fallen fast asleep.

Chapter Twelve

After their gentle ride along Selborne's lanes and bridleways next day, eating sandwiches bought at the pub, then past the site of the old Priory towards Oakhangar, back towards Blackmoor and home, Heather and Kathie presented themselves expectantly at the gate of the Walled Garden...and waited. After ten minutes or so when they began to wonder if Stewart had thought better of his peace being disturbed, they both lifted their heads and sniffed the air.

'Can you smell burning?' Heather asked Kathie and at her anxious nod, Heather led her round to the back where she'd squeezed in on her previous visit. This time she found the gap had been widened and the tangle of trees which had blocked her way before had been cleared and, as the two women ventured in, they were set upon by Dizzy and Dotty, tails waving, barking enthusiastically. They spotted Stewart a few yards away tending a large bonfire, heaving cut branches onto the blaze with a garden fork. He advanced towards them, nodding a welcome then indicated the improved access he had made just that morning.

'Better?...Better?' he asked, putting down the fork for a moment and rubbing his hands together.

'Much better,' replied Heather, 'thanks a million, Stewart. Did you do that just for us?' He nodded and, turning back to the fire, he picked up a billhook and proceeded to slash at the wall of dead weeds blocking their view of the interior of the garden.

'Don't tell me you've already been in here,' Kathie said, accusingly, picking up a rake and beginning to clear up the dead stalks and chucking them on the fire. 'Trespassing! I ask you!' then turning to Stewart she said, 'you'll have to put up a notice saying 'Private' to keep her out otherwise she'll be in here every day bossing you about. She trained as a gardener once, you know!'

That won't keep me out, thought Heather, thinking back to her childhood days when such a notice presented her with an irresistible challenge.

'Come...come,' Stewart said, waving his hand around, 'go...look, look for....' he struggled a few moments for the words, 'glass...careful...f-foot.' Kathie put down the rake and followed Heather up the overgrown path then along what had once been a wide grassy walk towards one of the side walls. Fallen branches blocked their way from time to time, but they were able to make out a line of disintegrating bricks, a collapsed wooden door and, as they soon found out by the sound of crunching below their feet, the shattered glass walls of a long rectangular greenhouse. Heather pointed at the bottom of the wall where a tumble of bricks and a rusty pipe was all that was left of the old Victorian heating-system which former Franklins must have installed with great pride and hopes for the exotic fruits of their labour.

'According to the old photos,' murmured Heather, 'there were two greenhouses, filled with grape-vines and other gorgeous fruits.' She picked her way along the remnants of the wall, scraping at the ground with her foot then stopping with a little cry of success.

'See here, Kathie? They always planted the vines outside so their roots were cool, then trained them to go inside so the fruit got as much heat as possible. And look, here's the remains of one of them, quite a hefty root, and a bit of it left.' She bent down and scraped at the stubby bark with a fingernail.

'Still just alive,' she said thoughtfully, 'so it can't be that long since Mr Franklin – as I suppose I'd better call him – had to abandon the garden after his heart-attack. It must have been awful for him to realize what was happening to his pride and joy and not to be able to do anything about it...the shattering of dreams.'

Kathie stood beside her and lightly touched her elbow, her expression uncharacteristically solemn.

'Your daughter's dad...if only Stewart would let us in to tidy all this up it could be a sort of memorial, not only for him and for Gwen but for you too, to remember him by.'

'But mostly for Stewart,' Heather said, 'I can remember John Franklin every time I look at my daughter. But Stewart's children used to play in here...and he showed me a special tree Jenny and he planted not long after their marriage, a *liquidamber,* still thriving and it will come to its full glory in a few more years.' She heaved a sigh. 'So much to be done. I can't bear to see the whole place going to rack and ruin.'

'Well,' said Kathie, standing with her hands on her hips, 'I don't know much about gardening, but I'm strong and willing to learn and there's always Bob and Harry to do the heavy work.'

Heather smiled regretfully and turned away back towards where Stewart was still heaping dead wood onto the bonfire.

'It's such a tempting thought,' she murmured, 'but when I've finished sorting out Mr Franklin's papers, which won't take much longer, I'll be out on my ear. That's the only thing I was engaged to do, after all.'

Kathie sniffed and shot Heather a determined look.

'We'll see about that,' she remarked shortly, 'all we have to do is get Stewart on our side then make Gwen see that Westhangar Hall can't possibly function without you. Who will help me exercise Conker if you go? And you've got Stewart talking again, not much I grant you, but he's so much more...more alive since you came. As soon as Adrian comes back, I'll get to work on him, he seems to like you.'

'And I like him, very much,' replied Heather, 'there's a lot more to young Adrian then meets the eye, whoever his father was.'

They strolled back along the paths and watched Stewart at his work, breathing in the rich, smoky smell of burning wood and leaves. As the dogs retreated to a safe distance, he heaped the debris up into a mound, then came over and all three of them watched the plume of thick smoke rise into the air.

'You're doing a grand job here, Stewart,' said Kathie, gesturing with her arm, 'Now...can you remember a time when the greenhouses still had fruit in them?'

Stewart looked solemn for a moment, then nodded and clasped his hands.

'Very good...good grapes...p..p...peach...mm...mm,' he paused, struggling a bit, frowning with determination, 'm.m.m...melons...good, good,' and he patted his stomach to emphasise the point.

'Well,' said Kathie, in her decided fashion, 'I'm looking forward to the day when we can have peaches and melon and bunches of grapes again without having to go into Alton for them - and wine! And I'm sure Gwen would like some orchids for the drawing-room when she has guests.'

Stewart looked puzzled for a moment, gazing in the direction of the derelict greenhouses with a frown.

'All broke...broke,' he said eventually, a look of distress passing over his tired face, 'glass...all broke,' then he added, 'sorry...sorry...' and looked at the two women with such sadness in his blue eyes that Kathie took him by the elbows and gave him a little shake.

'Don't be sorry,' she said briskly, patting his arm, 'what's broken can be mended, can't it, Heather? Won't be easy...but we can all help.' Then, turning away she said, 'the bonfire's woken up, it's blazing away now. We won't disturb you any more today, Stewart, we can see you've got a lot of work ahead of you, but thanks...'

They picked their way back to the gap in the wall and entered the main garden once more and the two women looked at each other with glee.

'Think we've sown the seed?' asked Kathie, as they glanced back at Stewart, getting to work with the billhook again, slashing and chopping with all the energy of a twenty-year-old.

'Almost literally,' answered Heather, seeing in her mind's eye the glasshouses rising from the ground again, the vines sprouting, and the rest of the garden cleared, the well-chosen trees allowed to reach their full potential without being choked by invasive weeds. 'But now I must have another go at Alicia's letter before supper. Just got to an interesting bit but it's too faded to read, so I'm popping down to the Library to get it enhanced.'

While she was in the Library Heather looked up the Parish Records for Selborne for 1853 to see what had caused the deaths of John and Alicia so soon after their return to England. Goodness! Typhus fever! Both of them! Whatever could have caused that, she thought frowning? She hadn't come across any other mention of the dread disease in Mr Franklin's records. Bad drainage? Contaminated water? But if it had been either of those reasons there would have been other deaths from typhus in Selborne at the same time, but there were none.

There was a mystery there. For the moment, however, there was no way she could solve it and folding her copy of Alicia's letter into her handbag she set off back to Westhangar and that good supper she knew Elsie would have prepared for them all, thanking Gwen silently for having arranged for her to stay later for the few days she expected to be away. Kathie was willing and good-hearted but didn't know one end of a pork chop from the other and Heather had been secretly dreading having to endure her slapdash cooking for days on end.

There was just time before then for her to have a look at the last page of the cross-written letter, much enlarged and clearer than before. It was full of Alicia's excitement at her and

John's imminent homeward voyage and her hope that her trunk would eventually arrive safely.

'We'll be spending a few days in Liverpool before we travel down to Hampshire,' she'd written, 'with some good friends we've made out here. They live quite near the docks, very convenient for when we arrive. We've never visited Liverpool before so it will be quite an adventure for us.'

Hm…Liverpool docks…probably not the most salubrious part of the country in the mid-nineteenth century, she pondered. Could that be where they picked up the disease that killed them?

Still a bit more to read and she crossed the room to put on the light.

'I've kept the most exciting news until last!!!' Alicia had written, the writing disintegrating into hurried scrawl. 'Our pitch came good at last; a really rich seam and John's been working it night and day with me holding the lantern and a pocketful of candles, both of us living in a tent and he's had to pay for extra guards to keep the jackals away.' Not real jackals, Heather surmised, but humans, sometimes murderous ones, keen to benefit from other people's hard work. 'We're so excited! We plan to pack the gold amongst my clothes, and we pray to God that the trunk doesn't end up on the bottom of the ocean. It'll have to go into safe keeping at the East India docks until we can arrange for it to be transported to Selborne. I shan't be easy in my mind until I see it again. Also, John has managed to sell our pitch to a fellow prospector and got a splendid price for it, paid in gold sovereigns. Oh, won't it be thrilling to get home, settle down in lovely Selborne and show our spoils to all our friends and relations!! We thought we might donate some of the money to the church to buy a bell for the church-tower or whatever they really need. We cannot wait to get home!! Your very affectionate cousins, John and Alicia.'

Heather's mouth went dry with excitement, and she gazed at the trunk at the bottom of the wardrobe with renewed respect. We *must* find that key! There could be a fortune inside! Her heart thumping with anticipation, she quickly changed into a blouse and skirt, squirted on a spray of perfume and ran down the steps out into the courtyard and into the house.

'You look as if you'd dropped sixpence and found a guinea, Miss Heather,' remarked Elsie, glancing at Heather's flushed cheeks and bright eyes as she took her seat around the kitchen table. 'Won the pools?' She reached into the range and brought out a large earthenware dish from which a tempting waft of steam arose. 'Chicken casserole OK for everyone?'

A general cheer went up from them all causing Elsie's face to break into a huge grin and a contented silence reigned for several minutes as they savoured the tender meat and vegetables. Kathie leaned back in her chair, wiped her mouth with her hand, blew out her cheeks and patted her stomach in a most unladylike way.

'Got a feeling I recognised our supper,' she announced cheerfully, with a broad wink at Heather, 'There were only four Light Sussex with Cock o' the North in the henrun this morning instead of five as Champ and I went by. But she must have died a beautiful death knowing how good she was going to taste.'

Elsie flushed nervously and stirred the pot around with a wooden spoon to hide her discomfiture.

'Gwen told me a coupla days ago that this one was egg-bound and to get one of the gardeners to wring its neck. So that's what I done. You'll get no curry tomorrow if you're going to turn your nose up at good food.'

As the others laughed, assuring Elsie that it was just a joke, Heather asked her who had taught her to cook.

'That were my Mam, Miss Heather,' Elsie replied, looking a little happier, 'remember those cakes she used to bring up to your Gran's every week? Your brother used to be hanging out of the front door waiting for us when we come to do the cleaning.'

'She taught you well, Elsie, that's all I can say. By the way...
I'm trying to locate another key, a big one this time, probably
old and rusty, to fit that cabin trunk in my study. It's nowhere
in my flat and I just wondered...'

It was Doris who fetched a chair and opened a cupboard
door high up on the kitchen wall, peering into the dark
interior, frowning.

'Somewhere here...I remember seeing a bunch of old keys,
been there donkey's years, I shouldn't wonder...'ere...catch,'
and she tossed three rusty iron keys tied up with a bit of
brown string covered in cobwebs, down to Elsie who held
them under the tap for a minute or two.

'That's better,' she said, rinsing her hands at the sink. 'Now,
who's for rhubarb crumble and custard? Or do you want to
try the key first?'

After their pudding, they trooped across to the stables and
helped Heather slide the trunk out from the bottom of her
wardrobe and Elsie, forward-thinking as usual, armed with a
small tin of oil and an old rag, cleaned all three keys, then
poked the rag into the keyhole, twisting it for a few seconds.

'Now,' she said sternly, regarding the keys, 'one of you'd
better fit, or I'll eat my hat! Want to try, Miss Heather?'

'Well,' she said, doubtfully, 'I feel it should be Gwen or
Adrian to do the honours...but, as they're not here, I suppose
one of us could...'

'Go on,' urged Kathie, impatiently, 'you found the letter
and went to all the trouble of deciphering it...you try.'

Holding her breath, Heather slid one of the keys carefully
into the keyhole, where it stuck and wouldn't move. She tried
again with another one and this time it slipped deep inside the
keyhole and, as she tried to turn it, Heather felt it give just a
little, then turned slowly, grudgingly. After a wiggle or two
and a bit of brute force it clicked, the lid parted just a crack
and she was able to push her fingers into it. Cautiously, she
lifted the lid by gradual degrees, just in case any Australian
wildlife might still be lurking there. Unlikely after a hundred

and thirty years, but one couldn't be too careful. She would hate to be the one to spread a hitherto unknown bacterium or virus amongst the good people of Selborne and be responsible for a further visitation of the Great Plague.

'Have to take that risk,' she muttered grimly under her breath and eased the lid up into a vertical position as they all peered in, to gaze at the contents.

'Alicia was right,' Heather said, glancing round at her curious audience, 'and so was Elsie, partly. Full of ladies' dresses, hats, gloves and underpinnings. You'll have to avert your eyes, Stewart. Now... she said in her letter that she'd hidden a tin box amongst her underwear so...it should be somewhere...here!'

Her fingers had touched something hard and, as they all held their breath, she drew out an oblong object, tightly wrapped around with oilcloth. Heather looked at it then around at the others.

'Do we dare?' she said doubtfully, 'it feels...wrong somehow. Alicia wrapped this up in 1853, expecting to be able to open it herself...but now...What do you think, Stewart? What would Gwen think? Would it be very wrong of us to open it?'

Thus appealed to, Stewart flushed with embarrassment but curiosity obviously getting the better of him he struggled to utter a word or two, then, more clearly came the one they had all been hoping for.

'Open,' he said, and Kathie patted him encouragingly on the shoulder. Fetching a vegetable knife, Heather slit the oilcloth along the top and sides and eased it off to reveal an old tobacco tin, the lid further sealed with candle wax. She looked at the tin for a moment, a nagging suspicion forming in her mind ... the wax seemed broken along one side. She gritted her teeth, frowning as she looked at the others.

'I've a nasty feeling the jackals might have got here first after all. Some of those so-called guards couldn't be trusted an inch,' she said slowly, looking carefully again at the oilcloth wrapping. Had it been slit open once before and inexpertly, possibly hurriedly, cobbled together again? 'Those dockhands too must have had a pretty good idea of which luggage came from the goldfields…don't get your hopes up yet, folks.'

They all crowded round to watch Heather open the tin box. What feelings of excitement and apprehension must have assailed Alicia, she thought, as she anticipated the day when she could reopen the carefully wrapped package and she and John could realize their dreams for themselves and for the village?

'Get a move on,' urged Kathie, handing Heather the knife again, 'the suspense is killing me.' Heather, her hands shaking, slipped the knife round the edge of the tin, easing off what was left of the wax and, at last, they were all able to gaze on the contents.

There lay half-a-dozen roughly shaped objects, wrapped in decaying brown paper, from which the gleam of gold could be seen through small tears, and, as one, they all drew breaths of pent-up excitement. These items lay embedded amongst a layer of red sand, gleaming in the light, the tin heavy in Heather's hands. For a minute or two they were all speechless, then Kathie found her voice.

'Get the paper off, quick! Let's see what it looks like! We could be looking at a small fortune there, what d'you think, Heather?'

Heather's expression grew solemn, even fearful as the implication of the discovery hit home.

'I'm really not sure,' she said slowly, 'never seen gold nuggets before…nor much gold at all come to that. Mightn't be worth anything much at all.' As she carefully removed the crackly paper from the first lump, she gave an almighty groan, echoed by the others as flakes of gold paint fell into the trunk to reveal a nugget … not of gold but of hard-baked clay!

'Those jackals,' muttered Heather, gritting her teeth with dismay and fury. 'I could murder every last one of them!' She unrolled the rest of the little bundles, almost weeping as each one disintegrated into crumbly clay in her hands.

'Well,' she said, leaning back on her heels, 'well...what...'

She knelt there, lost for words, cold disappointment washing through her like ice. 'I'm so sorry, all of you,' she said at last, biting her lip. 'But just so glad that Alicia would never have seen this. Just imagine how she would have felt...all those months and years in the goldfields gone to enrich some thieving...' she stopped, then uttered a startled 'Oh!'

Her expression changed as she noticed a second layer of thick waxed paper lining the bottom of the box. Holding her breath, she slid the knife underneath and began to lever it off. It peeled slowly sideways as they all held their breath, then gasped as they stared at a layer of gold sovereigns covering the most beautiful necklace of deep green emeralds separated by sparkling diamonds on a golden chain with earrings and a brooch to match.

'Well!' whispered Heather when she could manage to speak, 'at least these have survived. But this necklace! Did you ever see anything more beautiful?'

'Are they really...real, Miss Heather?' asked Elsie, her eyes round with astonishment, 'not just some cheap stuff the jackals 'ave put there to fool everyone?'

'Can't be absolutely sure...but I think they *are* real,' murmured Heather, lifting the necklace out and holding it to the sunlight streaming in from the window. The emeralds glowed, throwing dancing green lights across the walls and the diamonds glittered with white fire. Her heart beat rapidly and her stomach constricted as she gazed at them. 'And there's a note here too.'

Handing the necklace carefully to Kathie, she unfolded the brittle paper carefully, screwing up her eyes to read Alicia's tiny writing.

"This is my most precious and beloved possession, the necklace my dear husband bought for me to celebrate our first find of gold. God willing, it will arrive safely in England for me to wear again on our return."

Silently, Heather returned the necklace to the box then turned to face the others.

'Not a soul must know of this,' she impressed on all of them in the room, 'until Gwen or Adrian comes back and can tell us what they want to do with it. If anybody else found out, we might all be murdered in our beds.'

'Not all of us,' announced Kathie firmly, getting up and moving towards the door, 'just you, my dear. We're off, aren't we, Elsie and Dorrie?'

'Thanks a lot,' said Heather in disgust, surveying the torn oilcloth and wax scattered all over the floor. 'And who's going to help me get this wretched thing back?' She had already decided to return the tin re-sealed and re-wrapped to the trunk in the bottom of the wardrobe and she'd keep the three keys under her pillow. But first she took some flash photographs, one or two just of the box and contents, then of the interior of the trunk to show exactly where she had found it.

Stewart came to her rescue, helping to wrestle the trunk back into place. When he'd left, she covered it with a rug then sat in the easy chair, thinking, thinking over the events of the day.

What a lot had happened since they'd waved Gwen off on her holiday yesterday morning …and now this! This dilemma! She had seen jewellery like the necklace amongst the collection of a cousin of her mother who had been born and brought up in Ceylon and she had no doubt that it was genuine – and valuable. And not mine to dispose of, she reminded herself, it should go to a member of the Franklin family as Alicia had clearly intended. But John Franklin was dead; Adrian was not his real son, not 'a child of his body' and as far as she could remember without looking at the family trees again, John had had no siblings and no cousins.

It should be Gwen, Heather supposed, as the wife of Alicia's most closely related descendant. Then a curious thought struck her. Did 'a child of his body' necessarily have to be a legitimate one? Might Sally…if it could somehow be proved…? What would be the law in such a matter? Who would be able to advise her? Whom could she trust?

Only one person fitted the bill – Chris! He might know nothing about jewellery, but he might know about the ins and outs of inheritance. And he could be trusted. She'd ask him tomorrow.

For some time, she simply sat in the armchair, thinking... and worrying. Then she edged the trunk out of the wardrobe once more, unlocked it and lifted the lid just enough for her to pull out the tin. She withdrew the diamond and emerald brooch and one of the sovereigns and put them in her pocket before replacing the tin and the trunk carefully as before. She put the brooch into her handbag alongside the keys, then placed her pillow on the top. As she fell into bed after the hastiest of showers, she lay awake, staring up at the stars her mind whirling with apprehension and excitement but unable to rid herself of disturbing feelings of doubt and guilt.

It was not just the reservations she felt about having opened the trunk, but also the uncomfortable feeling she had that, now the whole household knew what was inside, she'd felt impelled to hide the key from a group of people she'd come to regard as the best of trustworthy friends. The fact that she couldn't bring herself completely to rely on them not to try and help themselves to what might be a considerable fortune was the most disturbing thought of all.

It was well after midnight before she finally fell asleep, only to be awoken after what seemed a mere five minutes by Cock o' the North crowing joyfully at the crack of dawn a mere few yards from the stables. Cursing to herself, she leapt out of bed and wrenched open her door.

'You'll be next for the pot!' she threatened, racing down the staircase in her nightwear and shooing it out of the courtyard down the drive. 'You'll be Coq au Vin if I catch you again!' Unable to relax and knowing she'd be unable to fall asleep again, she decided to use the time before breakfast to carry on with John Franklin's coded letter and see if any more shocks and surprises could possibly be in store for her!

Chapter Thirteen

Heather sat up in bed watching the sky lighten for a few minutes then found the place in Mr Franklin's secret diary where she had left off a few days before and settled down to deciphering the coded pages. That should be simplicity itself now she knew the key.

Even so, it was tedious work, plodding through his account of preparing for his trip abroad, catching his flight...but then something gave her pause for thought and she hitched herself over onto her side the better to read and transcribe his tiny script. 'I hope Greece will live up to its reputation and that I shall meet some alluring dusky maidens there,' she read and suppressed a giggle. 'Naughty man...you've only just got married,' she thought, but, of course, it was the word Greece that had caught her eye and sent a shiver of delicious recollection down her spine.

A few pages of lyrical description of the Greek countryside, olive groves, the heat of the sun, the azure blue of the sky, white houses with vine-covered terraces and trickling fountains, dusty visits to majestic ruins, all standard poetic cliches, nevertheless sparked off delightful memories of her own impressions of that wonderful country all those years ago; the rich scents of thyme, marjoram, sage and other aromatic herbs that arose from the ground on every excursion into the hills, the rough-haired goats that cropped the thistly vegetation, the bold stares of their dark-eyed shepherds and always, always that hazy blue line on the horizon that was the warm, inviting Mediterranean Sea.

She sighed, leaning back on her pillows, glancing up through the Velux window to notice that dawn had well and truly broken, then returning, with some reluctance, to the diary. Would he have mentioned their stolen encounter below the Judas trees that night after the gymnastics display and the crazy, drunken dances that followed? Or was that an episode he might have regarded as best forgotten, unaware of that living legacy he had left behind?

Ah...here it was. Oh, God! She felt her body tighten as she deciphered his account of meeting the naval cadets, 'a rather undisciplined shower, but I'll soon lick them into shape' and the plans he had made for their display beside and across the swimming-pool. 'Hope it works!!!,' he'd written, 'don't want to make the Navy into a laughing -stock.' Then followed a few notes about the display itself which, according to the diary, 'went off very well until that idiot man stood up and left the circle just as I was about to leapfrog over him, and I crashed into that poor girl. She took it very well...and the idiot man did me an unintentional favour as that led to the most brilliant bang I'd had in years!'

Heather grew hot with extreme embarrassment.

'Oh, my God!' she said in horror and, although she was quite alone, she buried her face in her hands as her body shook with shock and a sinking feeling of guilt and dismay at the way the episode, which she remembered with such tenderness and joy, had been described as just one 'bang' amongst many others in Skip's experience, which, she gathered, must have been rich and varied. Was that all he'd thought of her?

After a few minutes, when her breathing had resumed its normal rhythm and she could hold the diary, the key and her biro without trembling, she cautiously worked out the next few sentences, gratified and saddened in equal measure by their content.

'I must say, she was utterly splendid, no tears, no demands of me. What a pity I didn't meet her months ago. Don't suppose I'll ever see her again, ships that pass in the night and all that.'

And then he forgot me, sighed Heather, my lovely Skip, off to pastures new and then back to England...only to find that his new wife had been having her own adventures with an old flame who must have been just waiting for his chance to pounce.

Heather couldn't face any more transcribing for the moment as the sun was already creeping above the trees, lighting up the rooks' wings as they swooped above her roof and sending the clouds hastening across the sky. It was going to be the most beautiful day.

'Two ships,' she repeated in her mind, as she pulled on her clothes, rather relishing the comparison, 'that met, saluted, then sailed away to their own worlds.' But, as a result, two children, Adrian and Sally, had been conceived, two children born that might, by a series of extraordinary coincidences, be about to meet again – very soon.

Before going down for breakfast Heather lifted down the photo album containing the pictures of the Walled Garden and had a look again at the one of the glasshouses built against the walls. 'Oh...and there were peacocks!' she cried aloud – not real ones but topiary, beautifully detailed with tails spread like fans and crests on their small, proud heads. So, somewhere in the garden there must be at least two unkempt bushes of box which could, possibly, be brought back under control to grace the walkways once more.

She sighed with a mixture of happiness and regret. If only she could stay at Westhangar long enough to see the garden transformed... it was a big 'if'. Gwen would soon be back, her work on the Franklin papers would only take about another couple of months then there'd be no good reason for her to stay. In the meantime, she must see Chris, tell him of their disappointment over the fake gold, then show him the sovereign and, emerald brooch, then – if he could discover if they had any value – try to discover who they should belong to. That should be plenty to keep her mind from drifting back to that 'brilliant bang' of twenty-three years ago. And ... some other astounding news was about to add to her turmoil and shake her to the core.

As she approached the kitchen, she became aware of an unruly uproar from within. Elsie was screeching, Kathie was bellowing with laughter and the dogs had decided to join in with furious, excited barking. Heather stood in the doorway, mouth open with surprise, gazing at them all with wonder in her eyes.

'Oh, Miss Heather,' gasped Elsie, her hand on her heart to steady her nerves, 'You'll never guess...in a million years!' before lapsing into more shrieks of laughter or distress, it was hard to tell which.

'What on earth...?' queried Heather, 'what's got into you all? Is it Adrian?' she said, with a sudden clutch at her heart. A quick glance at the crossbow, still safely on the wall reassured her, then Kathie came across and unceremoniously pushed her into her chair, grinning a maniacal grin.

'Elsie took a phone call this morning,' she said, 'from our sainted employer, Gwen – from Tenerife!'

'Tenerife?' echoed Heather, staring from one face to the other, shaking her head in disbelief, while both Elsie and Kathie tried to answer her together.

'And... she's getting married!' Kathie's voice came out strongly, 'to Adrian's father – his real one, I mean! They've got a special licence, Adrian's going to be Best Man then he's coming back here while Gwen and lover-boy go swanning off round the Canary Islands on their honeymoon.'

'I should've known she were goin' to do summing like that,' broke in Elsie, anxious to get her word in, 'as she asked me to pack her best dress and jacket and some 'igh 'eeled shoes, but I'd never 'ave guessed...this!'

For the first time in her life, Heather fully understood the words 'struck dumb' and could do no more than sit staring at them as her head swarmed with questions that her lips refused to utter.

'I...I...' she tried, then was spared the effort of saying anything more by the arrival of Stewart, who ambled in and took his usual seat by the table as if nothing out of the ordinary had happened.

'Do we tell him?' Kathie mouthed across to Elsie, 'do you think he knows?' then both looked at Heather to indicate that she had been recruited, unwillingly, to pass on the news.

'Er...er...Stewart,' she began nervously, turning her chair to face him squarely, 'er...do you know where Gwen has gone? And why?'

Stewart managed the ghost of a grin and nodded, hiding his mouth behind his hand.

'Tole me...tole me...y...yes...'he gulped hard, concentrating on the next difficult word, 'y...yes...t..t..terday!' He held an imaginary phone up to his ear, 'Getting m...m...ma...married!' and he almost grinned again, looking triumphantly at the three women staring goggle-eyed at him.

'And you never said a word!' said Kathie accusingly, 'and what do you think of your sister getting hitched again?'

Stewart nodded, dug his spoon into his boiled egg and took a piece of toast, buttering it liberally as he considered his answer at his leisure.

'Good...' he uttered at last, 'v...v...ver good. Gwen happy...happy,' then settled to the serious business of enjoying his breakfast. Doris appeared, in a flurry after running through the village and the news had to be told over again to her squeals of amazement, her hands holding her rosy cheeks in surprise and joy.

'Pity she couldn't 'ave waited till she got 'ome,' she remarked, donning her apron, 'then we could all've been bridesmaids – always wanted to be a bridesmaid,' she added wistfully, 'always wanted Elsie 'ere to get wed but she never... and neither did I so never got to wear the big posh dress.'

Kathie gave Heather a painful prod as she passed her chair and whispered, 'don't you forget that Miss 'Eather, when you get wed,' before helping herself to a huge bowl of cornflakes and swilling in milk, rich and creamy, from one of the tenants' farms. 'Off to see Chris today, are we?' she added archly, raising her eyebrows, catching the crust of bread Heather aimed at her and throwing it back where it landed in her hair. Stewart, catching sight of this tomfoolery and, perhaps for the first time in five years, threw put back his head and roared with boyish laughter.

'Good... shot!' he called, without hardly a trace of hesitation or a stammer, 'damned... good... shot!' which reduced them all to helpless, joyful laughter. Heather put on a severe expression to answer Kathie's loaded question.

'As a matter of fact, I am,' she said primly, looking down at her bowl, 'seeing Chris today, I mean, to ask him what we should do about Alicia's jewellery and the sovereigns. Now,' she added, decisively, changing the subject, 'how can we send our congratulations to Gwen? Do you have a phone number for her, Stewart?'

It turned out he did. He'd had the presence of mind to make a note of it when she'd phoned him yesterday with her glad news.

'I wonder where they'll live after their wedding,' Heather mused, 'her new husband might not want to come here where she's been married to another man for over twenty years.'

'Might 'ave a grand 'ouse of 'is own,' speculated Doris, waving a tea-cloth about, 'somewhere in Park Lane...or summat,' she added lamely, having come to the end of her entire knowledge of the smarter parts of London.

'Or Bishops Avenue,' put in Kathie, to help her out, 'Millionaire's Row that used to be called. What do you think, Stewart?'

For a moment he gazed into space, considering his answer, while Doris put another slice of warm toast in front of him.

'Near...here... hope. Near...me,' and Heather noticed his cheeks had flushed up and he was blinking rapidly. Kathie noticed too and, standing behind him she clasped her arms around his neck and kissed the top of his head.

'She won't desert you, Stewart,' she reassured him, '... and neither will we. We'll look after you just like we always have, me and Dorrie an' Elsie. We love you...and don't you forget it.'

Stewart sniffed, blew his nose, arranged his face and settled to his breakfast once more, looking a little happier. Heather got up, calling 'I'll be back in a tick,' and trotted off back to the stables. She returned with the photo-album, opening it at the page showing the pristine glasshouses and the topiary peacocks. She propped it up where Stewart could see it but far enough away to save it from any stray bits of butter or marmalade that might accidentally come its way. The others all crowded round with oohs, aahs and wows of amazement, and Heather realised that probably none of them round this table, apart from Stewart, would have seen the garden looking like the photographs as Mr Franklin had had his first heart attack, which stopped his gardening activities, some years ago.

'I'd no idea it looked like that,' said Elsie at last, 'I 'ardly ever gets into the garden, too busy waitin' on Missus to gad about lookin' at flowers. I never knew there was anything be'ind that brick wall, thought it were just a wall! But this...' she said, pointing at the album, 'this is just...amazin'. Look at them fountains, just like a Stately 'Ome.'

Stewart had turned a page or two, drawing in his breath as each view of the garden reminded him of times past. He stopped to gaze at one picture that showed a small garden chalet in one corner and his breath came in short, sharp gasps and tears began to pour from his eyes. He looked round wildly from his audience back to the album and, with a shaking hand, pointed to the chalet, mopping his eyes all the while.

'That...that...where my chil...my children... play.... sorry...sorry,' and, pushing back his chair, he stumbled out of the room, shuffling down the corridor towards the door and into the open air.

Nobody could speak as they were all too busy mopping their own eyes. Then Elsie found her voice, rather shaky and punctuated by sniffles. 'Gwen told me once that Stewart 'ad never once cried for 'is family since the funeral, nor spoke again proper either. Bottled it all up, see...bad for 'im.'

'Perhaps,' put in Kathie, serious for once, 'this will have helped him let out his emotions, at last...after five years!'

'Yes,' they all agreed, and they finished their breakfasts in sober silence.

'I'll take this album to the library next time I go,' Heather said, when they had all had time to recover themselves, 'and get some copies made. We can give them to Stewart and this precious thing can go back in the study. Might inspire him to get on with his tidying up,' and she told Elsie and Doris how he'd invited her and Kathie in and they'd found him chucking dead wood onto the bonfire. Then Kathie offered to phone Gwen in an hour or two to offer their congratulations and Heather went to collect her bag containing the precious key, the brooch and the sample sovereign to show Chris, promising to exercise Conker later that day.

When she knocked at the door of the Vicarage, the door was opened by his elderly housekeeper, who told Heather she'd find Chris in the church, preparing a group of teenagers for their confirmation in the Autumn. To fill in time, she wandered round the churchyard again, noting names she recognised now after four months in the village, which gave her a comfortable sense of belonging. There were all the Franklin graves of course – and she stopped for a special thoughtful moment before that of Alicia – then there were the postmistress's parents, the milkman's mother, Chris's housekeeper's husband – and Stewart's family. Was I right, she asked herself, to revive memories that perhaps he might have been able to forget, given time? And yet, as Elsie and Kathie had agreed, confronting him with images from the past might have been just what was needed to help him emerge from the thick fog of mere existence that had enveloped him for all those years.

Hearing giggles and chatter coming from the church, she dodged past the exiting teenagers and managed to waylay Chris as he was moving bundles of parish magazines from a cardboard box into the porch in preparation for their delivery by volunteers.

'Could I ask you something?' she said, 'when you're not too busy.' His quick smile of real pleasure when he saw her reassured her and he thrust a pile of the booklets into her hands along with a handful of rubber bands.

'If you could sort these into bundles of twenty and stack them here then I'm all yours,' he answered cheerfully, 'I've got a few posters to put up and some to take down so we should be finished about the same time.'

They worked quietly together for a few minutes then he closed the church door and they wandered out into the churchyard together.

'Now,' he said, 'is this business or pleasure? OK out here?' and at her nod, he led the way towards a wooden seat amongst the trees that she hadn't spotted before. A brass plaque was screwed onto the back of the seat.

'In memory of my dear husband, John Franklin, who worked so hard for this village and who will be forever in my heart. Placed here by his widow, Gwendoline Franklin, in the year 1984,' she read aloud, glancing up at Chris, a dubious expression on her face.

'Not quite so sure about the forever,' she murmured and at Chris's enquiring look, she continued, 'Did you know she's gone off to Tenerife with – with an old friend – and they're getting married!'

Chris looked startled and stared at Heather in utter amazement. 'Are you...absolutely sure?' he stammered out at last, 'I'd have thought she'd...' he paused a moment before continuing, 'well, I've known Gwen...and I knew John, for years! I simply can't believe it!'

Heather told him what had occurred that morning, watching his expression change from shocked disbelief gradually to doubt and then annoyance.

'I think,' he said slowly at last, 'and this is just between you and me. I think it would have been...more considerate for her

to have given us...just a little warning. As her vicar...' he let
the remark die away until another thought struck him. 'And
what will Adrian have to say about this? He's a sensitive lad –
as you once reminded me, Heather – and this may hit him
hard so soon after...'

Heather stopped him with a laugh, her hand on his arm.
'No need to worry about Adrian,' she said merrily, 'it's his
real father that Gwen's marrying and Adrian's going to be
Best Man! We were all a bit shocked, I admit, there was no
warning, no suspicion of...,' then she paused a moment,
remembering Kathie's jokes about lover-boy, 'actually, I think
Kath had some suspicions. But...not about actual marriage!'

Chris got up from the seat and took a few steps away,
composing himself. It must have been sobering, she realised,
for him to realise that someone he had supported with
sympathy and prayer after John Franklin's death, could take
such a serious step without his knowledge or advice.

'And it's so soon,' she heard him mutter to himself before
returning to the seat and flopping down beside her again. 'Just
a few months...and there's her poor brother still mourning,
grieving for his loss, after five years.'

'Well,' began Heather tentatively, looking down at the
grass where a bee was busily helping itself to the nectar in a
patch of white clover, 'I think...that perhaps we're making
some progress there.' She told Chris how Stewart had reacted
to the old photographs of the Walled Garden. 'And I also
think, despite her hearty disdain for anything approaching
sentimentality, that Kathie's more than a bit sweet on him,'
she added mischievously, 'but that's just between you and
me too.'

'Well, I don't know...I'm not often lost for words, but...'
he trailed into silence again and they both laughed as words
failed him again. Heather turned to him with a hint of mischief
in her eyes.

'Can you stand any more shocks today, Chris?' she said, 'a
good one this time, at least I hope it will be.'

He sighed resignedly. 'Go on then...surprise me...if you can!'

'I think I can!' she returned, decidedly, 'but you'll have to come over here first,' and she led the way to the Franklin area of the graveyard and stood him in front of Alicia's tombstone.

'I finished reading Alicia's letter yesterday,' she said and explained how Doris had found the key to the trunk, their excitement at finding the tin box, followed by bitter disappointment that the gold nuggets were mere clay, then elation again as they gazed on the sovereigns and emerald necklace.

Chris regarded her with astonishment.

'What a mercy Alicia never knew they'd been cheated,' he said with a sigh, 'some of those prospectors would stoop at nothing to make their fortunes.'

'I'm afraid you're right,' said Heather uncertainly, 'somewhere during their trunk's journey, robbers – jackals as Alicia called them – managed to replace their gold with gold-painted rubbish. And Alicia and John and their heavy luggage were on different ships, no chance to keep an eye on it in their cabin....or perhaps they were too trusting or simply not careful enough. I think the robbers were disturbed before they could pinch the whole lot so I brought this sovereign to show you in case someone could test it somehow, assay it or whatever you do to find out if it's real. Clever Alicia managed to hide a whole stash of them, payment for their pitch that they sold before they left Australia. And,' she continued, delving into her bag, 'she'd hidden this brooch and a magnificent matching necklace and earrings underneath them at the bottom of the tin. Now this, my instinct tells me is genuine, possibly bought in Ceylon – Sri Lanka now – on one of their holidays from Australia. What do you think?'

Chris studied the gold coin first, scraped at it with his forefinger, turned it over two or three times then shrugged his shoulder.

'Well, I'm not a mineralogist – but it's certainly not painted clay. But this…!' As he held the brooch in his hand, turning it so that it caught the light, he drew in his breath then whistled softly between his teeth. 'This is a real treasure, almost, *almost* sure of it.' He was silent for a moment, turning the lovely item over in his hands. 'And I know someone who could tell us, a jeweller in the Burlington Arcade, Piccadilly. Could you entrust this to me for a few days so that I could take it to him, rather than trust the post?'

Seeing the slight doubt in her eyes, he added, hastily. 'I'll give you a signed receipt for it, never fear, if you don't mind popping into the church for a moment where I can find some Diocesan - headed notepaper.'

She followed him inside, trying to fight down the nagging feeling that it might be unwise to let it out of her sight, so sat down in front of the Gilbert White Memorial window, counting the birds to calm her doubts while Chris scribbled his receipt. As he approached her again, she looked up at him anxiously.

'I do trust you, Chris, really I do…and I don't know whether to hope they're genuine or not. The trouble is,' she said as she handed the little objects over to him, 'is that once one finds something of value one starts to suspect everybody of trying to relieve you of it. I did some work for an archaeological society once and heard all sorts of stories about people slipping little treasures into their pockets on the sly.'

Chris held the sovereign and brooch out to her, inviting her to take them back. 'If you just want to wait a few days…' he said, looking into her eyes, 'I promise I shan't be in the least bit offended.'

Heather gently pushed his hand away and, smiling a little shamefacedly, prepared to leave the church with him. To her surprise he blocked her way and placed both hands on her shoulders and just stared at her silently for a moment.

'There's something I've wanted to do almost from the first moment I saw you,' he said gruffly, tightening his hands, 'and...I don't think I can help myself...but, if you don't want me to...please, please...just say stop and I will.' With that, to her amazement – and utter delight – he pulled her to him and kissed her on the lips, gently at first then with increasing fervour, wrapping her in his arms and rocking her to and fro. Unable to believe at first quite what was happening, she felt herself relax into his strong body, revelling in his warmth and closeness, a delicious sense of safety and security sweeping through her as his arms tightened around her. As they gradually pulled away from each other he smiled... she smiled at his smile and taking her arm he led her into the open air, pausing for a moment at the porch door, giving her a searching look.

'You're not just any Heather, you know...you're a lucky heather. I knew you'd be good for Selborne,' he said, a little huskily, 'I had that feeling...the same feeling I had when I held that brooch and sovereign in my hand, convinced they were genuine. That's what you are, Heather – genuine. You're a catalyst; you change people; for the better.'

Heather looked at him, amusement dancing in her eyes. 'Well, Chris,' she said, still flushed from their encounter as they walked towards the gate, 'I've been called some things in my time...but never a catalyst. I suppose I should be flattered. And another thing...' She stopped him before they could reach the road, amused to see a flicker of worry cross his face. 'That,' she said, 'that's the first time since my wedding to Jerome that I've been kissed by a vicar ... and it was lovely.'

For a moment or two they stood together silently. Then Chris found his voice.

'I'll phone my jeweller friend now and see if I can visit him later today,' he told her, glancing at his watch as they parted to go their separate ways, 'might just catch the eleven o'clock train. And I'll drop by to see Stewart in a day or two – don't tell him I'm coming – I'd like to see how he is.'

'And you,' said Heather, cheerfully, 'will have to come and meet my daughter,' she laughed, 'she'll be here in a day or two...can't wait!'

Chapter Fourteen

Walking on air! That phrase so beloved of romantic novelists described exactly how Heather felt as she left the churchyard, her lips still burning and her heart thumping from that unexpected embrace. Had it really happened? Had she imagined the whole thing?

So engrossed was she as she re-lived those wonderful moments that she was hardly aware of the sound of hoofs ringing down the road towards her and only looked up at the last moment. There she saw, to her utter surprise, Kathie on Conker following Champion ridden by...Stewart! He looked quite at ease on the big horse, his long legs confidently resting in the stirrups, the hint of a smile on his weather-beaten face, and he gave a shy wave as he passed by. Kathie slowed Conker momentarily as she reached Heather, leaning out of the saddle towards her, pointing at Chris's back view as he turned into the Vicarage just along the street.

'Up to no good in the church porch, I see!' she shouted merrily, causing Heather to touch her flushed cheeks in embarrassment and shake her fist at Kathie who kicked Conker into a rapid trot before Heather could think of a reply. She looked round hastily to check that nobody else had heard, then almost ran up towards the Hangar, mounting the Zig-Zag as if her feet had wings, to arrive at the Wishing Stone out of breath, her mind so full of astonishing thoughts that she had to grasp onto it for support. Chris...Stewart...Kathie...gold... emerald brooch! She held her face up to the sun shutting her eyes and knowing – but not caring – that she was being foolishly girlish, she circled the stone three times...and wished!

She made her way back to Westhangar Hall by a circuitous route, arriving at the same time as Stewart and Kathie, who stopped briefly in the courtyard to rub down the horses, before leading them back to the paddock. She waited for a few minutes until they returned.

'That must have been some ride,' she remarked to them both, 'never seen poor Conker break sweat before – and you both look in fine fettle, I must say.'

'Very good…good…happy,' replied Stewart, and he strode off, rubbing his legs and rumpling his hair, leaving the two women gazing after him with wonder in their eyes.

'However did you manage that?' asked Heather, her eyes round with astonishment, when Stewart was out of earshot. Kathie shrugged, gazing after him with a curious softness in her expression that Heather had never seen before.

'He…he just turned up,' she explained, 'you were nowhere to be seen so he caught Champion, lengthened the stirrups, stuck his hat on his head and took off. I followed on Conker in case he was out of practice and came to any harm. Then we saw you bidding Chris a touching farewell as you came out of the church – and had a terrific gallop over the Common, horses loved it. And so did I,' she added, still watching as Stewart disappeared into the Walled Garden, then turned towards Heather who grinned knowingly and gave a short, meaningful laugh.

'Does this mean I don't get any more riding lessons?' she asked, only half seriously but Kathie laughed, and reassured Heather that there would always be time for those to continue.

'Perhaps Stewart'll buy or rent another horse if he wants to carry on. There are those two empty stables below your flat. He was – almost – chatty on the way back from the Common and even gave Chris a cheery wave as we saw him drive out of the Vicarage.'

With Chris likely to be away all day and Kathie with a list of jobs to get through before lunchtime, Heather began excitedly to prepare for Sally's arrival. Elsie had already brought a fold-up bed and bedding across to the stables, so all she had to do was rearrange the furniture to make space for it, exulting all the while that she would see her daughter again so soon. With Gwen away she would feel no pressure to be seen to carry on with her work and there would be a day or two before Gwen would come face to face with Sally...so, to keep herself calm, she decided to tackle the remainder of Mr Franklin's diary which she had abandoned after reading the account of his 'brilliant bang,' there and then. She settled herself at her desk and unlocked the diary once more.

She let her eyes skim over that passage then, with greater speed now that she knew a good many of the corresponding letters by heart, she learned of the cadets' and his progress through the Greek mainland, next Turkey, then onto Italy where they gave several displays, Rome, Florence, Siena, Pisa...lucky young lads, she thought with a sigh, what an adventure for them...and what an education!

'Back home tomorrow,' she read, 'it's all been so wonderful. First chance I get I'll take Gwennie on the same tour, can't wait to see her again and tell her all about it.'

It was here that several pages had been torn out, probably burnt. Heather, her head in her hands, could only imagine the extent of the utter shock, fury, and devastating feelings of hurt and betrayal he must have experienced when he returned, bubbling over with excitement and happiness, only to learn that his young, attractive wife had, in his absence, conceived a child with another man.

And I had conceived yours, Heather told the diary, visited again by waves of guilt and regret...not for herself despite the tough decisions she had had to make twenty-two years ago, but for Skip, who was never to know his daughter. It was some time before Heather could compose herself sufficiently to leaf through the rest of the diary, which set out Mr Franklin's careful and considered plans for his, Gwen's and the coming child's futures.

'Not the fault of the child,' he had written, underlining the words twice, 'poor little bugger. But – to keep faith with my ancestors, the builders and guardians of Westhangar Hall, it *must* be a Franklin who inherits, anything else would be a denial of their hard work, good faith and their trust in future generations. I must pray that Gwen's child will be a daughter and that we then have a son or sons together, which will resolve the whole sad situation.'

But, as Heather knew, the sad situation never was resolved. As neither Mr Franklin nor Gwen found the right opportunity or courage to tell her boisterous, adventurous son the truth of his paternity, Adrian had been allowed to grow to manhood in ignorance. As Heather knew, his shock had festered and boiled and turned to bitter hatred as soon as he did find out and fired him with raging determination to revenge himself on his mother in the most horrible way that he could. Heather groaned aloud, pushing back her chair and walking around the room as she recalled once more those fearful seconds when she had watched the boy raise the crossbow to strike his mother dead…and the relief when she had caused him to stop and drop the weapon. She would never know if he would have stopped anyway…and she would never ask him.

She flicked through the remaining pages of the diary, written, to her relief, without the code, which ended when Adrian was about five years old. Probably another one somewhere – but it hardly mattered, there were unlikely to be any more revelations of such importance as the ones she had already read. Unable to settle to any more serious work, she frittered away the rest of the morning re-arranging the flowers her friends had brought her and checking her stock of tea bags, coffee, sugar, milk and biscuits. To fill in the time before lunch she decided to take another walk down the village to see if they had any magazines that might appeal to Sally and, glad to see that the sun was still shining, she wandered off down the drive again.

I wonder how Chris is getting on, she thought. Would that coin really turn out to be gold and the emerald and diamond brooch made of real gems? And, if genuine, who would be the lucky recipient? Occupied with these thoughts, she found she'd walked straight past the shop and, gazing around, realised she was almost opposite the Vicarage, standing proud at the bottom of a curving drive, lined with box hedging and a border of summer flowers and she stopped to have a good look at it.

It was a most handsome house, white painted with climbing roses adorning the walls, three bays with large arched windows – very appropriate for a Vicarage, she thought – but far too large for a single man, probably built in those days when vicars sired immense families like Anthony Trollope's Mr Quiverful, the badly-off but cheerful cleric 'blessed' with fourteen children, trying to support them all on £400 a year. As she chuckled at the contrast between the nineteenth and twentieth centuries, a most attractive woman appeared from a side door, dressed in a pale orange cotton skirt and matching jacket, straw hat on her head and a string of white beads around her neck, white handbag slung over one arm. Seeing Heather hesitating at the bottom of the drive, she approached, treating her with a generous, wide smile.

'Did you want to see the vicar? I'm so sorry, but he's gone out for the day, and I'm left holding the fort. Anything I can help you with?' As Heather seemed temporarily lost for words, she continued, 'I'm only staying with Chris for a few days so don't ask me anything about church matters, I'm an ignoramus as far as religion goes,' and she ended with a light, trilling laugh.

'No...no,' stuttered Heather in reply, trying to hide her shock and dismay with a forced, answering smile. 'I'd only meant to go to the shop and completely forgot where I was going.'

'I know,' replied the smart woman sympathetically, 'happens to me all the time – memory like a sieve. Chris is very disapproving – he's so well organised, thinks I'm a bit of an airhead, I'm afraid. Anyway,' she continued, 'I was about to pop into the shop myself to buy a little present for a friend in Gracious Street who's invited me, most kindly, to lunch as Chris had to go to London. Any original ideas? Flowers or chocs are so predictable, aren't they?'

Without giving Heather the chance to refuse, she slipped her hand under her elbow to guide them both across the street, while Heather's thoughts flew awry in turmoil. Staying with Chris? For a few days? A lovely woman like that? And apparently on the friendliest terms with him! Just after he'd kissed and hugged *her* with genuine warmth and feeling that very morning! Oh, Chris, she thought, disappointment flooding through her like a cold draught...whatever am I supposed to think now?

As they entered the shop, Heather spotted a rack of sketches of views of Selborne, the church, the yew tree, the Wakes, the pottery shop, the Zig-Zag and studied them with interest to try to quiet her troubling emotions.

'Hm,' she said at last, 'my daughter's coming to visit me tomorrow and I think I'll buy her one of these little pictures. They're really lovely, wish I could draw like that. Would that be an idea for your friend?'

For some reason, the shopkeeper, Mrs Johnson, gave a brief laugh and the smart lady came over to Heather and patted her arm.

'I'm *so* delighted to hear you like them. I'm the artist...and it's so encouraging to hear one's work praised.'

Whew! What a relief I didn't say something rude about them, thought Heather, then had to stifle a laugh as she noticed her new acquaintance pick up a box of expensive chocolates and a bunch of lavender and exit the shop leaving a waft of sweet scent behind her.

She selected a view of the Plestor with the church in the background and two figures relaxing on a seat in the front, then, with that and a copy of the Hampshire magazine and the

Radio Times under her arm, she set off back home. There was less gaiety in her step than before, as she wondered who that lively woman could be – and just how well she knew Chris. I could have asked Mrs Johnson, she thought, but didn't want to seem too inquisitive. After all, Chris can have whoever he likes to stay with him – *absolutely* no business of mine!

As she joined the others for lunch, she mentioned, as casually as she could, who she'd met coming out of the Vicarage that morning.

'I haven't seen her around the village before,' she uttered nonchalantly, 'but she told me she was an artist.'

'Ah', said Elsie, the fount of all local knowledge, as she cut a few more slices of bread, 'that'll be Vicar's sister, Charmian, she comes to stay coupla times a year. Got some smashin' clothes, according to Dorrie – she sees 'em when she does 'er room – and shoes! My eye! She's not short of a bob or two!'

The feeling of relief that swept over Heather was impossible to hide, and she found herself temporarily bereft of speech. Kathie shot her a sharp look, then slapped her on the shoulder, causing her almost to choke on the mouthful of lettuce she'd just manoeuvred into her mouth.

'Ha! You thought she was Chris's fancy woman, didn't you? Serve you right for having impure thoughts about our beloved vicar. I shall tell him one day!'

'Don't you dare!' replied Heather, then laughed as she saw Stewart duck his head as if to avoid any flying bits of food that might come his way.

'Don't worry, Stewart, I wouldn't waste it on her,' she reassured him and settled down to enjoy her lunch as her spirits soared once more.

As she noticed Stewart and Kathie wandering off towards the Walled Garden after lunch, dogs in tow, she thought it might be tactful not to follow them, so she started up Frog and drove to the apple-shop she remembered from her childhood, breathing in the delicious scent of ripe fruit and newly baked bread, and spent a indulgent half-hour selecting a few choice early apples, a box of dates, fancy biscuits and a bag of treats for Dizzy and Dotty. As it was still early afternoon, she took the road to Bordon then on to Alice Holt Forest, past the Garden Centre and Birdworld, making a mental note to take Sally there, looking about her with mingled excitement and regret, remembering times past when she and her family had travelled this route in the Rolls Royce, feeling like royalty, she and Craig sometimes cheekily waving to passers-by who often stopped and stared...just wondering!

She returned via Alton, unable to resist the temptation to take Frog on a small detour to pass the railway station door just in case she might spot Chris getting off the Waterloo train, even though her common sense told her it was far too early to expect him. But that's the sort of thing one does when one's falling in love, she thought, then braked a little too sharply. Oh God! Did I really think that? Far too soon to even consider such a thing after just one little kiss, especially as he was a vicar, and she was a sceptical heathen! But she could not deny that feeling of utter relief and joy that had swept over her when she'd heard Elsie describe that attractive woman as his sister. Sister! Oh, joy! And perhaps one day sister-in-....! No! She mustn't even allow herself to think it! Far too old at nearly forty-five! Be your age, Heather!

To keep such tempting thoughts at bay, she sang as many of the songs that she and Craig used to sing in their childhood on car-journeys at the top of her voice with her window wound down. As she drove through Alton High Street towards the Butts, where the fair arrived every Spring and Autumn, churning up the grass and filling the town with music, flashing lights and good cheer, her voice faltered a little and she found herself fumbling for a tissue. Laughing one minute – weeping the next – what could possibly be the matter with her?

When she'd parked Frog, she ran up her staircase to put her purchases away, then strolled over to the Walled Garden to see how Stewart and Kathie were getting on, letting herself in by the back gate. She was met, as usual, by the two dogs and wished she'd remembered to bring the dog-treats. Stewart and Kathie were busy in one corner, prodding the earth with garden forks and clearing weeds and debris away from the bases of four tumbledown walls, two of which had gaps in them where windows must once have been. Pieces of rotting timber lay in a heap next the walls besides the tattered remains of what once must have been a thatched roof.

'The Chalet,' called Kathie as soon as she saw who it was, 'not much left of it now, I'm afraid, but with those photos you found we should soon be able to re-build it. Your idea, wasn't it, Stewart?'

'Wheel...barrow,' Stewart articulated slowly in reply, 'bonfire,' and he indicated the scatter of rotten wood and the remains of dead plants heaped up at his feet.

'There's one propped up by the old greenhouses,' said Heather, 'I'll bring it over and give you a hand.' She stood back and surveyed the scene, envisaging what that corner of the garden could look like, given time and effort, pleased beyond measure at the ease with which Kathie had won Stewart's confidence. The wheelbarrow, red with rust, was smothered in clinging weeds but she manhandled it out, trundling it over to the remains of the chalet. It took them a good hour to hunt out all the rubbish and wheel it to the site of the bonfire, after separating the bricks and stones from the wood and weed stalks. From the house they heard Elsie calling them in for a cup of tea and gratefully left their work, planning to return the next day.

After washing their filthy hands in the kitchen sink, they settled round the table once more and, over mugs of tea and slices of fruitcake, exchanged reports of what they'd all been doing that afternoon.

'And tomorrow,' said Heather, her voice shaking with excitement, 'tomorrow I shall see my daughter. She'll be able to help with the chalet, Stewart, she's strong as a horse and almost as good looking.'

'And tomorrow,' added Elsie, 'we'll see Adrian again, he phoned me an hour ago.'

'Goodness,' said Kathie, holding up her hands in mock horror, 'so much excitement will kill me.' Then, looking hopefully at Elsie, she asked, 'will this mean an extra special celebration meal? What's his favourite pudding?'

'Ginger sponge,' replied Elsie promptly, 'with bits of real ginger in.'

'And... c.c.custard,' they heard Stewart say.

'Right,' said Elsie, 'ginger sponge and custard it will be and if any of you lot don't like it, you can lump it! Any objections?'

'Yes!' they all chorused, and burst into cackles of laughter, which faded away as they heard a tap on the door and Chris and Charmian peeped in.

'Somebody's birthday?' Chris enquired, looking around the table as the laughter died away, 'do you all remember Charmian? I gather you two met in the village shop,' he said, looking at Heather who nodded and smiled before turning to glare at Kathie. After a minute or two of pleasurable chatter, Chris asked what they'd all been laughing at as he and his sister came in.

'Favourite puddings,' explained Kathie, 'well, Adrian's anyway as he arrives home to morrow and Heather's daughter's coming to stay, so we'll be having a grand celebration while they're both here.' She turned to Chris, 'Could you and Charmian come to supper tomorrow?'

'Sorry...we'd have loved to,' replied Chris, looking genuinely dismayed, 'but we've already been invited to dinner in Winchester with a couple of Charmian's friends – could we make it another day?'

They all nodded their assent as Chris continued, 'and I may soon have some interesting news for you. My friend in London just needs some clear, close-up photographs of the necklace and earrings and he'll be able to give us a proper valuation. But he's had a look at this...' He drew the sovereign out of his pocket and placed it on the table in front of him. 'This is absolutely real and gone up in value tremendously after a hundred and thirty years.'

'Phew!', exclaimed Elsie and Doris in unison, their eyes round with surprise. Heather turned to Chris to explain that she had taken a photo of the necklace already so perhaps all it needed was to be developed and enlarged.

'If you let me have your camera,' he said, 'Charmian and I can go into Winchester tomorrow afternoon, find Boots and see if they can do an Express service for us before we visit our friends. And, in the meantime, would you have time to go through those Franklin family trees in the study and just check that Alicia and John had no close descendants, children, grandchildren, close cousins, nieces, nephews, anyone in fact who might have a better claim to her possessions than Gwen?'

It took Heather only a matter of minutes to race up to her flat, find her camera and run down again and for Chris to hand back the brooch.

'Hope your Sally arrives safely tomorrow,' he said as he and Charmian prepared to leave, 'we're both looking forward so much to meeting her. Must dash now – got some preparation to do before Evensong.'

As they left, Charmian turned and gave Heather a broad wink, which luckily her brother did not see. Having a specific job to do encouraged Heather to settle down to the wearisome task of studying the sheaf of handwritten family trees still waiting to be typed neatly so that they could be consulted in detail. This was a job she'd been putting off for days now, afraid of what she might find. Please God, she murmured to herself, even though I don't believe in you, please don't let me find evidence of a hitherto unknown married brother or sister of Alicia's or her husband, with a large, long-lived family with numerous descendants, who might all feel entitled to claim ownership of their ancestor's carefully concealed treasure – or, of course, the whole Westhangar estate. That would be too unfair.

Chapter Fifteen

Alicia…Alicia…now which family tree should she be looking for? There were so many, and Heather had looked at most of them whilst trying to find a connection between Arctic explorer Sir John Franklin and Gwen's husband, only ignoring those which were almost indecipherable or seemed too remotely connected to have much relevance to her work. That, however, was before she had seen Alicia's tombstone, read her cross-written letter and found the sovereigns and the glorious necklace in her trunk.

She fished out two or three documents she hadn't studied closely before, discarding two from the seventeenth century but found from one from the nineteenth, tattered and torn but which, with the aid of a magnifying-glass, she was just able to decipher.

Alicia Holmes had married John Frederick Franklin on 3 December 1820, at the age of 27, three years younger than her husband, one of two sons of John and Estelle Franklin, both born in 1783. Alicia and John had had three children, Charles, Richard and Evelyne, born two years apart in 1822, 1824 and 1826…but beside each date of birth was entered a second date. Charles died in 1826, aged four of diphtheria, Richard in January 1835, aged ten of smallpox, and Evelyne had not even reached her first birthday, dying at ten months, no cause given. Tears pricked Heather's eyes as she imagined the anguish of those parents as each child died, not unusual admittedly in Victorian times when the need for strict hygiene was unknown. Doctors did not wash their hands between visiting sick patients, water-supplies were often contaminated and those that lived in crowded cities could so easily catch virulent diseases from each other. They had no more children so possibly that might have influenced their decision to try their luck, along with thousands of others, in the goldfields of Australia.

So, Gwen's John Franklin must have been descended from John Frederick's younger brother, William John, born in 1795. Heather found a more recent family tree and ran her eyes quickly down the page. William had married Emily Gosling in 1835 as his second wife – his first died in childbirth – and Emily had produced twins, a boy and a girl in 1841, but the girl had died at two weeks. The boy lived long enough to marry Agnes in 1875 and they had reared three girls and, after a gap of several years, one son. Even though two of the girls had chosen to become nuns and the third had had no children, how they must have sighed with relief and joy when their son married, to know that the family name and ownership of Westhangar would continue.

This son, John Charles Franklin had been Gwen's husband's father. Heather sighed with relief. The direct line was clear, no need to go hunting for far-flung distant relations. And as John's widow, it was probable that it should be Gwen to decide the future of the necklace and the gold sovereigns...but the estate? The legitimate Franklin line had died out with her husband's death...what *would* Gwen do?

To keep busy until suppertime, she armed herself with dog-treats then strolled again to the Walled Garden to see what progress Stewart and Kathie were making. It was astonishing! A section of about six yards on three sides of the Chalet had been cleared – the other side backed on to the wall – revealing a half-buried, paved pathway leading from the main, central path of the garden and they had uncovered a selection of small stone animal ornaments, mostly intact, but covered in mud, which must once have lined the path or perhaps been placed in front of the little building. She must have another look at the photos in the study in case Stewart wanted to re-create the exact look of the chalet as he and his family must have known it. Kathie waved a grimy hand and stumbled over roots and clods of earth towards her, carrying a rake, glancing behind her to check that Stewart was out of earshot.

'Nearly had a relapse just now, I think,' she whispered anxiously, as Heather bent to hear her words, 'every stone animal we uncovered had to be wept over. I just let him get on with it, I'm afraid, and carried on clearing the jungle. Beginning to look a treat, isn't it?'

'Absolutely!' Heather agreed, then waved cautiously at Stewart. He trod gingerly across the cleared patch of ground towards her, a stone rabbit clutched in his hand, then shambled over towards the greenhouses, where he approached a rusty tap jutting out from the wall. After a few sharp taps and shakes he achieved a thin stream of dirty water and held the mud-caked model underneath it for a few minutes.

'Better...better,' he said and both Heather and Kathie nodded enthusiastically. 'Well,' continued Kathie, stretching her arms above her head, 'I'm off for a last look at the horses, then a shower before we see what delights Elsie has in store for us tonight. See you later, Stewart,' and, with a wave she and Heather walked together back towards the house. 'He'll be quite happy sobbing and reminiscing for another hour or two, do him good to get it out of his system.'

Heather glanced at her friend, striding in a determined fashion across the lawns and smiled a sympathetic smile. No nonsense Kathie, she thought, the ideal companion for a damaged man like Stewart.

Back in the study, she lifted down the album of old photographs of the Walled Garden. They pre-dated the arrival of the Chalet, but it was easy to see where it had been built, snugly against a north wall, sheltered from wind and rain. In her mind's eye she could imagine Stewart, Jennifer and probably Mr Franklin and Gwen too, pacing round the garden deciding on the right spot for the children's playhouse, confidently expecting they would have many years of fun and enjoyment ahead of them...all hopes to be snatched away by that dreadful accident, the chalet left to moulder, fall down and almost disappear beneath smothering weeds and shrubs.

Heather chased such gloomy thoughts out of her mind as she made her plans for the morrow. She'd go into Alton just after lunch, take the album to the chemist for photocopying, then drive to the station to meet Sally and introduce her to Westhangar and all her new friends. Then there might be a stroll round the garden, a wander down the village street and a peep inside the church at the bird-window, before home to one of Elsie's appetising suppers. But Heather was in for a surprise!

The next day went as planned until she arrived at the station and parked right opposite the door. She was early, of course, and paced up and down the platform awaiting that delicious moment when she'd hear the London train and know that Sally was *almost* within hugging distance.

Ah...at last! The train squealed to a stop. A few shoppers descended onto the platform, one or two office-workers, a gaggle of schoolchildren...then she heard peals of laughter and spied two figures sliding out of a First-Class carriage – First-Class, she thought, whatever next! There was bright-haired Sally, followed by...it couldn't be! There was Adrian, weighed down with two rucksacks, his curly hair more tousled than ever, struggling after her daughter.

Totally nonplussed, she wrapped her arms round them both, as together they tried to explain how they happened to be travelling on the same train, in the same compartment and seated opposite one another – in a First-Class carriage! She relieved Adrian of Sally's rucksack and led the way out to the car park, stowing both bits of luggage in Frog's small boot, then turned and looked at the pair of them, grinning from ear to ear.

'Well,' she said, at last, 'I think this calls for a cream tea. Come on – we'll have to get to the Station Cafe before the schoolchildren have bagged all the tables.'

Within ten minutes, they were all furnished with tea, scones, raspberry-jam *and* ice-creams and seated outside in the sun.

'Now then,' said Heather, looking from one to the other, 'who's going first?'

'Ladies first,' said Adrian, looking hungrily at the array of treats in front of him so Sally, after a swig of tea, leaned back in her chair and began the saga.

'Well, I arrived in rather a hurry on Waterloo station, hadn't bought my ticket, so got in the queue, then my rucksack slipped off as I was looking for my purse and half my belongings fell on the floor!' She took another mouthful of tea and bit into her scone. Sounds just like my Sally, thought Heather, careless as usual.

'So – while I was chasing things, this knight in shining armour leapt to the rescue, asked me where I was going and when I said Alton, he said...'

'I said,' Adrian interrupted, to give Sally the chance to swallow a second bite of scone, 'I said, well, so am I, so I'll get both tickets.'

'So then,' broke in Sally, 'we had to dash for the train, and I discovered he'd only gone and bought first-class tickets, which...' she glared hard at Adrian, who waved her away, 'I've told him I'll repay.'

'Then,' continued Adrian, 'the most amazing thing! She said she was going to Westhangar Hall where her Mum worked – so, of course, I knew exactly who 'Mum' was...and I thought...perhaps I can cadge a lift. Always wanted a ride in Frog. So, that's how it happened.'

The next few minutes were taken up with polishing off all the tea, scones and ice-creams, then Heather turned to Adrian.

'And how was the wedding, Adrian? No hysterics, no fainting, no scenes at all?' Adrian gave her a puzzled look.

'Course not...all very civilised...and Barry is super, looks like a rugby player and has hair just like me!' and he ruffled his own hair to emphasise the point.

Heather looked from one to the other, wondering how much Adrian had told Sally of his family's muddled background. She kept quiet for the moment, paid the bill and then they all piled in the car for the journey home, Sally sitting in the front.

'Thanks for the lift. See you at supper,' called Adrian cheerfully as he lifted out the rucksacks, carrying Sally's over to the stables. Dizzy and Dotty appeared from nowhere to smother Adrian with welcoming licks, then sat at Heather's feet, tails twitching, hoping for more snacks.

'Oh...can't they come in?' asked Sally as Heather uttered a stern 'No', sending them trotting off back to the Walled Garden, then, 'oh, I like this,' as she followed Heather up the staircase and into the large study, glancing up at the roof and peeping into the other three rooms.

'Hope this'll be OK for you,' Heather said, indicating the fold-up bed, 'Gwen said you could have one of the spare rooms in the main house – there are several – but I thought...'

'No! This is lovely...oh, just listen to the birds! And look at the trees, almost trying to climb in the window...I remember you quoting me a bit out of Gilbert White's book one day when we were planning a picnic up here. "The parish I live in is a very abrupt, uneven country, full of hills and woods and therefore full of birds", and it's still the same today. Lucky Mum, you won't want to leave here in a hurry.'

There was just time for a quick stroll round the gardens and to the paddock to pat Conker and Champion before it was time to foregather in the kitchen. Then came the introductions, to Kathie, and to Elsie and Doris – who had come along, ostensibly to help her sister with the extra catering but really to see if Sally remembered her. A few tears were shed as they all reminded each other of the years gone by, so many family members missing...no Gran, no Uncle Craig, no Jerome, no Elsie and Doris's Mum and Dad. Luckily, by the time Stewart arrived – late – the tears were dried so there was no danger of his being reminded of his own losses and he shook hands with Sally pleasantly enough, whilst studying her features with just a slight hint of curiosity.

'I brought these for you, Stewart,' said Heather, when there was a lull in the conversation and fumbled under her chair for the photocopies of the gardens, 'look at the peacocks! And the wisteria! And the fountains!'

'These...f.f. for me?' he asked, pleasure and surprise breaking out all over his face. 'Th...th...thank-you...keep... safe. Good...good.'

After supper, Heather and Sally pleaded tiredness for not staying after the meal for the usual jokes and chatter and plodded their way up the staircase to bed. Heather left her bedroom door ajar after she'd called good night, but Sally was obviously in no mood for sleep just yet.

'I've noticed something odd today, Mum,' she called from her bed, 'Everybody I've met looks at me curiously – not rudely – but you know what it's like when someone holds your gaze just a bit longer than really necessary so that you think you've got a huge smudge on your face or a pimple on your nose?'

'Mm,' agreed Heather, trying to sound casually non-committal while her heart began to beat a little faster – but Sally continued.

'And when I met Adrian on the station, he gave me a really startled look. Then, when we'd got onto the train, he stared again and said something like, 'Gosh, you look exactly like my...' but then he flushed up and looked out of the window. I'd only just met him so didn't feel I could ask him what he meant so we chatted about Selborne, Westhangar, the co-incidence of our meeting, all sorts of things. He's a really lovely guy, Mum and he likes you. Says you were really kind to him once but looked out of the window again before he could go into details.'

Heather sighed deeply, pausing awhile before answering and sighed again. Sally noticed, of course and, slipping out of her own she padded over to her mother's bed and sat on it, dangling her feet and glanced briefly at her mother's serious expression.

'Is there...is there something I should know, Mum?' she murmured quietly, 'something everybody knows – except me?'

Heather sighed again, then shifted over in the bed, patting the free side.

'Hop in,' she said and as Sally's warm, slim body slid in beside her, she put her arm around her, trying to control the tears that she knew she was about to shed.

'Haven't done this since you were about ten years old...and we were both crying for Jerome,' she got out at last and Sally sat up straight, tears of her own shining in her eyes at the sight of her mother's distress.

'There's so much you should know, darling,' Heather said at last, 'and I was planning to tell you all about it tomorrow... but...it seems, I ought to tell you here and now. But it's such a complicated – but rather wonderful – story, I'm afraid you'll be fast asleep before I finish half of it.'

'Try me,' replied her daughter, gazing at her mother with mingled doubt and excitement. 'Do *you* know what it was Adrian started to say in the train?'

Heather half-laughed. 'Certainly,' she said, 'that's also complicated, but, in its way, equally wonderful. In fact,' she continued, 'everything connected with Westhangar Hall is so full of extraordinary surprises that you couldn't make it up! You'll have to give me a moment to get my thoughts in order.'

She started by answering Sally's question. 'I think Adrian was going to say that you looked just like his father...but then he remembered just in time that the man he'd grown up thinking was his father...wasn't!'

'Bit like me,' Heather heard Sally murmur, 'but why...?' Her mother's explanation came out in a bit more of a rush than she'd really intended.

'Because, Sally, the man Adrian thought was *his* father was, in fact, yours!'

There followed a long silence during which Heather watched a whole range of emotions cross her daughter's face before relaxing into a final expression of relief.

'Oh! So you don't have to tell me that I'm Adrian's sister – or half-sister! Thank goodness!'

The look on her daughter's face was so comical that Heather threw back her head and laughed, guessing exactly what was in Sally's mind. She had come across the word 'consanguinity' occasionally in old documents, when not only brothers and sisters (which included half-siblings) but also first cousins had been forbidden by the Church to marry and had wondered just how many 'matches made in Heaven' had been denied for fear of inheriting some dread disease or deformity.

'Adrian is absolutely no relation of yours, I can assure you,' she said dreamily, then paused again. 'But there's more to tell…such a lot more.'

Owing to Heather's lengthy narrative and Sally's urgent questions, it was 2 a.m. before Sally scrambled back into her own bed but neither mother nor daughter managed more than a couple of hour's real sleep. It was Cock o' the North, escaped again, who roused them just in time to swallow a cup of tea, get dressed and arrive in the kitchen in time for breakfast. Afterwards Heather asked Elsie if it would be all right for her to show Sally the portrait of Mr Franklin in Gwen's bedroom.

'Go ahead,' she replied, 'shan't need to do any tidying or cleaning in there for a while. Gwen phoned to say she and her new husband will be away for a fortnight, they're leaving Tenerife for Lanzarote today.'

Heather breathed a sigh of relief, glad that Gwen wouldn't have to be confronted with the result of her husband's 'brilliant bang' for the foreseeable future and they made their way up the stairs to the row of bedrooms. She paused a moment, her hand on the door handle, before turning to her daughter.

'Remember I wrote you a letter years ago about my – my encounter with a really exciting man when I was working in

Greece, who I only knew as 'Skip' and then never saw again. Well – just in case you've ever imagined him as some glamorous film star – you'll be able to see what he really looked like ... in here.'

Together they tip-toed into the room and Heather turned Sally round to see the portrait of Mr Franklin, dressed in a white shirt, a blue cravat casually knotted around his suntanned neck...auburn-haired, blue-eyed, with a roguish smile. Sally pointed, breathlessly, to the cleft in his chin, then just stared at the portrait before turning to her mother and gasped out,

'Oh Mum, thank-you for giving me such a lovely-looking father! And he lived *here* ...in this very house! Slept in this very room! We used to come to Selborne, didn't we, to visit the Wakes and run up the Zig-Zag to the Wishing Stone? We might have seen him in the street... or in the church when we were looking at the bird-window! Oh...I wish...I just *wish*... I'd known!'

'Don't forget, darling,' said Heather, trying to suppress the rush of guilt that had suddenly overwhelmed her, 'that I didn't know anything about him either. And I was always determined to keep Jerome's life as pleasant and uncomplicated as possible, knowing how ill he was. It would only have made trouble if Skip, as I knew him, and I had found each other again as, of course, he was a married man. But I have to admit that, when I saw that portrait and realised that I had discovered the name of your father, I was really sorry that he had already died.'

She forebore to tell Sally of his description of her conception in his diary...there were some things too private and personal to tell one's child and, having written it in code she was quite sure Skip had intended it to remain secret.

'We must take a photograph,' Sally announced, 'so that I'll be able to show *my* children who their grandfather was. Was Adrian terribly upset when he found out that Mr Franklin wasn't his real father?'

'He was far more upset to discover that it had been kept secret from him...and that he had been disinherited.

The shock affected him very badly. He went missing for several days, Gwen was desperately worried. Mr Franklin must have been an immensely proud man, proud of his ancestry, proud of sharing the same name as Sir John Franklin, the Arctic explorer, and he simply couldn't countenance the idea of the child of his wife's lover inheriting Westhangar Hall.'

Sally blew out her cheeks in an irritated pout. 'Goodness! What a fuss! Probably been dozens of the wrong children inheriting wealth and property all through history, even kings and queens! Quite soon, there will be a way to be sure of one's parentage, called DNA I think, I was reading about it the other day. Sounds amazing – there'll be no secrets then!'

As they walked back to the stables to fetch Heather's camera, she suddenly remembered she'd lent it to Chris yesterday, then spied the man himself flying up the drive, waving as he saw them, puffing and panting as soon as he reached them. Chris, our local vicar, Heather explained hastily to Sally.

'And this must be your daughter,' Chris said, shaking Sally's hand with vigour, eyeing her carefully, then pausing, eyebrows raised, to shoot a questioning glance at Heather.

'It's OK, Chris,' she said. 'she knows...she'd just been to see his portrait.'

'Well,' he said cheerfully, 'hope you were impressed. He was a fine-looking man and there's certainly a clear resemblance. You may get a few curious stares as you walk down the village street, my dear.' He turned to Heather, 'I phoned Gwen this morning, explained a few things – and I told her I'd drop a word or two to Mrs Johnson so there'll be no need to tell anyone else.'

'Mrs Johnson keeps the village shop,' explained Heather to Sally, 'and knows everybody. That's where I bought your little picture.'

'It's sweet,' said Sally, 'I remember the Plestor from when I was a little girl.' She turned to face Chris. 'Mum and I were wondering if we might have actually seen Mr Franklin years ago without knowing who he was.'

'Ah,' said Chris, frowning slightly, 'I suppose it's possible. By the way, Heather, has Sally met Adrian yet?'

The whole story had to be re-told, Chris looking from one to the other, his smile widening as each detail was added.

'What a relief he wasn't upset – or jealous,' he said, sighing thankfully, 'that could have been tricky with you living in the same house. Well,' he continued, handing Heather's camera back to her, 'Charmian and I got several good close-up prints of the necklace and I'll post them to London today, so we should know something soon. Will you and Kathie be out riding today?'

'It all depends on whether Stewart gets to the paddock first,' laughed Heather, 'he's really come out of his shell now, lovely to see him happier every day. It's all Kathie's doing.'

'And yours, don't forget,' said Chris, rubbing his hands together enthusiastically, 'Perhaps he'll soon be ready to move back into his own house – but we won't rush things. Well, Charmian wants me to drive her to Frensham ponds this morning to do some sketching, so I'd better get moving. Bye, Sally, lovely to have met you,' and with that he charged down the drive again waving his hand.

'Wow,' said Sally, looking after him with wonder in her eyes, 'is he always in such a tearing hurry? Bit undignified for a vicar, don't you think?'

'Not in the least,' replied Heather shortly, then turned to look her daughter squarely in the face, 'and, if you must know, I think he's rather…dishy.'

'Mum, you're blushing! You can't possibly be thinking…,' then as Heather made no reply, she added, relief in her voice, 'anyway, no chance…he's married, I saw his ring and he kept mentioning Charmian. Can't have my mother marrying a vicar for goodness' sake!'

It took several minutes before Heather could stifle her giggles as they made their way towards the village, pointing out places they had known in days gone by and, by common consent, they entered the church to stand in front of the Memorial window and count the birds.

'You always used to tell me I'd see a hoopoe one day, if I was really quiet and patient,' said Sally, looking accusingly at her parent, 'I used to spend hours, eyes skinned, in our garden and along the lanes at home.'

'Well...you might!' said Heather, chuckling to herself. 'Keep looking! Come on now, let's go to the shop and give Mrs Johnson something to think about. It'll be fun to see her face!

Chapter Sixteen

'By the way,' remarked Sally, on their way back to the house later that morning, 'what did the vicar mean about a necklace and photographs when he saw us this morning?'

'Ah,' replied Heather, 'that's another long story,' and as they wended their way back along the village street, she told Sally about finding the cross-written letter from Australia and the disappointing discovery they'd made in the trunk in her bedroom.

'Except that it wasn't *all* disappointing – most of the gold had been pinched but then we – I – found a stash of gold sovereigns and a stunning diamond and emerald necklace, earrings and brooch sealed under some paper right at the bottom of the tin. I suspect the thieves, jackals as Alicia called them, must have been disturbed before they could remove the whole lot. Chris has a contact in the Burlington Arcade, he's verified that the sovereign is genuine, but he needs some really good close-ups of the jewellery to see if he can tell if that's the real thing and what it's worth.'

'Golly! How exciting!' Sally's eyes glowed. 'Just like an Enid Blyton story! The Famous Five Find a Fortune! Can I see it?'

'I'll show you the brooch when we get back,' her mother told her, 'but the necklace is locked up in the trunk again and...,' she gave Sally a mischievous smile, 'I'm the only one who knows where to find the key. If it does turn out to be valuable, it'll go into safe-deposit at the bank until Gwen decides what to do with it. My gut feeling, for what it's worth, is that it *is* the genuine article – it's utterly beautiful and we should soon know.'

'Hope it won't take as long as seeing a hoopoe,' said Sally, then, 'Oh, look, there's one!' pointing at a magpie sitting on the telegraph wire just above their heads. Momentarily taken in, Heather turned sharply, looking upwards in amazement, before they both doubled up, laughing. Oh, how wonderful it was to have her daughter with her, the only member of her family left to laugh and joke with.

They decided to return to the house via the Zig-Zag – not forgetting to let Sally pay homage to the Wishing Stone – then down through the woods to the top of the drive.

'Better show you the Walled Garden,' Heather suggested, 'see how Kathie and Stewart are getting on.' The dogs frisked joyfully round Sally, her presence still a novelty for them, as they edged their way in by the rear door. They were greeted by a veritable working-party as besides Stewart and Kathie, Bob and Harry had been roped in to help and there was Elsie, wearing a pair of wellingtons too big for her, her hair done up in a scarf, wielding a rake with more gusto than skill, while Adrian, armed with a saw, was energetically tackling the lower dead branches of a group of fir trees.

'Glad you've come,' called Kathie, dropping her billhook and dusting off her hands. 'If Sally could come and help Adrian clear some of those branches out of the way and stick 'em on the bonfire, then you and I can exercise the horses, haven't got round to it today. Stewart's busy over by the chalet and we've all got an invitation to the Vicarage for tea tomorrow afternoon, so it's now or never.'

Sally snorted derisively. 'You'll never get my Mum onto a horse in a million years – she told me once they bite one end and kick the other.'

'Your mother may surprise you,' remarked Kathie, with a grin, as she eased her way out of the thicket and dusted herself down. 'Oh, by the way, Stewart said I must be sure to show you the tulip-tree, says it's the best he's ever seen it. And the *liquidamber* is a picture.'

Heather and Sally obediently made their way to the centre of the garden and, after admiring the tulip tree, smothered now in pale yellow flowers, alive with bees, the branches slightly stirring in the breeze, they walked the few yards across to the acer, its leaves already beginning to develop their Autumn colours.

'It's like the one in our garden, Mum. Is there something else special about it, apart from being beautiful, of course?'

As she turned to go out of the gate, Heather explained that Stewart and his wife had planted the tree soon after they were married, just as she and Jerome had done. 'But they take a long time to mature, so she never saw it looking like this. He must always think of her whenever he sees it as it's a memorial, a constant reminder of what he's lost.' She sighed, then turned a more cheerful face towards Sally. 'You go and help Adrian, so you don't have to watch me make a fool of myself on Conker and I'll see you later.'

'Not if I see you first,' rejoined Sally happily and Heather smiled to be reminded of that old family joke, looking after her daughter with affection as she busied herself gathering up the fallen branches, raining down from the fir-trees one by one.

'What time are we expected to parade at the Vicarage?' Heather asked the others at lunchtime the following day, 'are we going to march down the street in a body?'

'About half-three,' said Elsie, 'but Dorrie and I'll be there a bit early to give a hand setting out the tables in the garden. There'll be about a dozen or fifteen of us altogether if they all turn up. It's Charmian's idea of course, she does love the chance to entertain. You're going to come, aren't you, Stewart, I've made some of your favourite cheese scones and drop cookies.'

'Of course he's coming,' said Kathie firmly, ignoring the doubtful look on his face, 'because he's coming with me! We'll go down with you and Sally if you like, Heather. Has Chris any news of the necklace?'

'It's too soon,' Heather replied, 'he only sent the photos off yesterday. Anyway, he wouldn't want to broadcast any exciting news to half the village, would he?'

Kathie turned to Sally and gave her a broad wink.

'We'll have to keep an eye on those two...all sorts of places in the Vicarage garden for intimate conversations,' and, giggling, she escaped with Stewart through the kitchen door before Heather could find anything handy and unbreakable to throw at her, leaving Sally looking after them with surprise.

'Soooo,' she said, eyeing her mother suspiciously, 'there really is something more than meets the eye with you and the vicar. I'll have to mind my ps and qs in future. Whatever does his wife think about this?'

'No wife – she died...years ago. Charmian's his sister...and to be honest, I did make the same mistake about her myself. And don't be ridiculous. I've told you...I'm nearly forty-five. Far too old for romance and all that rubbish. I just like him, that's all. And now...I promised to show you that brooch and then we'll get ready for our afternoon of wild excitement.'

They both had problems deciding what to wear. Since April, Heather had been happy to live in jeans, polo tops and cardigans, but she decided to sport her only smart blouse, pale blue with a ruffled neck, teaming it with a navy cotton skirt and navy waistcoat, and, after a glance at the sky, which had clouded over since the morning, draped a light cagoule over her arm. Sally looked a picture in white cropped trousers and knitted green sleeveless top, a pale green wrap floating around her shoulders and a white bandeau round her bright hair.

'Never been to a vicar's tea-party before,' she said to her mother, 'so I hope I'll pass muster...wish I could wear the emerald brooch, it would just go with my outfit.'

'Well, you can't,' said Heather, 'we'd spend the whole afternoon losing it in the grass. Anyway, you look stunning as you are.'

And the image of your father, she thought, feeling a shiver of apprehension run through her as she wondered how many of Chris and Charmian's guests would look at her daughter – and herself – with disapproval once they'd got over their first initial suspicion of who she might be.

Deal with it, she heard her father's voice echoing down the years, face it head on…if you can't change it – deal with it! Right – between us and with the support of our Westhangar friends, we'll get through the afternoon, she told herself. At least there would be Elsie's cheese scones and drop cookies to enjoy…*and* she would be seeing Chris again.

By the time she, Sally, Kathie and Stewart ventured down the Vicarage drive, the garden was already well filled with chattering villagers and there was a noticeable hush as they arrived. Heather and Kathie held firmly to Stewart's arms as they sensed his reluctance to cross the lawn, but he was given no choice to escape as Charmian advanced towards them and hugged and kissed them all.

'And this must be your daughter,' she said to Heather, running her eyes appreciatively over Sally and holding both her hands, 'and a beauty into the bargain. Well, my dear, I'm sorry there aren't many young people here, but Adrian's promised to come along later and we're all, *all* young at heart. Now, Stewart, there's someone I want you to meet, she's a bit deaf so you may need to shout. She wants your advice about camellias as hers won't flower.'

Stewart allowed himself to be towed away and Heather and Kathie watched as Charmian sat him beside an elderly lady armed with a walking-stick and soon she was patting his knee and laughing at something he had said – or tried to say – and Stewart himself had broken into a broad grin. Charmian was just hurrying back to them when Doris, resplendent in a pink summer frock, reached them and bore them off to a table beneath a wide-spreading cypress-tree. A smartly dressed, slightly balding middle-aged man instantly stood up and shook hands with them, blushing a little as he gazed hard at Heather.

'You've forgotten me, haven't you, Miss Heather?' he said, 'It's Timothy, Doris and Elsie's brother. My wife wants to meet you, heard such a lot about your family.'

'Ever felt you weren't wanted,' Heather overheard Kathie whisper to Sally and the two of them drifted over to another table where Kathie had noticed Mrs Johnson deep in conversation with another 'lady of a certain age' and boldly introduced Sally to them both. Heather was just in time to notice them both give a self-conscious start before remembering their manners and inviting her to take a seat beside them.

'I remember you now,' she assured Timothy, 'but of course I remember your mother better, can still taste those seed cakes she used to bring us in exchange for my Gran's cracked eggs.'

'Ah...it was the duck eggs she liked best – they never saw the inside of a cake tin. I keep a few ducks now, you know, our kiddies love feeding them.'

At the sound of his voice and rich Hampshire accent, Heather felt herself overcome with an unexpected wave of nostalgia and sat down rather suddenly on the chair he proffered. They spent several minutes reminiscing about their old lives, before Elsie joined them, wiping her hot forehead and puffing out her cheeks.

'The whole clan 'ere now,' she remarked to Timothy, 'pity you didn't bring your littl'uns, Tim, they'd 've loved rolling about all over this lawn.'

'Yes, that's what I was afraid of. They're quite happy being spoilt to death by Betty's Mum,' Timothy reassured his sister before turning back to Heather, 'We're living in Winchester now, you now,' and the conversation rattled along cheerfully until they heard a brisk clapping of hands and noticed Chris standing on the steps which led up to French windows as he prepared to address his guests.

'Shush,' said Doris loudly and crossly to no-one in particular, 'Reverend's speakin,' and all heads turned obediently.

'Welcome to you all to the first of my summer garden teas,' he began, 'and I'm very pleased that my sister Charmian arrived just in time to do all the hard work for me.' Polite laughter and a little scatter of clapping followed, as Chris looked round at all the tables. 'And I want to take this opportunity of introducing those of you who haven't already met her to the most recent addition to Westhangar Hall - their archivist, Heather La Fontaine. Where are you, Heather? Ah, there hiding under a tree, come out so that we can all see you...'

Surprised at the unexpected elevation of her job-description, Heather emerged from under the cypress-tree, where Charmian hastened to stand beside her.

'Those of you,' continued Chris, 'who came to the Mother's Union meeting last Tuesday will already know that Heather discovered, during her research, the exciting news that she had an unexpectedly strong connection with Westhangar and the Franklin family. Consequently, her daughter Sally also has a strong connection, and I would urge you all to welcome and support them both for as long as they decide to remain in Selborne.'

Everyone clapped again politely and smiled their agreement, most of them drawing their own conclusions about the 'strong connection' and began murmuring amongst themselves.

'And some of you may also know,' he continued, 'that Mrs Franklin was very recently married to an old acquaintance of hers and is at present on her honeymoon in the Canary Islands but plans to return to Westhangar with her husband, Mr Falkland, in the very near future.'

This announcement drew several surprised responses as the guests looked at each other in mingled astonishment and dismay.

'Adrian Franklin,' continued their vicar, 'has met his mother's new husband and fully supports her in what she has done. It would, however, be greatly appreciated, if you have any questions, if you could apply to me and respect the privacy of the Franklin family and the staff of Westhangar Hall for the next few weeks while certain legal proceedings take place.

Now... the news you've all been waiting for. Tea is served in the dining-room, but you're welcome to bring it out here if the rain holds off. If you need anyone to help carry your tray, just ask...'

As Heather and Sally offered their services to those they thought needed them, silently blessing Chris for his tactful yet informative explanation, the hook-nosed, stout, formidable-looking lady, whom Heather recognised from the May Fair as 'important' Mrs Grierson and who, in spite of her unwieldy walking frame had managed to take first place in the refreshment queue, pulled Heather by the sleeve and indicated Sally.

'Thought I detected a family likeness,' she said in her unmistakeably loud voice, 'how exciting to find you're related to our dear Mr Franklin, he was very much respected in Selborne.'

'So I gather,' replied Sally diplomatically, 'just a shame my Mum couldn't find any proof that he was descended from the famous Sir John Franklin. He would have been rather disappointed.'

Well done Sally, thought Heather, clever of you to sidestep any more questioning – the truth, or as much of it as necessary, will gradually filter through *via* the village grapevine and in no time at all, our curious connection will be old news.

Chris, Heather noticed, acted the perfect host, chatting to all his guests but to none of them too long and Adrian arrived in time to do the rounds of all the guests, shake hands and exchange a brief word with everyone. After filling his plate with sausage rolls, cheese scones and gingerbread and holding a large mug of tea in the other hand, he joined Sally and Heather at a table with Charmian and a couple she introduced as 'my friends from Gracious Street' adjacent to the table where Stewart, Kathie, Elsie, Doris, Timothy and his wife Betty were sitting.

Just before she sat down Heather noticed that Mrs Grierson was having a struggle to hold both her tray and the walking-frame and hurried over to her, taking the tray from her.

'Not easy, is it, on this rough grass?' she said and stayed beside her until she, the tray and the frame were all safely delivered to her table and Mrs Grierson comfortably seated in her chair. 'Hope I didn't spill any of your tea.'

'Not a drop,' replied Mrs Grierson and put a shaky hand on Heather's arm. 'And thank you, dear, very kind.'

'Scrumptious scones,' she heard Sally say as she returned to their table, leaning towards Elsie, who blushed like a girl to hear her cooking praised and blushed even more when Charmian's friends pronounced them to be the best they'd ever tasted.

'She could walk round the village with a tray on her head and sell them just like a muffin-man,' joked Kathie, as they were joined by Chris and made more room by pushing the two tables together, while Adrian found a spare chair.

'Used to sing a song about the Muffin Man when I were at school,' reminisced Doris, a dreamy look in her eyes, 'never learned much at school – but I do remember summing about Droory Lane...never bin to Droory Lane. D'you think 'e still does?' she enquired in all innocence, at which they all began to sing,

> 'Do you know the Muffin Man,
> the Muffin Man, the Muffin Man
> Do you know the Muffin Man,
> who lives down Drury Lane?'

which elicited a burst of ironical applause from the other tables. Mrs Grierson raised her considerable voice to announce to the assembled company that she could distinctly remember muffin-men from her childhood in London.

'That's because she's at least a hundred years old,' Heather heard Adrian murmur *sotto voce* to Sally, who almost choked over her ham sandwich and had to swallow a large mouthful of tea before she could safely take another bite.

After more agreeable chat and more tea and cakes, heavy drops of rain began to fall, causing a general gathering up of handbags, opening of umbrellas and hurried thanks and 'good-byes' as the garden rapidly emptied. The Westhangar contingent retreated with Chris and Charmian to the shelter of the cypress-tree, huddling together for several minutes until, almost as suddenly as it had started, the rain lessened and stopped.

'Hope they don't all come back again,' said Kathie as they stepped over puddles to collect dirty dishes and cups, tip-toe-ing up the steps into the house, Doris leading the way to the kitchen and beginning to fill an enormous Butler's sink with steaming water.

'No need for you all to stay,' said Chris, 'everything still out in the garden can wait there for the present...but I just want to have a quick word with Heather. If it rains again, I'll run her back in the car.'

'I'll go back with Kathie, Mum,' said Sally, 'if you'll let me have the key. Haven't really finished my unpacking yet. See you in a bit.'

'Not if I see...' Heather began but Sally was away, her red hair bobbing merrily up and down on her neck, so Heather scoured the garden for pieces of cutlery or the odd plate that had been overlooked and took them into the kitchen.

While Elsie and Doris got the washing-up under way, with Charmian in charge of the drying and putting-away, Chris led Heather into a study alongside the kitchen and sat her down on a well-worn leather chair.

'I've some good news,' he said, 'although quite who it will benefit, I'm still not sure. My jeweller friend has had a good look at all those photographs of the necklace and is about 99% certain that all the stones are genuine. He can't be *absolutely* certain until he's seen the necklace for himself, but you can take it from me, Heather, that he knows a good thing when he sees it.'

Heather beamed with delight and relief, gazing at Chris with the brightest of eyes.

'So...what do we do now?' she asked, trying to remember all the things that Alicia had planned to do with their hard-won – and then stolen – gold. 'I mean...we know she had no close blood relatives. What a terrible shame all her children died.'

'I wondered if she and her husband had left wills,' said Chris, 'I phoned in a request to the Family Records Centre in London for a copy, but they could find no record of anyone of that name. It's my guess they were planning to make new ones once they were settled back in Selborne, but...'

'They died before they had the chance,' finished Heather, frowning with concern while Chris drummed his fingers on his desk.

'It's unlikely they would have left them in Australia as they always intended to return to England. So, I think we're back with Gwen,' he said slowly, 'not a descendant but the wife of the nearest blood relation – but now she's remarried. We'll have to get Mr Grundy to sort this one out, I'm afraid and hope the cost isn't greater than the value of the goods. In the meantime, better put the necklace and the sovereigns in a safe or in the bank. Which would you prefer?'

'Well,' said Heather, considering, 'I suppose anywhere's better than the bottom of my wardrobe ...even though they've been safe there for over a hundred years!'

Chris leaned towards her, taking one of her hands in his, a quizzical look in his eyes.

'As a rough estimate, he thinks that all three items, necklace, brooch and earrings...are worth upwards of £75,000,' he said. 'The value of the gold coins changes from day to day but the bank-manager will be able to let us know that. Just think, Heather...suppose you'd never taken the trouble to read that difficult letter...suppose Elsie hadn't found that key...suppose you hadn't thought to look in the bottom of that box. If it hadn't been for you, they wouldn't have been found at all!'

'Don't belong to me though,' Heather uttered slowly, thoughtfully, 'and yes, we'd better go to the bank tomorrow and then on to the solicitor, I really don't want the responsibility of keeping it in my room any longer than strictly necessary.'

'So, when you say 'we' you mean you'd like me to come with you?' Chris said at which Heather nodded eagerly.

'Please, Chris, I'll need a bodyguard. I'd be too nervous driving into Alton on my own, might get mugged.' But that's not the only reason, she admitted to herself.

'Right,' he said briskly, getting up from his chair and reaching for the phone, 'I'll make both appointments here and now. Then I'll come in the kitchen and hope to find all the work done by Charmian and her team!'

Heather returned to the kitchen, her head reeling with the news she had just heard and seeing that the sun had come out strongly, she grabbed her cagoule and bade the others goodbye.

'Must get back a.s.a.p.,' she called, 'and tell Chris I won't want a lift – I'm going to run all the way!'

Chapter Seventeen

'Afraid I've got to love you and leave you this morning,' Heather told Sally as they got ready to go down to breakfast the following morning, 'taking the jewellery and sovereigns to the bank for safe keeping. Will you be OK here on your own?'

'Kathie said she'd give me a riding lesson if I wanted, and Stewart said he hoped I'd help a bit more in the Walled Garden – and I've got to buy a certain person a birthday card. You'll let me have a peep at the necklace before you take it away, won't you, we never got round to it yesterday?'

An hour later, Chris's car arrived in the drive, and they drove off towards Alton, Heather's precious cargo clasped in her hands and a copy of the most recent family-tree to show Mr Grundy.

'The party went well yesterday,' she remarked as the big car ate up the miles between the grassy banks along the curving lane to Alton. Already the fields were beginning to glow with midsummer fertility, the oak-tree leaves were darkening and hazel nuts, still green, showed in abundance in the hedges. It would soon be harvest time – amazing to think she had been at Westhangar for nearly five months.

'And there weren't too many embarrassing remarks, were there?', said Chris with a quick glance at her.

'Several curious glances,' returned Heather, 'and a bit of muttering, people trying to work out what exactly the 'close connection' really meant, but I think they were much more surprised by Gwen's hasty re-marriage.'

'By this time next year, it'll be past history,' Chris reassured her, 'and there won't be many people in the village who haven't got a family skeleton hidden in their own cupboards. I've found during my ministry, that people, on the whole, are tolerant of other people's behaviour so long as they're not actually evil or criminal. When I lived in Newcastle, hardly anyone commented adversely when my wife left me even though I could tell that opinion was divided on who was to blame. And after my bishop gave me his backing and even came to preach at our church, there was no question of my having to move to a different parish, even though I offered to go. After she died, so tragically...that was a different matter; then I felt I had to go. Has anyone told you what happened to her?'

Heather nodded and looked out of the window. Chris paused a while then continued.

'Of course, I'd never have wanted anything like that to happen to her. One hears of these terrible tragedies, but you never expect anyone you know to be involved, particularly not your own wife. But...' he sighed, catching his breath slightly. '... if she'd lived there would have been a messy divorce and I would most likely have felt obliged to leave the Church. It's a dreadful thing to feel relief at someone else's death – but I can't deny that I did.'

Heather felt a cold chill run down her back at the thought that she might never have met Chris if he hadn't come to the quiet country parish of Selborne and for once in her life she could think of absolutely nothing to say.

Chris slowed the car as they entered the town and parked in the old market square, then sat quietly for a minute or two.

'We mustn't let any of these sad memories spoil our day,' he said, chafing her hand in his, 'it all happened a long time ago. And we have our futures to look forward to, don't we?'

Our futures? Was Chris already confidently expecting that she would be sharing the future with him? How should she answer such an enigmatic question? Heather merely smiled, cradling the precious package carefully as she exited the car, and they approached the bank in companionable silence.

There were few formalities to be gone through at the bank, although Heather felt a pang of regret to see the jewellery handed over and a receipt and numbered key given to her instead – but at least she had the photographs. Very shortly, she and Chris were seated before Mr Grundy's large desk as he inspected the family-tree and listened to their explanation of how Heather came to be in possession of the jewellery and to have so much knowledge of the Franklin family background. He already knew of Adrian's parentage, but Heather and Sally's connection with Mr Franklin was news to him and he called in Miss Hibberd to witness Heather's sworn statement about Sally's conception and birth.

'Well,' he said at last, his beady eyes inspecting Heather over his half-spectacles, 'this is a situation worthy of a rather sensational novel, isn't it? A very knotty knot indeed! Bit of a change from our usual run-of-the-mill work, eh, Miss Hibberd? Of course, when Mr Franklin wrote those words into his will, 'the child of my body or a blood relation,' insisting on that old-fashioned terminology, he had no idea that such a person already existed, merely hoped that he and Mrs Franklin would one day produce one – but that was not to be!'

'You do realise, don't you, Mrs La Fontaine,' he continued, 'that it's the Westhanger estate that is at stake here not just the ownership of the jewellery you found? There will need to be more investigations before we can be sure who'll inherit. When your daughter was born, you were married to...' He looked at the papers in front of him, 'to Jerome La Fontaine, so she was legitimately his. Your daughter will have to submit to a blood-test just to rule out the possibility that Mr Franklin was *not* her father. Not possible yet to prove without doubt that he *was*...though that may be possible within a few years. We'll need to advertise in the press – just a discreet message in a part of the paper nobody ever reads in case anyone else believes they have a better claim, which, I assure you is *extremely* unlikely.'

'I have been through as many family-trees as I could find in my study ... and can't find anyone who fits the bill. All the relevant ones are there,' she indicated the small pile of papers on his desk, 'but how far back in history does one have to go? And what will your investigations cost?' asked Heather after a moment or two as calmly as possible despite the whirl of thoughts and possibilities that had suddenly crowded into her brain.

'If what you say is true...and we have no reason to doubt you, the notice in the papers will suffice. We'll give you an estimate in two- or three-days' time,' he said, while Miss Hibberd scribbled down a few notes, 'you'll be at the same address, I take it?'

'And thank you both for coming in...we'll be in touch. Are you, by any chance also related to Mrs La Fontaine,' he said to Chris as he rose to indicate that the consultation was at an end. Was he joking? With that inscrutable expression, one couldn't be sure.

'Not yet,' replied Chris, with a roguish grin at all three of them, 'but who knows what else this 'knotty knot' might yet throw up?'

'I think we should call him my spiritual advisor,' Heather answered quickly, 'and today he was also my driver and bodyguard.'

They were both aware of two pairs of eyes regarding them curiously as they left the office and Chris made a point of taking Heather's arm as they made their way down the High Street. 'Well, Mrs La Fontaine...what now?'

'Coffee and a doughnut,' replied Heather promptly, 'there used to be a really good café round here,' she added, 'and I'll treat you, Chris, to say thanks for coming with me.'

'I think I know the place you mean,' he said, leading the way around a corner and they settled themselves at a table by a window to watch the world go by.

'What muddles we human beings get into, don't we?' Heather mused as they waited for the coffee to arrive, 'far better to be a dog or a horse. And the worst of it is that we don't just make trouble for ourselves but for the innocent people we accidentally create. Take Adrian and Sally. They're the ones this affects the most and they had no choice in the making of it.'

'Never be sorry for having Sally,' Chris said, frowning slightly, 'she's quite obviously been loved and loving all her life. Adrian too until...well, you know...but he seems to have accepted his situation very well once he got over the shock.' He paused, sighing, and gazed out of the window as a huge removal-van rumbled by, then turned back to look steadily at Heather.

'He told me, you know,' he murmured so that no-one could overhear. 'What you did for him that day up on the Hangar. Poor boy – he must have been feeling absolutely desperate.'

Heather looked shocked as she bit into her doughnut and stared at Chris. 'I...I didn't think he'd ever tell anyone...a secret between him and me if he promised never to try such a thing again.'

'I think perhaps he wanted... extra reassurance... and maybe, even though I don't suppose he has any religious leanings – yet – he even felt the need to confess. People don't always see me as an ordinary man you know...they see the dog-collar and believe I'm from outer space ...and did you know you've got sugar all over your face?'

Heather tried to laugh while fumbling for a tissue. 'And so have you!' she said, 'we're both making pigs of ourselves. And...for what it's worth...I see you as a man first and a vicar second.' As she stuffed the tissue into her pocket, Chris leaned forward and gently wiped away a few grains she had missed, then sat there, just looking at her.

'Am I fit to be seen now?' she enquired, feeling herself blush at his gaze. Instead of answering straightaway, Chris took a quick glance around the café then laid his hand on her arm.

'I could look at you for ever,' he said shortly, 'even if you were covered in mud instead of sugar - and I'm glad you think of me as a man first. And I need to confess…that I think about you almost all the time, ever since …,' and to avoid continuing, he took another bite out of his doughnut and a spout of red jam dribbled down his chin and onto his plate.

'Oh dear!' said Heather, unable to stop herself laughing, 'doughnuts weren't such a good idea, definitely danger zones. I'll go and ask for a few more tissues.'

'Was it a surprise to you when Mr Grundy mentioned the estate?' Chris asked when she returned, armed with a damp cloth and a whole box of tissues and they had both finished their doughnuts without further mishap. Then, before she could collect her thoughts, he said, with some regret, 'oh, dear, I think we've been spotted! That's the trouble with sitting by a window looking out on the world. The world comes along and looks at you. It's Mrs Grierson… keep smiling!' and as the lady with the loud voice and walking-frame entered the café with a friend, he rose politely, helped keep the door open for her and invited them to join them. They seemed extremely eager to accept and darted numerous inquisitive glances at them both.

After a few minutes polite conversation during which Heather explained that she was no stranger to Alton and that she was so pleased to see that her family's favourite café still existed, she and Chris finished their coffee and left. She noticed him glancing at his watch and then he suggested a walk around the nearby park.

'I've got someone coming to see me about a baptism later this morning,' he said, 'have to admit I prefer those to funerals. But we've got time to go for a stroll. Do you remember this park?'

'I remember the bandstand and the swings,' she answered, 'Don't suppose Mrs Grierson and her friend will be coming to have a go on the see-saw, will they?'

Chris threw back his head and laughed aloud, stopped in his tracks then laughed again. He slipped his arm through hers, squeezing it companionably and they made their way slowly round all the flower beds, with Heather naming every bloom and every shrub. They approached the Mound, where she and Craig had so often raced each other round the circular path to the top, then took a moment to catch their breath and look across the park at the view.

'Can't see them,' he said, shading his eyes. It took Heather a second or two to realize that he was looking across to the playground ... then it was her turn to double up with giggles. As she straightened up, she found herself clasped in a bear-hug with Chris rocking her to and fro, his face buried in her hair.

'Oh, Heather, if you only knew...you're so good for me... you make me feel...like this!' and he lowered his lips to hers, holding her close and they swayed together until they were both breathless.

'Pity we can't stay here all day,' he murmured at last, 'there's nowhere else I'd prefer to be, in this lovely park, on a sunny day...with you.' As Heather drew back her head to look into his face, she was surprised to see traces of tears in his eyes and had to blink rapidly herself before trusting herself to descend the Mound safely.

They made their way slowly back to the car hand in hand, swinging their arms together, keeping an eye out for the two old ladies and quietly, thoughtfully got into the car. Before fastening his seatbelt, Chris leaned across and indulged in one more long, delicious kiss, before starting the engine and pulling out of the car park.

'And I don't care a rap who sees,' he declared, staring defiantly from side to side, almost as if he were hoping they'd had an audience.

It was only when they were well on their way back to Selborne that Heather remembered his last question and turned towards him.

'About the estate, Chris... the idea that Sally *might* inherit did cross my mind – but I reasoned that the circumstances of her birth and all the other complications, 'the knotty knot' would have ruled her out. In any case, the question of inheritance won't arise seriously for years, will it, as the estate will be in Gwen's hands for many years to come?'

Chris pursed his lips doubtfully. 'I'm really not qualified to answer that. As Mr Franklin's widow, that would certainly be the case. Now that she's married again...oh, I really don't know! But I do know that solicitors earn every penny of their fees, sorting out other people's lives for them, don't you agree?'

Heather nodded and fell silent as she gazed out of the window, seeing in her mind's eye the hop fields she remembered from her childhood and, her emotions still aroused from that passionate embrace, unexpectedly found herself overwhelmed by a great wave of nostalgia, sadness and regret. Seeing her fumble for a handkerchief, Chris pulled into a quiet side-road and waited until her shoulders stopped heaving and her breathing steadied.

'Have I upset you?' he asked anxiously, 'is it because...?'

'No...no...just...my Gran, my mother – and my brother – used to come along this road so often,' she said, trying to speak, wipe her eyes and blow her nose all at the same time, 'and now... they've all gone.' Her words ended on an involuntary hiccup.

Chris said nothing for a while but simply cupped her hand in both of his.

'But you have Sally,' he said quietly, 'and you're the Mum. And sometime Sally will have children and you'll be the Mum *and* the Gran...'

'And I'll be able to bore them all to death, mumbling through my false teeth, about how I used to see and smell the hops and meadowsweet and that things were so much better in my day. Oh, Chris, why do we all have to get old, lose the people we love and then...'

'I know,' he said, sighing, 'I know...it's just...inevitable. And, believe me, Heather, I see a lot of people close to death and the fear and worry that oppress us when we're young, seems gradually to disperse, becomes less important and death…somehow more…well, desirable, if you can possibly believe that.' He leaned towards her and holding her arm, very gently kissed her wet cheek and started the car again.

They were both silent until they reached the sharp bend just before the village and Heather ventured to speak again, her voice now well under control.

'How long's Charmian staying?' she asked, 'I do like her, she's so friendly and so tactful.'

'About another week. She comes two or three times a year to make sure I'm eating properly and not wearing the same shirt week after week. Our parents died recently so she still feels she ought to keep an eye on me. She's quite a young widow and like you, her husband was ill for a long time … Parkinsons, such a cruel disease. Her two boys, twins, are at Cambridge studying something scientific and totally incomprehensible to me. They're just a bit younger than Adrian.'

'No children of your own then?' Heather asked tentatively, hoping she wasn't veering onto delicate territory. Chris shook his head regretfully.

'Moira – my wife – it turned out, didn't want children…but somehow it slipped her mind to tell me. That was partly the reason why she left me…. didn't want to be persuaded against her will, I suppose…that and the fact that she'd found somebody else far more fun than a staid old vicar.'

Although he was staring straight ahead, concentrating on his driving, Heather could see by the set of his lips and frowning forehead that this event must have hurt him more than he cared to show. She wished now that she and Kathie hadn't treated his wife's desertion with such levity all those months ago – and it did just make her wonder. Was forty-five too old? … before mentally slapping her wrist.

Before she could betray her thoughts, they arrived back at Westhangar and she turned to Chris again.

'I think it would be as well not to mention what Mr Grundy said about the estate, even though we know nothing would actually change for years. But...if it were to become common knowledge, it might make Sally a target for...well, for unscrupulous men, gold diggers.'

He held his hand out and shook hers warmly. 'I think Sally's far too smart to be taken in by that sort of character. And don't forget, she's got a very astute, protective and sensible mother to ward off any unwelcome advances.'

After she'd changed into comfortable clothes, Heather was greeted by a scene of almost frenzied activity when she made her way down to the Walled Garden. The working party was again at full strength and full stretch. Kathie and Doris, armed with strong leather gloves were searching out broken glass and bits of twisted metal by the derelict glasshouses and chucking them into the wheelbarrow; Bob and Harry were laying about them with scythes and shears and tossing debris onto yet another bonfire; Stewart and Kathie had cleared more of the area in and around the tumbledown chalet and were seated on a pile of rescued planks, studying the photograph of the area that Heather had given Stewart.

'We could easily re-build it,' she heard Kathie say, 'there'd be room for chairs and a picnic table and somewhere to put a camping-stove to make our coffee to save Elsie the trouble of coming out here with a tray – ah, speak of the devil – oh, it's only Heather. How d'you get on?'

Heather perched herself next to Stewart before replying.

'Well, the necklace and coins are safely in the bank, Mr Grundy is in charge of sorting out the future of Westhangar, Chris and I have had coffee and doughnuts in the Market café with Mrs Grierson and her friend so there's nothing to worry about until Gwen comes back. And,' she added, looking round at all the activity around her, 'how come Adrian and Sally are getting out of all the hard work?'

'Adrian decided he'd give her a riding lesson,' Kathie replied, 'so they're both down in the paddock. Don't worry, he's a competent rider and I made sure they both had hard

hats. Seems to me like the beginning of a beautiful romance…
what do you think, Stewart?'

Stewart looked a little startled, then, gathering Kathie's
meaning, he nodded and grinned.

'Good…good…that would be…very good,' he said at last
and fell to studying the picture of the chalet again, as a little
flush of colour rose in his cheeks. Heather nudged Kathie and
murmured below her breath.

'He thought for the moment you meant you and him,' she
said, then noticing Kathie's discomfiture, nudged her more
firmly in the ribs.

'Now *you're* blushing,' she accused her, before getting up
from her uncomfortable perch, 'Right - I have a bit more tidying
up of my research to get on with,' she added and wandered, still
partly in a dream, back to the stables, where she opened Mr
Franklin's diary once more and stared at the pages of scribble
before her. No good trying to concentrate as the words danced
and dazzled before her eyes, swept back in time first of all to
that unforgettable moonlit night when she and Skip lay together
under the Judas trees and began the life of her beloved daughter.
Then, with a delicious shudder of anticipation, she dared to
think…what would it be like with Chris?

It took Heather until well after midnight to fall asleep that
night as she re-lived those blissful hugs and kisses on the top
of the Mound and in the car, her whole body flushing with
warmth and excitement as she recalled his words, the feel of
his face nuzzling her hair, pressing so hard on her lips, yearning
for those moments to come again.

Heather was woken next morning by a loud rendition of
'Happy Birthday to You' to find Sally bending over her with a
cup of tea in one hand, an envelope and a small parcel in the
other. Inside the parcel was a book of geriatric jokes and a
packet of condoms, reducing Heather to such a state of giggles
that she almost tipped her tea all over the duvet. Over the
suggestive name on the packet, Sally had pasted a fresh sticker
with 'Vicar's Delight' scrawled on it with marker-pen.

'Thanks a lot,' she said, giving her daughter a playful slap on the head, 'just what I've always wanted. You'll get these back for *your* birthday if you're not more respectful to your wise old mother!'

'Talking about birthdays,' said Sally when they were both up and dressed, 'mine and Adrian's are almost the same – just a week between them in September. Isn't that a co-incidence?'

Heather looked at her daughter and began to laugh with delight.

'Absolutely not!' she said, 'work it out for yourself!' and she couldn't stop chuckling all the way down the stairs and into the kitchen, where she was greeted by another rendering of the birthday song and a pile of packets balanced on her plate. There was a small china horse from Kathie, a hand-knitted pair of mittens from Elsie (and from Dorrie, she explained, as they had made one each), a book about trees from Stewart and Adrian had given her a colourful beaded bracelet he'd bought in Tenerife.

'Goodness knows how you knew the date,' Heather gasped, wiping her eyes, then noticed a small pile of cards which had disappeared under some discarded wrapping-paper.

'Always helps to know the postman,' explained Kathie, 'we've been saving these up for the last couple of days when we discovered someone had given the game away.'

On the back of one of the envelopes one of her old college friends had written in pink, 'All the best for the 20th of August, you ancient old cow!' with a row of crosses beside the message.

'So, it wasn't exactly hard to put two and two together,' explained Adrian, 'then we passed the news around.'

'Does that mean the whole village knows?' gasped Heather, her face a picture of anxiety, but Adrian reassured her that they'd only told one or two. As if on cue, once they had all finished their breakfasts, there was a tap on the kitchen door and in walked Chris and Charmian who both treated her to a warm hug and kiss.

'Any excuse,' Heather heard Kathie murmur as they handed her a card and a rectangular packet.

'Whatever's this?' Heather wondered, feeling it all over and glancing up at the brother and sister who stood watching her. She unwrapped it carefully, then uttered a long hoot of surprise and delight as she gazed on a large, charcoal sketch of Westhangar Hall taken from an angle which also included the stables and the window of her room, with the two horses' heads poking out of the stable doors below. She'd captured the simple dignity of the old house perfectly.

'It's...it's... absolutely gorgeous!' she said at last, looking at Charmian with wonder in her eyes. 'Whenever did you find time to do this?'

'Chris told me he'd keep you away in Alton yesterday for a few hours, so I sneaked up here and did a quick drawing which I worked up later in the day. Had to guess a bit doing the horses but at least I knew roughly what they both looked like. Luckily, we had some unwanted pictures in the Vicarage, so we were able to use one of their frames.'

'Hope they weren't gifts from grateful parishioners,' remarked Kathie, 'who'll be extremely upset when they can't find their carefully-selected present in prime position on the wall.' Chris assured her that they'd been there since the vicar before last or even before that so there was little danger.

'Unless it was Mrs Grierson's,' whispered Adrian to Sally, not, unfortunately, quietly enough to escape Chris's sharp ears.

'I'll have you know, young man,' Chris said with mock seriousness, 'that Mrs G. is a very generous woman, a great supporter of the Church – and where would we be if she wasn't there to lead us all in the hymns?'

'This picture will remind me of Westhangar and Selborne for ever,' Heather said quietly, wrapping it up again and tucking it under her arm. 'And now, Sally and I are going to visit the Wakes and pay homage to Selborne's most famous son. Then I'll come and do my share of slaving away in the Walled Garden.'

She was as good as her word. After spending a couple of hours looking at old copies of the *Natural History*, stuffed animals and birds in glass cases, skeletons and sketches of birds, then sitting in Gilbert White's barrel seat in his garden and looking up at the Zig-Zag, they returned to Westhangar to see what progress had been made since yesterday.

Chapter Eighteen

A week later, news came through that Gwen and Barry would be arriving at Westhangar in three days' time. This elicited a frantic tidying-up and cleaning and scrubbing of the kitchen, dusting, polishing of furniture and a good deal of baking. Adrian made a 'Welcome Home to Mum and Dad' sign to put over the front door while Heather played her part by sweeping the drive and courtyard, already becoming littered with the first of early Autumn leaves. She, Kathie and Stewart found the time to attend a coffee-morning at the Vicarage to say farewell to Charmian and it was towards the end of the gathering when most people had left, that she managed to draw Heather aside for a quiet moment.

'Promise me you'll look after Chris when I've left,' she said confidentially, 'vicars can get quite lonely despite all the contact they have with their parishioners, who expect him to have time for them all. Sometimes it's the vicar himself who needs comfort and support. His wife let him down disgracefully, but he's always had the guilty feeling that it was his fault she left him, so his fault she died so tragically.'

At Heather's nod, she continued. 'It's been many years now since that disaster, I thought he might never get over it – but I've seen such a change in him since you came here, so much more relaxed, more optimistic and much more fun.'

Heather smiled and sighed, regretfully.

'I'm really fond of Chris,' she said guardedly, 'I suppose that's becoming obvious. But, Charmian, I've been thinking hard about...about him and me...and I know I could never share in his religious beliefs, not with real sincerity. If we could remain as...as just close friends...that wouldn't be a problem. But...with him being a vicar, with his parishioners looking up to and respecting him...we couldn't just live together, could we?"

She heaved another sigh and frowned distractedly. 'But...I know...I just *know*, Charmian, that he wants us to become more than that. If he seriously mentioned marriage, I simply don't know what I'd do. He's just the sort of man I could love, 'till death us do part' and all that jazz, like a healthy, strong and active version of my late husband Jerome, kind and thoughtful.' And with beautiful manners, she thought to herself, considering how much her mother would have approved of him. 'But it would be under false pretences, Charmian. Surely, a vicar needs a real believer at his side to help with his ministry.' She managed a slight, ironic smile, 'a younger version of Mrs Grierson, perhaps!'

'Heaven forbid!' Charmian laughed, 'spare him that! And, Heather, I know my brother well enough to know that he would never force his beliefs on you. As far as I know he doesn't judge me, and he knows I have mixed feelings about religion – any religion. It can be divisive, cruel, murderous even and encourages people to stop thinking for themselves and leave it all to God. Well, as far as I'm concerned, there's nobody upstairs smiling down on us, so we have to shift for ourselves. And my dear brother would be a far better, more tolerant and forgiving vicar if he were happily married. There...I've had my say!'

She paused a moment and gave Heather's hand a quick squeeze.

'And I'll really look forward to seeing you again in the New Year. You've brought a breath of fresh air into Selborne, Heather, and especially into that little community at Westhangar. *Promise* me you won't go and run away before then.'

Heather smiled without making any such commitment. For how could she possibly tell where she'd be in another four months? Having doubts about her future, now that, after twelve years of widowhood, she had found a man she could really love was little short of agony. Oh, why did religion have to get in the way and spoil everything?

After the coffee morning, she, Kathie and Stewart made their way, as usual, over to the Walled Garden, almost unrecognisably the same jungle that Heather had first seen all those months ago. The brick foundations of the glasshouses had been exposed with new bricks filling the gaps where old ones had crumbled away. Their interiors were now cleared down to central brick pathways and matching empty beds each side, just crying out to be filled with tender plants and fruits. A pile of new timber, window-frames and a door had been delivered and were stacked beside the remains of the chalet. Unruly scrub and shrubs had been rooted out or trimmed and the sites of the once-trimmed peacocks had been identified.

'Hope Gwen will be pleased with our work,' remarked Heather, looking round her with satisfaction. 'It's amazing what we've managed to achieve in just a few weeks with us all working together.'

'Knowing Gwen,' remarked Kathie acidly, 'she probably won't even notice. Gardening wasn't her strong point, it was all left to Stewart after John died, and he'd already lost heart since Jenny and the children died. And we'll have to do without Bob and Harry now too, a shame as they've been an absolute godsend, but they need to get back to their regular jobs in the rest of the garden. Gwen won't be happy if there isn't the usual show of bedding-plants and bulbs in the formal gardens, she does like that sort of thing.'

Heather heaved a deep sigh but said nothing even though her imagination was working overtime.

'The chalet's coming on a treat,' continued Kathie, 'Stewart ordered a bag of ready-mix from the ironmongers to patch a few gaps in the base, a roll of roofing felt *and* some preservative paint, being delivered tomorrow, so all's well.'

'Did he do that himself?' Heather asked with surprise and Kathie nodded.

'I stood by in case he was suddenly lost for words, but he managed. Did you know he's been visiting a speech therapist?' Heather shook her head. 'Chris has been running him into Alton once a week for his appointments then he gets him to walk up and down the High Street and go into one or two shops. He's improving every day.'

'He's a good soul,' murmured Heather quietly and Kathie gave her a sharp glance. 'Chris...or Stewart,' she asked mischievously, then returned to the subject of the chalet.

'Once the base is mended, probably later today, we can all muck in with the actual building – and, with a bit of luck, it'll be finished, painted and glazed by the time the honeymooners arrive back. Elsie's found some old carpet in the attic and one of us could rig up some curtaining.'

Heather could already see in her mind's eye a row of potted geraniums and small conifers along the outside walls, a water-butt to catch rain from the roof and perhaps they could heave one of the neglected stone statues over to stand guardian by the door.

'It'll look splendid,' she said, 'and of course I'll help, much more fun than being shut up in the stables in this lovely weather. And,' she added, 'in a week or two it's Sally's and Adrian's 24th birthdays - a few days apart but they're planning a joint party.'

Heather returned to her study feeling suddenly light-hearted and enthusiastic after her encouraging chat with Charmian, the good news about Stewart's progress and the work going on so well in the Walled Garden, which inspired her to get out the old photo-album once more, mulling over the 100-year-old black-and-white pictures. No chalet then of course but what really excited her were two rows of wooden pergolas running along three sides of the garden, hung with laburnum, rambling roses and possibly clematis clinging to the posts very much in the style of Lutyens and Jekyll – no trace of them at all now, but surely the bases would still be there? To fill in the time before lunch, she pulled out a clean sheet from her pad of typing paper and began a rough sketch of how some of the old features could be re-instated, her heart beating fast with excitement. Throwing away the first two efforts, she made a fair copy, filling borders with colourful perennials, annuals in front, just as she had learned at college all those years ago.

She leaned back in her chair, her hands behind her head and heaved a sigh. She *must* find some way of remaining at Westhangar – in the five months since her arrival it had become her home, the staff had become the only family she had besides Sally. And she could hardly bear the thought that all the renovation work in the Walled Garden would be going on without her. She pinned her sketch of its possible transformation onto her notice board, then fell to wondering what she should do about Mr Franklin's diary.

So far, she was the only person who knew that it contained his frank description of the stolen episode that had given her Sally, the only evidence that would help to prove that she was his daughter, should more be needed besides her obvious resemblance to him and her own sworn statement. It hardly mattered that Chris knew; he could be trusted to inform people – if he felt they needed to be informed – in a tactful manner. But, even if he kept his promise to intercept Gwen before her arrival and warn her of Heather's brief fling with her husband, what would be her attitude to Sally, the living evidence and result of their folly? And how would Gwen, and Sally herself feel if the exact circumstances were to be made known to a curious, gossip-loving public? Speculation was one thing – truth was another, especially with many of the village residents having been well known to Gwen and her husband and now to herself.

How could Mr Grundy prevent that happening? What would the great and good of the village think? She could imagine Mrs Grierson's reaction! And all because of herself. If she had never come to this house, Skip's and her moment of madness in 1961 would never have been known. Heather, however, would never have been able to name the real father of her child and Sally would never have known her true parentage. Even though Sally had never set eyes on her father, she had told her mother that just knowing who he was and seeing his portrait had given her some sense of where and to whom she belonged, and that was a good thing. But Gwen... how would she react? Should she and Sally leave, quietly and unobtrusively, before Gwen's return?

And yet...her mind kept swinging this way and that...all her friends at Westhangar had accepted the situation with understanding. Perhaps...with all their support and Chris's tactful explanations, she could stay and face the music, 'deal with it' as her father would have advised. But this *still* left her with the problem of what to do about the diary. Should she destroy what could be the evidence she needed to help prove Sally's parentage if it proved necessary? It was against all her instincts to dispose of records especially when there was only one copy. Oh, she sighed, her head in her hands, why did life have to be so complicated?

There came the sound of footsteps on the stairs, followed by a light tap on her door and there stood Chris, causing her heart to leap as it did now every time she saw him.

'Just seen your daughter and Adrian exercising the horses,' he remarked, glancing around the room. 'He must be a good teacher or else she's a very quick learner as they were both cantering around the paddock like a pair of professionals.'

Heather smiled wanly, then sighed before replying.

'It's lovely to see them getting on so well together – and so hard for me to stop building castles in the air... those two together. I have to stop myself encouraging them, but don't want to put them off!'

Chris stood behind her, wrapping his arms around her waist and kissed her head, burying his face in her hair.

'My advice...if you need it,' he said, 'is simply to let nature take its course. They're not teenagers, after all.'

Heather nodded but her expression was serious, and she wore a worried frown.

'It's not how they feel about each other that's the problem,' she murmured, clasping his arms with her own, 'but *who* they both are. They're not just two strangers who happened to meet on a train, although that's what they think they are. Just suppose...'

Chris disentangled himself and pulled a chair closer to the desk, the better to listen to Heather's worries.

'Just suppose,' she repeated, 'just suppose Mr Grundy decides that Sally would be the right person, the blood relation, to inherit Westhangar, how would Adrian feel about her when he must still think it ought to have been his? And Gwen? What's she going to think about Sally and me anyway once she knows of our – our connection with her husband? I really think, Chris, I *really* think it would be better for all concerned if Sally and I just slipped away quietly before Gwen and Barry arrive. Sally, I hope, would understand...eventually.'

Chris jerked upright in his chair and gripped Heather's upper arms quite fiercely, painfully, and shook her, frowning.

'No! Don't even think of it!' he almost barked, 'I never thought of you as a coward! Just because you don't think you could face Gwen, you're prepared to ruin the future happiness of your daughter and the boy she's falling in love with? If Adrian was hurt again so soon after his parents' betrayal of him, I don't know what he would do. It would be...' he drew in his breath, 'it would be criminal to separate them now.' He got up, scraping the chair sharply and stood over her, scowling.

Shocked by his sudden vehemence Heather sat staring straight in front of her rubbing her arms where his fingers had dug into her, unable to speak or even think straight, appalled that anyone should accuse her of cowardice when her intention had been to help solve a problem rather than worsen it. She turned her head slowly and looked at him nervously, biting her lip, afraid of what she might read in his expression.

'I didn't mean...' she began, her voice husky with the difficulty of speaking, 'I just thought...it might be...for the best.' She gulped and cleared her throat. 'I don't want to leave

Westhangar one little bit, I love it here. But I just think...
I thought I *ought* to clear out.'

Chris's expression softened instantly as soon as he saw how
confused she was, and he drew her to him in a warm hug.

'I'm sorry,' he said softly, stroking her arms, 'I didn't mean
to shout at you, I was just taken by surprise – shocked! Also,'
he added, pushing her tousled hair back off her forehead,
'being entirely selfish, I don't want to lose you, Heather.
I don't want you to leave Selborne now...or ever!'

As they hugged together, she could feel his warm breath on
her neck and his arms tightening around her.

'Please...,' he said, his voice urgent, intense, 'don't go away,
Heather. Can't you see I'm falling in love with you more and
more every day? I know exactly how those two young people
feel,' he waved a hand in the general direction of the paddock,
'even though I'm nearly fifty! I never thought I'd feel this way
again, never dreamed I'd have the chance to feel...young!
Please tell me I'm not just someone to keep you amused for a
few weeks. I don't think I could bear it!'

'Chris,' Heather began in a low voice, glancing at him,
distressed to see the fearful expression on his face, 'of course I
don't think that! And I do, I *do* feel the same, except...'

'Except?' Chris muttered, gritting his teeth, as if he didn't
really want to hear her answer, 'must there be an 'except'?'

Heather took a deep breath before replying.

'Except that I'm really not sure I'd be the right person to
share your life...I can't suddenly become a believer, I'd be
living a lie if I pretended, just to be able to live with you.'

'But you *could* live with me? Is that what you're saying? If
my religion wasn't a problem?' he urged, hope suddenly
springing back into his eyes, 'and if I said I didn't give a damn
about your beliefs or lack of them? Truly, Heather...I just
want *you*! I want you to marry me, you can have as long as
you like to think about it. I couldn't give up my beliefs any
more than you could adopt them under false pretences. But it's
not unusual nowadays for vicar's wives to follow their own

interests, their own careers…it needn't be a problem unless we make it one, I promise you.'

Heather stood up and lifting one of his hands to her lips, kissed it gently.

'Listen,' she said, ushering Chris firmly but politely to the door before her resolve weakened, 'first let me deal with facing Gwen and Barry – and there's Sally's birthday coming up fast and I haven't bought her a present yet. And Adrian's too. And I have to decide what to do with Mr Franklin's diary. And if it's any comfort to you, Chris, I'm not likely to go off and marry anyone else…I promise you that at least.'

He stood at the top of the stairs, looking back at her for a moment, a slight smile playing around his lips.

'I shall have to be content with that, then, I suppose,' he agreed, 'but I'm warning you, Heather, I shall ask you again when you're least expecting it,' and he went off down the stairs, leaving her in more of a state of confusion than ever.

Any hope of deciding what to do with those compromising diary entries was completely shattered by what had just occurred. She'd suspected, hoped even, that Chris might propose at some stage in their relationship. This sudden, fierce declaration, however, had rather knocked her feet from under her. Jerome, she recalled, had prepared the ground carefully, thoughtfully, with a delicious meal in a semi-lit restaurant, Greek music playing seductively in the background, with a bouquet of flowers delivered to their table, his beautifully worded proposal nestling amongst the blooms.

To clear her head, she packed up her work, locked the door and wandered down to the paddock to see if Sally wanted to come into the town with her to choose her own present and stood for a moment gazing up at the Hangar. The beech trees were beginning to turn from dark, shiny green to a mixture of beige and yellow and the far-off drone of tractors cutting the wheat fields beyond the paddock broke in on her troubling thoughts. Swallows were beginning to gather on the telegraph wires, twittering to each other, preparing for their long migration ahead and she realised with a pang of regret how much she would miss waiting for their return next Spring if she left Westhangar now.

She stood watching Sally and Adrian as they dismounted, sending Champion and Conker across the field with a slap on their rumps, pulling off their hats as they came towards her waving cheerfully, a tumble of dark curls escaping from Adrian's, red-gold ones from Sally's, a lovely sight.

'See you later,' Adrian called to Sally with a cheerful wave at Heather.

'Not if I see you first,' she replied automatically, then turned her attention to her mother. 'He's got an appointment with the estate-manager,' she explained, dusting down her trousers, 'and then this evening we're going to the cinema in Alton, but at the moment, I've got nothing to do."

'Want to come out for a spin in Frog?' Heather asked, at which Sally nodded vigorously.

'So long as you'll let me drive, I'm longing to have a look at our old home again.'

'Of course,' replied Heather, altering her plans in a split-second. There'd still be two whole days to get her a present – in any case she might prefer money to buy her own. 'Got your licence with you?'

Heather was pleasantly surprised at how well and carefully Sally drove, especially as it was some time since she had driven her mother's car. They spent the journey pointing out well-known landmarks to each other, sighing to remember the picnics in the Rolls Royce and pausing for several minutes in front of the drive leading up to their former home, each occupied with their differing memories of the happy but often turbulent years they had spent there, Heather thinking of Craig and Sally of her kitten that had been lost for days, then found, alive but very thin, caught in a tangle of wire in the wood at the back of the garden.

'What will I do without her when she goes back to Hatfield?' sighed Heather soberly, as they swapped places so that she could drive back, then cheered up as she realised that it would only be six weeks until the half-term holiday and with Adrian as an inducement, Sally would be sure to want to spend it in Selborne again.

After an early supper she drove the two of them to the cinema and arranged that they should come back by taxi. It was such a beautiful Autumn evening that she decided to stroll up the Hangar to the place by the Wishing Stone where she had first seen Stewart, then took the path to that part of the wood where she had first encountered Adrian, her heart beating strongly as she remembered the horror of that first meeting. She sat down as close as possible to the same spot, looking down on the long grey roof of Westhangar Hall and thought back across the months at all that had happened since; seeing the stables, her own little world; meeting Kathie, soon to become such a down-to-earth, amusing friend; and Elsie and Doris, arousing such surprising, pleasant memories of her childhood; glimpsing and later entering the neglected Walled Garden which had tugged at her heart so powerfully; sitting beside Adrian in front of the Gilbert White Memorial window; learning of Stewart's family tragedy and watching his gradual recovery; her friendly acceptance by the people of Selborne; her riding lessons on Conker. Then the shock of finding Mr Franklin's diary...seeing his portrait... and the growing suspicion, followed by conviction, that he and she had met before; the cross-written letter from Alicia that had led, first to disappointment when the hoped-for gold turned out to be mere clay, then sudden elation at the discovery of the gold sovereigns and the diamond and emerald set of jewellery.

And then there was Chris. Heather leaned her back against a tree, rays of low sun darting between gently moving branches, forcing her to close her eyes, the better to re-live every moment of every meeting she had had with him, every look, word, touch and kiss. Would she be able to overcome her doubts, her feelings of unease at the prospect of joining her life to a man of such conviction and sincerity, which would inevitably result in her becoming involved with church affairs? And would that be enough to satisfy her? Although she had loved being married to Jerome and he, she and Sally had been the almost perfect family, she couldn't deny that she had also appreciated her more recent years of independence, able to choose her occupations, her jobs, where she lived, her holidays...and there had always been Sally as the anchor to her life, away perhaps for weeks and months at a time when she was at University, but who'd always returned to their home in Hatfield to enliven her mother's days and keep her abreast of modern ways and modern thinking.

But... Sally would not be with her for ever. At almost twenty-four she would already be later than most young women at flying the nest, and with Adrian in the picture, it was more than likely that, any day now she would be hearing her say, 'By the way, Mum, I'm thinking of...' and that would be the end of their closeness. A sudden prospect of her impending loneliness, the thought that nobody then would need her, brought on a flood of unexpected tears.

So much was going to depend on Gwen's reaction to her knowledge of Sally's parentage. If she proved hostile – and who could blame her? – Heather could never feel comfortable at Westhangar or even in the village. As she rose from the undergrowth beneath the beech trees and made her way slowly down to the road, she tried to note every house, every garden, tree and footpath, imprinting them as closely as possible on her mind. She would soon have to come to a decision that would inevitably alter the course of her future life.

Chapter Nineteen

Next day Sally surprised her with the news that she and Adrian had decided to celebrate their birthdays half-way between the two dates, 24 September, with a day out at a nearby Stately Home and that anyone from Westhangar would be welcome to accompany them.

'And you can bring Chris,' she said to Heather, 'so long as he's not visiting the sick, baptising, marrying or burying anyone that afternoon.'

During the general cheer that went up round the table, Heather's muted contribution was hardly noticed, as she secretly wondered whether she would be a welcome member of the party...or the skeleton at the feast? She would soon find out.

Gwen and Barry were expected to arrive in mid-afternoon and Chris was taking Adrian to meet them off the train. Heather tossed and turned throughout the night before, trying not to wake Sally, worrying and wondering what the morrow would bring. After her morning ride on Conker, she sat staring at the neat piles of papers in the study and went over and over in her mind what she would say and do if confronted by a furious, tearful Gwen.

'I'm so sorry.... had no idea... never knew his name... such a shock to me... would never have come here if I'd known...!' All possible explanations sounded implausible, feeble, and she tried to prepare herself for shock, anger, instant dismissal... disappointment for Sally and Adrian, the misery of having to say goodbye to all her new-found friends and Westhangar. Kathie, noticing her preoccupation and the dark circles around her eyes, with quick understanding, offered to take Sally for a riding lesson to co-incide with the couple's arrival which would lessen the difficulty of the confrontation a little.

'The horses won't mind a second ride out,' she assured Heather and slipped a comforting arm around her shoulders, 'and if there's any trouble with Gwen I'll threaten to resign. She can't do without me so don't worry about a thing!'

But how could she help worrying? She spent the couple of hours after lunch pacing round and round her rooms, mentally packing up her belongings, trying to plan what to do about Mr Franklin's diary, wondering what Mr Grundy would make of her and Sally's sudden departure and how it might affect the future of the estate, all the while listening anxiously for the arrival of Chris's car in the courtyard.

At last, she heard the crunch of tyres on fallen beech leaves, voices, laughter, the slamming of car doors and felt her stomach heave with nervous sickness. She peered cautiously out of the window, looking down on the cheerful little group below, watching as Chris helped unload suitcases and straw baskets out of his car.

'Couldn't resist a few souvenirs,' she heard Gwen say merrily, packets of this and that tumbling out of her arms, 'oh, thank-you Chris,' as he bent to retrieve a soft parcel that had almost rolled under the car, 'skirts for Elsie and Doris and a whole heap of jazzy T-shirts, even one for you, Vicar, with a bee-eater on it. We'll tip them all out on the kitchen table just like a jumble-sale. Now, Barry,' Heather heard her exclaim, 'welcome to Westhangar!'

Heather craned forward the better to see the new addition to the family, not tall but sturdy, sun-tanned from his holiday and with a tumble of dark brown curly hair streaked with grey and heard him reply with a deep peal of laughter. There could be no mistaking whose father he was, especially when she caught sight of Barry and Adrian standing close together, deep in conversation. She swallowed hard, hating the thought that this happy homecoming might soon become unpleasantly acrimonious and watched as the little group disappeared into the house.

To her surprise, after less than ten minutes, Gwen emerged, waving goodbye to Chris and headed straight towards the stables. At the same moment, Kathie and Sally arrived, swinging their riding hats by the straps and, to her astonishment, Heather saw Gwen take one look at her daughter then threw her arms round her in a tight hug and give a laugh of delight.

'See you both at lunch,' she said, leaving Sally looking stunned at this unexpected show of affection, 'must have a word with your Mum,' and, while Kathie tactfully bore Sally off in the direction of her rooms, Heather waited with trepidation as Gwen's footsteps sounded on the staircase. At her light knock, she drew in her breath, opened the door, gritted her teeth and looked directly into her employer's eyes.

'Don't shirk – deal with it!' she heard her father's words in her mind, then felt her elbows grasped as Gwen held her firmly, backing her into her room.

'No need to look so scared,' she said, her eyes crinkling with amusement, 'not going to eat you! And don't worry – Chris has explained everything to me. I just find it completely hilarious to think of you dallying with my husband almost at the same time as I was...well, enjoying Barry's company. And just look at the two splendid people we produced between us! And I must tell you this...may I sit down a moment?'

Heather gestured towards the spare chair and sat down herself, weak with relief, staring at Gwen, who leaned towards her, merriment in her eyes and took both her hands in hers.

'When Adrian greeted me at the station,' she said, breathlessly, 'he hardly had time to give me a peck on the cheek and say 'Hi' to Barry before he gabbled out, "Mum! I've met the girl I want to marry!" to which I replied, totally taken by surprise, "Well then, Adrian, go for it!" without thinking that she might be somebody entirely unsuitable. So, I looked at Chris and said, "Do you know this girl?" then Adrian chipped in before he could answer, "Of course he does, she's the daughter of the woman that *he* wants to marry, so she's my fa...John Franklin's daughter!" And then he said, looking suddenly worried, "I would be allowed to marry her, wouldn't I, Chris, not forbidden by the Bible or anything?" Then Chris said, "well, you'd better ask her first, that's the most important thing. And she's no relation of yours, no need to worry about consanguinity. And if she says 'yes' you'll both have my blessing" Then, on the journey home he went on to explain yours and my – extraordinary – connection, very keen to emphasise the fact that you arrived at Westhangar in total ignorance of who my husband was.'

Heather sat back, trying to take it all in, her head swirling with a torrent of surprises. How could it be that, in the space of a few hours, her plans had changed from packing up and leaving Hampshire with all its memories and connections with her childhood, to staying here in Selborne, close to all the friends she had made, close too to Sally if she chose to marry Adrian? It was all a bit too much to take in.

'A co-incidence made in Heaven, I believe,' Gwen said, 'and another thing. Since Adrian had blurted out the fact that you and Chris were becoming...close, Chris said he felt you were having doubts about becoming a vicar's wife without status or a career of your own. So that gave me the most sensational idea! Heather, I intend to appoint you as Head Gardener of Westhangar Hall with a budget to allow you a free hand to do what you will with the gardens here. I'm told you've already inspired my brother to take an interest again in the Walled Garden and if Bob and Harry won't mind taking their orders from you instead of me – well, I'd be very relieved! John was always the gardener, not me, until his heart-attack. My idea of Heaven is to ride around our beautiful countryside, visit a friend for coffee, eat one of Elsie's delicious little lunches, then sit in the garden with a G and T and admire someone else's hard work.'

There was a long silence. It was all so tempting and so totally unexpected.

'That must have been some car journey from the station,' Heather remarked at last, at which Gwen laughed again.

'Yes...I think we drove about five times round the Butts,' she admitted, then rose and headed for the door, 'now I must go and see Elsie and Kathie and meet your daughter properly. And no need to make any decisions about anything yet. We need to sort out all manner of legal details with Mr Grundy concerning the estate and that'll take time. But that can all wait...let's just enjoy today. I want to show Barry round everywhere and he needs to meet Stewart and the horses, and I want to see what you've all been up to in the Walled Garden ... and then ...' Her voice trailed off as she trotted off down the stairs, still chatting and Heather watched out of the window until she was out of sight.

Overcome with amazement and relief, Heather felt suddenly faint as the room began to revolve around her and, stumbling into her bedroom, flung herself onto the bed and lay there gasping, hardly knowing whether to laugh or cry. She'd been worried sick in anticipation of Gwen's reaction to the news of her husband's dalliance, then equally shocked to discover that she seemed to regard their two escapades as one enormous joke. Had Gwen had absolutely no compunction about breaking her marriage vows so soon after her wedding?

Had Barry swept her off her feet in much the same way that Heather had been on that warm Mediterranean night? Had he seduced Gwen in a similar way, underneath a velvety sky studded with stars, caught up in a fever of excitement and desire? And if so...could Heather think worse of her than she did of herself?

Another thing...it seemed that Chris's attachment to her was now common knowledge, which he had done nothing to refute. Was there a conspiracy amongst the people of Selborne to marry off their vicar? Had Charmian been secretly campaigning on his behalf? Had Mrs Grierson and her friend, after seeing them together in the café in Alton, been spreading rumours about them at the Mother's Union, WI or at the latest beetle-drive? Did all these people in the village know what was good for her better than she knew herself?

Suppose she did marry him and discover, too late, that they were incompatible? Suppose he insisted on wearing his socks or eating cream crackers in bed? I suppose I could ask him, she thought and suddenly rolled up on the bed, convulsed with laughter. I *can't* ask him for a test drive – can I? Not a vicar – surely!

At that moment, she heard Sally's footsteps on the stairs and, after the lightest of taps on the door, she flew into the bedroom, astounded to see her mother flat out on her bed, still shaking with unstoppable giggles.

'You OK?' she asked, looking down on her with genuine concern, 'are you laughing or crying? Shall I get Kathie?'

Heather pushed herself up onto her elbow and wiped her eyes on a corner of the sheet, then heaved herself into a sitting position and regarded her daughter thoughtfully.

'Now, Sally,' she said, 'you know all about modern life. Is it done these days for a woman to ask a man to spend the night with her, just so that she can check that…that everything is in working order?'

Sally looked at her mother aghast, her mouth opening and closing as she sought for the right answer and there were several seconds' silence.

'Well!' she said at last, flopping down on the bed beside Heather, 'I'm sure it's OK for *some* people – but I can't believe you'd ever have the cheek to ask Chris! Suppose he said no! You'd feel incredibly rejected…and humiliated! And, after all, Mum, think about it. You're forty-five, not a teenager! I mean…!'

'You just wait until you're forty-five, young lady and been single and celibate for over twelve years…the feeling of longing never goes away. Not until you're at least four-score and ten… or is it three-score? Can't remember, have to ask Chris!'

'While you're checking his equipment!' spluttered Sally, letting out a lusty laugh, then standing and pulling Heather up by both hands. 'You've made me laugh so much, I've almost forgotten what I was going to tell you.'

She tried to compose her features into something nearing normality. 'Now listen, Mum, this is serious stuff. Adrian and I want to get engaged, I mean, as soon as we've heard what Mr Grundy has to say about the estate, who'll own it, who'll manage it, will Gwen and Barry want to continue to live here...oh, a hundred things!'

Heather shouldn't have been surprised by this announcement, especially as she had predicted it ever since her first meetings with Adrian but nevertheless it came as a shock.

'Well, darling,' she said at last, 'you've only known him for a fortnight! How can you be thinking...?'

'That's why we don't want to get engaged yet,' broke in Sally, 'but...we feel so sure and wanted you to know first. I know it's crazy, but we're prepared to wait a while, perhaps until the Christmas holidays. We surely should know by then. And you would approve, wouldn't you, Mum, he's such a darling? And if he finds out after all that he won't inherit the estate, surely there'd be some way we could stay here, an empty farm cottage or a flat somewhere? The local school might have a job for me or there's sure to be something in Alton. Oh, please say you'd like him for a son-in-law, I know he likes you – ever so much!'

Heather gave Sally a tight hug, smiling with affection as she noticed a few blades of hay in her hair. I wonder how they got there, she thought idly, then sat Sally down in the chair in the study and faced her squarely.

'A few months ago,' she began, 'I found Adrian sitting in the church, still desperately upset that neither of his parents had had the courage to tell him that he was not Mr Franklin's real son. He struck me then, and he strikes me still, as a lovely young man, warm-hearted and sensitive and I remember telling him that, if I'd had a son, I'd have liked one like him. So, I could hardly object to him becoming my son-in-law, could I?'

Sally leapt out of her chair and treated Heather to a warm, firm kiss on the cheek.

'But I think you're sensible to wait a while,' Heather said, her expression solemn, 'Keep your engagement a private matter between you and Adrian and me now of course, as there may be hazards along the way with this business of the estate which neither you nor Adrian may have foreseen. I think Mr Grundy is going to have his work cut out to untangle this muddle – and solicitors' time doesn't come cheap. But if you'd be happy enough in a farm cottage then I think that proves that you and Adrian really do love each other, and I'd be happy for you.'

As Sally went down the stairs, whistling cheerfully, Heather leaned back in her chair, her hands behind her head, an affectionate smile on her lips. Farm cottage indeed! Even if, by some mischance, it was proved that neither Sally nor Adrian would gain any benefit from the estate, dear Jerome had made sure that Sally would never have to go begging for her bread. At the thought of Jerome, wasting away in his last years but never losing his courage or good humour, Heather felt herself suddenly overwhelmed with sadness, regret and a little guilt. Did I show him I loved him enough, she wondered, did he really understand how much I relied on and appreciated his goodness, patience and wisdom...and how much I was going to miss him when he died? Would it be disloyal to his memory to marry again?

The following day, Gwen and Barry decided to take Adrian and Sally out for a drive into the New Forest, so, pleased to be alone for a while, Heather walked down to the Plestor, then into the churchyard, sitting awhile on Mr Franklin's memorial seat. If you only knew, she mouthed silently to the man she'd only known, until recently, as 'Skip', what a legacy of complicated relationships you left behind you, perhaps you'd never have led that misty-eyed, happily intoxicated young woman out into the garden in Athens all those years ago. But do I regret it, she asked herself? Perhaps – at the time – but now, seeing those two young people so happy and optimistic about their futures how could she possibly wish it had been otherwise?

With Sally safely away for the day, Heather drove into Alton to look for birthday presents for her and Adrian, completely baffled as to what young men in their twenties would like. Passing a rather superior gentlemen's outfitters, she spotted, amongst the tweed jackets, plus-fours and deerstalker's hats, a smart leather riding-crop and went in boldly to ask the advice of the proprietor, who agreed whole-heartedly with her choice. Swallowing hard to cover her shock at the price, she paid by cheque then planned to give Sally the equivalent in cash for her to make her own choice. I might have made one mistake, she thought, don't want to make two.

After heavy rain the night before, which hampered the bringing in of the harvest for a day or two, the date of Sally's and Adrian's joint birthday celebration dawned clear and sunny. When they assembled in the courtyard after an early lunch to be sorted into carloads, they laughed to see each other arrayed in jazzy Lanzarote T-shirts, Elsie and Doris wearing their new cotton skirts, Stewart and Chris in bright, patterned blazers, Gwen and Barry in matching white trousers and blue tops. Heather, Sally and Adrian travelled in Chris's car, Elsie had room for Doris, Kathie and Stewart while Barry and Gwen had hired a large car *and* driver for the afternoon. They all cheered and waved out of the windows at each other as they set off in convoy *en route* for their destination near Basingstoke.

'Just like a Sunday School outing!' said Sally ecstatically, holding hands with Adrian in the back seat, while Heather, after a quick, happy smile at Chris, gazed out of the window.

'Glad I opted not to drive Frog,' she said, as they sped along the broad main road, easily overtaking all those vehicles in the inner lane, 'Will Stewart will be OK travelling by car?'

Chris nodded and murmured his reply.

'He's been out with me or Gwen a few times to dental appointments, get his hair cut and recently to the speech therapist, and he's sensible enough to realise that he can't walk or bike or go on horseback everywhere.'

'Not like Gilbert White and his flock,' replied Heather, 'imagine what it must have been like with no telephone, no radio or T.V. nothing faster than a horse and cart to carry you anywhere. No gas cookers, no electricity.'

'Well,' said Chris, 'it's what they were used to, a slower pace of life, plenty of time for a learned curate to wander about and look and listen to wild nature all around him and wonder endlessly where the house-martins and swifts went in winter. I sometimes wish I'd lived in the eighteenth-century with time to stand and stare! And every generation is living in the modern age, as far as it's concerned. Just imagine what people five hundred years from now will think of us poor savages while they're all translocating to outer space, subsisting on pills instead of roast beef and apple-crumble, no need to talk to each other as it will all be thought transference.'

'Wonder how they'll have babies,' Heather and Chris overheard Adrian mutter to Sally but before they had to enter into such speculation, they approached the environs of Basingstoke, then reached their destination in another ten minutes.

It was an idyllic day, the Autumn sunshine moderated by a gentle breeze, the flower beds full of late roses, chrysanthemums, heleniums and dahlias, Virginia creeper on the old bricks of the Stately Home just turning to fiery red, yellow sycamore and field maple ablaze in the woodland walks. The united and excited group of ten who emerged from the three cars as they arrived, gradually loosened and separated into smaller ones, meeting round corners from time to time or, in the case of Elsie and Doris, simply relaxing, sprawled on the grass, eyes closed, faces turned towards the sun. As Heather and Chris strolled past them, Heather regarded them both with a sympathetic smile.

'They work so hard, those two,' she confided to Chris in a low voice, 'they hardly ever have time to sit in the gardens at Westhangar. They must be loving every minute of this.'

'Isn't there a lake here somewhere?' she said a few minutes later, looking around her, 'shall we try and find it?' They took a winding path through one of many shrubberies, spotting Kathie and Stewart in the distance and emerged onto a wide grass pathway bordering a long expanse of water, almost perfectly calm, reflecting the blue of the sky and the small white clouds drifting across it. A few ducks dabbling in the reeds at the edge and the occasional fish rising to the surface to catch an unwary flying insect, were the only living creatures they could see. As they stood there, silently gazing at the prospect before them, Heather felt Chris slip his arm around her waist as he guided her towards a rustic summer house, artfully situated at the head of the lake. A few swallows skimmed across the surface, catching mosquitos as they went.

Brushing a scatter of dead leaves off the timber seat inside, Chris sat Heather down then settled himself beside her and together they looked out onto the water, rippling gently now as the ducks swam into the centre, dipping their heads, turning upside-down, causing them both to laugh at their antics.

'Good to hear you laugh,' Chris said quietly, 'you've had a lot on your mind recently, haven't you, my darling?'

Heather nodded, looking at him anxiously.

'I was so worried about Gwen and Barry's return from their honeymoon,' she confessed, 'once they'd realise who Sally was...then amazed when they took it so well. My mind has been in utter turmoil for days with despair, hope, joy... everything!'

'Yes,' murmured Chris as they both stared into the distance, 'I know'. He took her hand and turned her slightly towards him.

'And now,' he said, huskily, 'I'm going to make your life even more complicated.' He paused nervously, darting anxious glances at her, 'because you know what I'm going to ask you, don't you?'

Heather looked down at their two hands clasped together and said nothing. Chris continued, daring to smile, 'and if you say 'no', I shall jump into that lake.'

Heather laughed then and looked into his teasing eyes.

'Go on then – I dare you!' she said.

Chris left the seat and struggled down onto one knee, groaning a little, then took her hand again.

'Mrs La Fontaine ... Heather,' he said, almost solemnly, 'do I dare ask you to do me the honour of becoming my wife? Or would you rather see me drown in that muddy water?'

'Well,' replied Heather uncertainly, 'it would be rather fun to see if you can swim –but a shame to see you spoil your new blazer. So,' she said, with a sigh, 'I'm afraid it's going to have to be 'yes'.'

'Oh! Thank God!' Chris almost shouted and Heather genuinely believed he meant every word. He grabbed her hand again, pulling her upright and started off across the lawn with her in tow then stopped again suddenly, an anxious frown wrinkling his brow.

'You did mean that, didn't you?' he asked, 'not just teasing?' and he veered a little closer to the water, threatening to fall in. Heather grasped his arm in case he overdid the theatricals and burst out, 'Of course I meant "yes"! You just wanted to hear me say it again, didn't you?'

'Over and over again,' Chris said, clasping her to him and burying his face in her hair, 'as often as you like until I really believe it.' There followed the longest and loveliest embrace she could imagine then, too breathless to speak, they began to make their way back through the shrubbery towards the main lawns. As they approached a huge cedar-tree, they both jumped in surprise as Kathie, Stewart, Elsie, Doris, Adrian, Sally, Gwen and Barry appeared from behind it, waving their hands in the air and cheering, causing a group of surprised passers-by to join in by clapping and cheering too.

'You can't fool us!' carolled Gwen, 'we knew what you'd be up to the minute you disappeared down to the lake. That summer house has a reputation, you know. They call it the Pop the Question Pavilion because so many couples have plighted their troth there.'

Doris's eyes widened as she considered what that could possibly mean until Chris explained, 'just means getting engaged,' at which she smiled her approval, then, looking down at Heather's hand remarked abruptly, 'well, where's your ring then?'

Chris and Heather looked at each other in confusion. Then Chris stooped to pick a piece of long grass which he twisted into a circle and slipped onto Heather's finger.

'Just temporary,' he said to Doris, who had looked askance at this unorthodox offering, 'just until we go to buy the real one. Anyway,' he said looking around the little group, 'we mustn't forget that this is supposed to be a celebration of Sally and Adrian's birthdays – we don't want to steal their thunder.'

'Thunder?' repeated Doris, nervously looking up at the sky and Elsie gently drew her aside for a moment while the others drifted over to the picnic area where Gwen and Barry had already pushed together a couple of tables and were unpacking a large hamper, throwing bright gingham tablecloths over them and doling out paper plates and matching napkins.

'Well, why don't 'e say what 'e means?' Heather overheard Doris say plaintively to her sister, but she brightened up when she saw the preparations for the birthday feast.

Adrian and Sally volunteered to order drinks for everyone and went off hand-in-hand to the kiosk. The others arranged themselves on the benches in anticipation of the treats in store and cheered as they made their way back towards the tables without mishap. Then Gwen raided the hamper and brought out packets of cheese sandwiches, sausage rolls, tiny orange tomatoes, chunks of ham interspersed with cheese on sticks and a Jumbo-sized bag of crisps. As the *pièce-de-resistance*, she carefully lifted out a large birthday cake, divided into two curving halves, one iced in blue, the other pink with twenty-four white candles in silver foil holders arranged around the edge of the cake-board. Everyone rushed to get out their cameras, getting in each other's way until one of the ladies from the kiosk offered to take as many pictures as they liked with their own cameras to make sure everybody featured in at least one of them.

'We're used to this,' she said cheerfully, working her way round the table, 'with people getting engaged an' that. Now, tell me, who are the twins having their birthday today?'

As they all laughed and tried to explain, she got several shots of them with their mouths open, then left them to enjoy the picnic, eyeing the cake whilst trying not to look too envious.

'Almost a shame to cut it up,' said Elsie, 'are we going to take a slice home each just like at a kiddies' party?'

'We'll eat half now, then take half back for tomorrow's tea,' decided Sally, 'as that'll be my last teatime with you before I have to go back to school.'

Amongst the groans that accompanied this announcement, Heather overheard Doris whisper in surprise to Elsie, 'she still at school, then? Thought she were older'n that,' before Adrian offered to sacrifice his half that day and even wielded the cake knife, cutting it into twelve evenly matched slices.

'Can't count!' said Doris loudly and tactlessly, before Adrian wrapped up one slice in a paper napkin for the obliging photographer and handed the other to Gwen, 'for your driver.' Then they all tucked in and scattered blue crumbs all over the table.

As they trailed back to the cars, exclaiming to each other that that was the best birthday outing *ever*, Heather felt her hand gripped tightly as Chris drew her a little way behind the others.

'Thank you so much for saying yes,' he said, looking anxiously at her, 'promise me you won't regret it and that we'll be together for ever?'

At the sight of his worried expression, surprised at such evidence of his insecurity, she stopped and gave him a shake and cuddle.

'Til death us do part,' she promised, 'and let's hope – and pray if you like – that that won't be for a long time yet!'

Chapter Twenty

Heather suffered further turmoil of mixed feelings two days later as she drove Sally to the station, knowing that she would be feeling anxious and lonely for the next few days, but determined not to show it. Nevertheless, as she slowly stripped off the camp bed, folded up the bedding and threw the sheets in the laundry basket, she had trouble keeping the tears at bay as she realised just how much she was going to miss her.

The clatter of hooves in the courtyard, a brisk knock on her door and a cheerful call from Kathie broke in on her doom-laden thoughts.

'How about a ride? Conker is champing at the bit,' Heather heard her shout, and she ran down the stairs to see her friend holding both horses by the bridles. 'Thought you might be feeling a bit blue so I'm taking you out on the Common for a gallop – well, a gentle canter anyway. Get your gear on and leave tidying up until later.'

Such a beautiful morning…just enough slight chill in the air to remind Heather that Autumn, her favourite time of year, had really arrived. She felt a slight tremor of trepidation as they headed out onto the Common. Conker lengthened her stride and flew energetically over the rough ground, her mane flapping as they raced to catch up Champion, several yards ahead. She was prepared this time for Conker to slow to an awkward trot as she and Kathie reined in both horses and they were able to gaze at the wide view below, the trees touched with gold and rich brown, the fields, shorn of their ripened crops, ready for the plough.

'Absolute Heaven,' she remarked, realising with a start that she hadn't thought about Sally for well over an hour. Would she ever stop thinking and worrying about her, she wondered? I'm sure nobody worried about me at the age of twenty-four.

'We'll deliver the horses back to the paddock,' said Kathie as they trotted through the village, 'then, unless you've any pressing work to do, we can get on with the chalet. I left Stewart painting all the woodwork yesterday, so it's going to be all hands needed to put the whole thing together. Are you handy with a hammer and nails?'

'Pretty good,' replied Heather, glancing about her as they passed the Vicarage and the church but there was no sign of Chris. She did spot Mrs Grierson, however, making her way carefully towards the village shop and they both slowed the horses and gave her a wave as they passed.

'Hope your daughter got off safely this morning?' she called up to Heather, 'you'll miss her, won't you? And from what I hear, so will young Adrian, they make a pretty pair.'

Heather returned a friendly, non-committal answer then urged Conker into a faster pace, pondering on the impossibility of keeping anything secret in a village where everybody knew everybody, and the village shopkeeper knew everything. She wondered whether Chris would ever tell her more about Moira or if it was a subject he'd prefer to leave buried in the past.

As they put Champion and Conker back in the paddock, drank a quick coffee and made their way over to the Walled Garden, suitably garbed for the task ahead of them, they saw Elsie just ahead of them.

'Oh, Miss Heather, there was a phone call from your daughter to say she's safely arrived and there's masses of weeding and leaf sweeping to do in the garden as well as preparing all the registers for the start of term but that she'd had a brilliant time here and can't wait to come again at half-term. Phew...remembered every bit!'

Heather thanked the God she didn't believe in, then threw herself into helping Kathie and Stewart erect the newly painted chalet, fitting the door, and puttying the windows into place. Next came the challenge of cutting the roofing felt to size, folding under the edges and tacking it firmly into place. They gave Stewart the honour of fixing up the finial and all stood back to admire their handiwork.

'Looks good,' came a voice from just inside the wall and there stood Adrian carrying a bottle of wine and a few glasses. 'Topping out ceremony,' he announced, and they all flopped down on the grass just as Chris came through the gate to add his congratulations, lead them in three cheers and share the bottle with them. Then Gwen and Barry, attracted by the noise arrived, armed with champagne and a box of salt crackers and the ceremony had to be repeated all over again.

'Fetch Elsie,' someone suggested, 'she mustn't be left out – I suppose Doris will be at the Wakes today, but we could save her some.'

'Don't suppose she's ever had champagne before,' remarked Gwen, 'mustn't lead her into bad ways. Stewart, darling, isn't this splendid? And...' as she looked round at the tidier beds and borders, 'what you've all done in here is little short of a miracle. John would be so pleased.' She choked a little on her champagne before Barry put an arm round her shoulders to give her a comforting hug.

'What really needs doing,' said Heather, casting her eyes over the parts of the garden that they hadn't had time to tackle yet, 'is to give all the roses a really hard pruning. I don't suppose they've been touched for some time, have they, Stewart?'

Stewart nodded and stood up, waving his arm around to encompass several neglected flower beds and part of the inner walls as well.

'Prob...probably not for ...three...four years,' he said at last, slowly. 'John did them in the Autumn...light...lightly then gave them a p...proper going over...in the...in the Spr...

Spring. But think…I think they need a real…really hard pr…
pruning now.'

'I agree,' said Heather and turned to Gwen. 'I thought that
now I've virtually finished all my research that I'd put together
a neatly-typed copy of everything I've discovered so that it
could be bound as a slim volume, say a dozen copies for the
family, the Library, Record Office, local Museum. If I could
divide my time between that and tackling jobs here in the
garden, would that be all right by you?'

'Excellent idea,' said Gwen, 'so long as you don't ask me to
help, I'd kill all the plants and leave all the weeds. And when
the copy is finished, we'll draw up a proper contract for you as
Head Gardener of Westhangar Hall.'

A general whoop of surprise issued from the little group
seated on the grass and they clapped enthusiastically. Heather
glanced anxiously at Stewart, who, she suspected might have
taken exception to a relatively new arrival at Westhanger to be
appointed to such a prestigious position, but he merely grinned
and pointed at his chest.

'All…all my idea,' he enunciated carefully, 'I tell Gwen…
you best person, you know…all about trees…flowers…'

'Oh, Stewart!' said Heather, resisting the temptation to
fling her arms around his neck, 'and that book you gave me
for my birthday will be such a help. Oh, dear…I think I'm
going to cry again…I thought I'd finished with all that!'

They drained their glasses and, as it was past tea time, they
decided to re-convene later in the kitchen for supper. Heather
headed for the stables and was surprised to see Kathie
following her.

'Mind if I come up for a minute?' she asked, and Heather
noticed her cheeks were rather flushed.

'You're welcome,' she replied, 'sit yourself down while I
tidy up a little. I don't think Sally left anything behind but…'

After a minute or two she slumped into the other chair and
looked at Kathie enquiringly.

'Fire away,' she said, 'what's the problem?'

Kathie was silent for a short while, then glanced at Heather shyly.

'Yesterday, while you were busy in here, Stewart asked me to help him do some sorting out in his house in the village as he's thinking of moving back in there before too long.'

'That's really good news,' exclaimed Heather looking at Kathie in wonder, 'he's ... he's getting on so well now, isn't he?'

Kathie nodded as her cheeks grew redder and her voice softened as she gazed out of the window, then turned to Heather again.

'And,' she went on, slightly hesitating, 'he's asked me to live there with him. Not to get married or anything...just live with him... look after him...keep him company.'

Heather's mouth fell open in utter surprise as she looked at the expression of tenderness on Kathie's face and she struggled to get her words out of her mouth.

'And...and are you? Are you going to?' she asked at last, astounded to see tears begin to trickle down her usually hearty, no-nonsense friend's cheeks. She handed her a tissue and leaned forward to catch Kathie's unexpected next words, which came out in a muddled rush.

'Nobody's ever...ever really needed me before,' she managed to blurt out, between wipes of her eyes, 'and I thought I didn't need anyone either, quite happy with horses and dogs. But Stewart...he was such a lost, unhappy soul when I first met him but he's...I expect you'll laugh, Heather, but he makes me feel...special. And I know I can make him happy again, not in the way that Jenny and his children did, but...I didn't realize this before, but I really need to feel of use to someone, not just Gwen, an employer, but someone...who I'd feel really belonged to me.'

On an impulse, Heather took one of Kathie's hands in hers and kissed it, then sat just looking at her with the widest of wide smiles.

'Kathie!' she said, surprised to find her voice husky with emotion, 'that is such a wonderful idea …I couldn't be more pleased.' She stopped a moment, chuckling.

'I expect it was re-building the chalet that did it,' she said, smiling, 'creating a little home from home…must have given him the idea.' Kathie nodded happily.

'Might even learn to cook now,' she said, 'I'd better buy a book.'

'Why don't I give you a few lessons, just some basics…in return for all those riding lessons,' Heather suggested, and Kathie nodded with enthusiasm.

'So…you'd still be able to look after Gwen's horses? You wouldn't really be leaving Westhangar?' added Heather with an anxious frown.

'We haven't worked out any details,' Kathie replied, 'but there's no reason why I couldn't carry on here, it'd only be a ten-minute run to get here, and I know Stewart wants to keep on working in the gardens now that you're going to be in control. Could he be your Under-Gardener?'

Heather laughed. 'I can't think of anyone better,' she said, 'not sure if Gwen would put him on the payroll though. But who cares…he'd be welcome any time. I still think of it as his garden.'

Later that evening, after supper, Heather finished clearing away all reminders of Sally's presence the better to digest this latest, most welcome news. Lucky Stewart, to have the prospect of a cheerful, competent partner to share his life… and lucky Kathie, to have someone to care for, to go riding with, and, best of all, she thought, hugging herself, lucky me to be keeping two such agreeable people here at Westhangar, who I'll be able to see and talk to every day.

Heather now threw herself with enthusiasm into preparing the text of the Franklin family history for Gwen's approval before she could approach a local printing firm to produce a few attractively bound copies for distribution to anyone Gwen so desired. After three weeks, it was ready and after giving the typescript to Gwen for her perusal, she planned a trip into Alton to find a suitable printer/publisher. There was another delicious job she had to do too as Chris had already approached a jeweller in Alton and asked them to prepare a selection of engagement rings for Heather to choose from – a tactful way to ensure she did not fall for something way beyond his means. She'd decided to keep the engagement and wedding ring that Jerome had bought her all those years ago as a memento of his love and regard for her, unable to even think of selling them or giving them away.

The night beforehand, as she listened to the wind howling through the beech trees and the constant clatter on the roof as beech mast and small branches were torn off, her thoughts turned to Sally and Adrian again, hoping that absence from each other for a few weeks would strengthen their attachment rather than diminish it. There'd been no word from Mr Grundy recently so the problem of the future of the estate still lay like a weight on Heather's heart, and she wished there was some way of resolving it before the two of them were married. The prospect of this happy event calmed her, however, and she allowed her imagination to run wild again as she speculated on the delightful prospect of becoming a grandmother at an age when she could still be an active participant in her grandchildren's lives. Whatever happened to the estate, she nevertheless had much to look forward to.

Grandchildren! Heather suddenly sat bolt upright in bed, uttering a sound between a strangled cry and a shout! Could that be the answer? A child of Sally's would surely be the blood-relation of Mr Franklin that he had insisted should inherit Westhangar Hall… surely? Oh dear, she thought, biting anxiously at her lip. Would a missed generation matter? A grandchild would still be closely related and carry the Franklin genes that Skip had been at such pains to ensure would continue his family line. Would this be enough to undo the knotty knot, would Mr Grundy see things that way? Always supposing, of course, that the two young people would want children of their own.

As Heather lay back on her pillows, she recalled the day when she had stood Sally in front of Skip's fine portrait and she'd wanted to take a photograph, 'to show my children what their grandfather looked like.' Yes...there was no doubt that Sally would want children and Adrian was so good-hearted that she could not imagine that he would deny her. Perhaps she could add a visit to Mr Grundy to her list of commissions next day and hear what his opinion on her midnight brainwave might be.

After thinking that she might not sleep any more that night, she suddenly awoke to the shrill cries of Cock o' the North and hastened out of bed to make her morning cup of tea and plan her day. The wind had dropped, and the sun was shining but the courtyard was littered with dead sticks and a thick carpet of beech leaves as she crossed to the kitchen. Stewart and Kathie arrived a minute or two after her with plans to carry on clearing and re-furbishing his house in the village and Gwen and Barry rolled in just as the rest of them were leaving. Heather explained that she had business in Alton that morning but that she'd start her rose-pruning in the afternoon.

'I'll need something like a really old thick shirt to wear over my clothes,' Heather remarked once Gwen and Barry were tucking into bowls of porridge and cream, 'otherwise I'll get scratched to bits and I didn't bring anything like that. Is there anything you were thinking of putting out for the jumble-sale next week that might do?'

Gwen nodded and, as Barry went to help himself to another cup of coffee, she dropped her voice to a whisper.

'I'm sure there'll be something in John's old clothes,' she said, 'I need to get rid of them, not very tactful to keep them now that I'm with Barry. I'll look out one or two likely things and leave them on your stairs.'

'Thanks very much,' Heather replied and went off to prepare for the succession of jobs she had to do in the town.

She called at the solicitor's office first and made an appointment for later that morning then visited the library, guessing that they would know who to recommend for the printing of the Franklin family history. They mentioned two names and seeing that one of them was close to the jeweller's shop, she decided to visit them first and as their terms were reasonable and they understood exactly what Heather had in mind, she left the typescript with them. After gazing nervously into the jeweller's shop window for a full five minutes, hoping she didn't look like a potential thief, she pushed open the door and explained her mission.

'Oh, yes...Mr Garland was in here only last week,' they remembered and fetched a tray of sparkling and beautiful rings with all their prices tactfully removed.

'Oh,' gasped Heather, 'they're all so lovely – however shall I choose?'

'Only allowed one,' teased the assistant and, although remaining in sight, moved away a little for Heather to make her choice. 'You can try them on and if you see one that doesn't quite fit, we can alter it before you come in again with your fiancé.'

She wanted one quite different from the sapphire that Jerome had bought her so, after much thought she decided on a half-hoop of small rubies with two little diamonds each side.

'Rubies; my birth-stone,' she explained to the assistant, 'and it fits perfectly, no need to change a thing.'

'Excellent choice,' the young lady agreed, nodding and put it aside in a velvet-lined box, scribbling something on the label.

As she left the shop, Heather was reminded of Alicia's emerald and diamond necklace and wondered whether anything had been decided about its future. She'd have to ask Chris next time she saw him.

She entered Mr Grundy's office with a bounce in her step and repeated to him the thoughts that had come to her in the middle of the night. After listening carefully, he considered a while, then pulled a book from a shelf and flicked through it, nodding and grunting a little, giving Heather no hint as to what he was thinking. At last, he snapped the book shut and looked at Heather with something like respect in his expression.

'Well, Mrs La Fontaine,' he said at last, 'the job of a solicitor is to attempt to carry out the wishes of our clients to the best of our abilities. We need to consider what Mr Franklin would have preferred...that the estate is handed on to a grandchild or fall into the hands of strangers with no connection to Westhangar by blood. I sincerely believe it would be the former, but...this is all speculative as of course your daughter and Adrian Franklin might not marry...and if they did, they might not have issue...but,' he paused dramatically and put his fingertips together, 'if they do and if they did, I see no reason to prevent a future grandchild from fulfilling the criteria of John Franklin's will, so long as there are no further claimants. We've had no response to our insertions into the newspapers.'

Gosh, just how long-winded do solicitors have to be to cover themselves, thought Heather but could not prevent a huge smile from breaking out on her face. Mr Grundy wagged a warning finger.

'Better to keep this information from the young people for the present,' he said, 'it wouldn't be fair to propel them into marriage and possibly too-early parenthood for the sake of an inheritance – tempting, I know, but far better to let these things unfold naturally. And, with Mrs ... er with Gwen likely to remain as chatelaine for many years to come, there would be no need to burden them with this knowledge for the foreseeable future. Mrs...er...Falkland,' he remembered, 'Gwen might have to make a new will, that's all, but that's quite usual after a death...and a re-marriage. Just reassure them – but only if they ask – that, when the time comes for young Mr Franklin to take over, there should be no problem as far as I can see at the present.'

Heather smiled again. 'You can't believe how much this has relieved my mind,' she said at last, 'it's been such a worry and of course I blame myself for... but how was I to foresee all these complications? As far as I was concerned, I was going to be just one more unmarried mother who had to make the best of things until dear Jerome took his chance to marry me.'

Mr Grundy leaned over, a twinkle in his eye and took both her hands in his.

'It's people like you, my dear, and the muddles you get into that constitute a large part of our bread and butter. Now, off you go and be happy. Nothing to pay, my mental stopwatch doesn't register until you've been here at least a quarter of an hour. Now tell me, my dear, how is that lovely spiritual advisor who looks at you as if he could eat you?'

'I've just been to choose my engagement ring,' she announced, with a broad grin, at which the portly Mr Grundy leaned as far across his desk as his stomach would allow and planted a most unprofessional, smacking kiss on her cheek and Heather swore she could see a moistening of his eyes as she left to fetch Frog.

There was no-one around when she reached Westhangar, so she made her way to the Walled Garden and tried to make out where those fine pergolas she'd seen in the old photographs had been. The area she had in mind was even more overgrown and derelict than the rest of the garden and it was hard even to see the wall, let alone any structures alongside. Looking inside the chalet she saw that someone had left some tools, buckets and tough gardening gloves there and donning a pair, she began to heave some of the thick growth of brambles out of the way, wishing she had a billhook or shears with her. Suddenly her foot struck a hard object and, clearing away a bit more brash she saw the outline of a stout length of timber, rather rotten but a good deal of it left and a length of rusty chain beside it. So, she thought, where there's one there should be about thirty more and if she could find the next...This was easier said than done, but she heaved away with a will and eventually uncovered a second post lying on the ground about three yards from the first. Good – now she had something to work on and tomorrow she'd come back armed with better equipment and see how many more she could find.

Returning the gloves to the chalet, she made her way back to the stables just in time to see Kathie and Stewart leading the horses into the courtyard and gave them a cheerful wave,

'After last night's storm we thought it was time for them to return to their winter quarters, so we've been clearing out their stalls and putting new straw in,' explained Kathie, 'so you'll be back to hearing strange noises in the night again. Think you could open their doors for us?' and Heather obediently yanked the two doors open and helped to guide the two lovely beasts inside.

'You look cheerful,' remarked Kathie, noticing Heather's satisfied smile as she prepared to mount her staircase, 'don't be late for lunch, think Elsie's made us a cauliflower cheese and we'd hate to have to eat it all ourselves,' and, with a last pat on Champion's and Conker's noses, she slipped her arm through Stewart's and led him off towards the kitchen.

On her hasty way up to her rooms, Heather almost fell over a soft bundle on the top step – and caught her breath as she realised that these were some of Mr Franklin's cast-off clothes. Picking them up almost reverentially, she clasped them to herself as she unlocked her door, then laid them on her bed and just stood...looking at them.

Skip's clothes...these had been on his body...next his skin... and she sat down suddenly beside them, her mind flooded with memories again.

Must be practical, she told herself sternly, choose the most suitable for the job. She selected a heavy twill shirt, the cuffs frayed and half the buttons missing, then drew out another in fine blue cotton, in better condition, too good for a jumble sale. I'll save this for Sally, she decided, the only tangible memento of her father and the rest can be thrown away.

As she was trying on the thick shirt, a small comb fell out of one of the pockets. She gazed at it for a long time…still got some of his lovely thick hair caught in it, she noticed and, trying not to feel foolish or guilty, she locked it up with some other small treasures in her suitcase, just as her phone rang. It was Chris, asking her if she'd chosen a ring and should they go and collect it tomorrow?

'You'll need to come in Frog,' he said, 'as I'll be going to the hospital afterwards on a pastoral visit – but I hope there'll be time for a quick coffee first.'

'You bet,' replied Heather, 'but no doughnuts,' and rang off, feeling just a little less emotional towards the twill shirt than she had been a minute ago.

On the way from the jewellers' shop to the café next day, her ruby ring on her finger, Chris informed her that they were both going to have to have an interview with his Bishop in the next few days.

'You have to be approved,' he said, 'particularly as this is a second marriage for both of us.'

Heather glanced up at him and frowned nervously. 'Will I have to go into details about Sally?' she asked, a sudden chill running through her at the thought that there might yet be some bar to her and Chris's marriage. He squeezed her arm reassuringly.

'No problem,' he said, 'as far as the Bishop – and everyone else who might wonder – is concerned, Sally was Jerome's child. He'll be more interested in your suitability as a prop and stay to your vicar than anything else.'

'Hm…that's what I'm afraid of,' said Heather quietly, 'what if he asks me if I believe in God?'

Chris gave a short laugh. 'He won't…but you could say… you do have doubts…he should accept that…as we all do, even him, I shouldn't wonder.'

Heather still felt uneasy and gripped Chris's hand tightly as they approached the cafe, then they both laughed as lo and behold, there sat Mrs Grierson and her friend in the window-table. They waved at them and, at their invitation, slid into the two seats vacant beside them.

'You order,' Chris asked Heather, 'must visit the Gents,' and he strode off leaving Heather, still discomposed at the idea of having to be 'approved' by the Bishop, to make polite conversation with the two old ladies.

'Tell me,' boomed Mrs Grierson as soon as Chris was out of sight, 'what was making you look so anxious in the street must now? Haven't had your first tiff, I hope.'

Heather bit her lip. 'No...nothing like that...but Chris just told me we've got to have an interview with the Bishop soon and I'm very far from being a 100% committed Christian – and I'm so worried he'll ask me if I am.' She took out her handkerchief and gave a quick dab at her eyes, before putting on her smile again for the benefit of the waitress who appeared at her side.

'Er...two hot chocolates, please, no extras,' she said and turned as she felt Mrs Grierson pulling at her sleeve.

'Now, you stop worrying *this instant!*' she said, luckily lowering her voice and her hand gripped Heather's arm quite tightly, 'Don't tell Chris I've said this...but you just leave the Bishop to me. There are things I know about my little brother that I don't think he'd want anyone else to know! There! Now...let's have a good look at that lovely ring of yours. Chris told me where he was off to today.'

Both elderly ladies were carefully examining Heather's hand when Chris returned, surprised and pleased to see her face wreathed in happy smiles once more.

Chapter Twenty-One

Chris and Heather's meeting with the Bishop in Winchester proved far less of an ordeal than she had feared, in fact he reminded her a little of the avuncular Mr Grundy. After asking after his sister – and did Heather perceive the slightest twinkle in his eye? – he merely asked her a few questions about her family, Jerome, her former connection with Alton, how long she'd been in Selborne...all perfectly reasonable questions with, she felt, no hidden agenda. His conversation with Chris took longer and her attention did wander occasionally until she realised the interview was at an end and, as far as she knew, they had the Bishop's blessing to plan their wedding as soon as they desired.

'So...have we passed muster?' she asked as they strolled down the High Street towards the statue of Alfred the Great, looking in all the shop windows as they went.

'We have,' he replied, 'passed with flying colours.' He paused for a moment beside a furniture-shop with a handsome double bed in a prominent position by the window, regarding it with keen interest.

'We'll be needing one of those,' he said, squeezing Heather's arm, 'new wife...new bed. You'll have to come and have a good look round the Vicarage to see what else we'll need. Men aren't always the best judges of interior design.'

'I'll wait until Charmian comes again,' said Heather, 'She has such good taste and I'd be happier with an expert opinion.'

'Trouble is, Heather, I'd like to buy that bed now...but I shall want to roll you up inside it straightaway – with me next you, of course.'

'And what would the Bishop think of that?' Heather rejoined quickly, to cover the fact that her cheeks were flaming, and she walked him quickly past the shop.

'He'd be jealous...but I suppose we'd better wait,' Chris said gloomily, 'ought not to set a bad example to my flock. But I tell you, Heather, we'd better name the day soon – very soon.'

They were both silent as they returned to Chris's car, then Heather brought up the subject of the gold sovereigns that they had found in the tin box in Alicia's trunk.

'I took them up to my jeweller friend in Piccadilly,' Chris replied, 'and at first he was a bit sceptical, but apparently many of the owners of pitches had insisted on being paid in British gold. So, they're English and altogether worth today about £60,000. I know, astounding,' he said, at Heather's gasp, 'but, as to who they and the necklace set belong to, I think we may have to go back to Mr Grundy for the answer to that.'

'Well,' said Heather decidedly, 'I think it should be for Gwen to decide about the necklace set to keep it in Alicia's family, but shouldn't the gold go towards honouring her wishes to benefit the church? They always seem to need new roofs or new pews or something.'

Chris sighed, nodding. 'Always,' he said, slowing as he reached a tight bend, 'and it's tough on a small congregation to be asked to give, give and give again. The people here, not just churchgoers, are very supportive and the Gilbert White connection brings in donations from quite surprising sources. But a generous lump sum like that would be a really great help.'

'So, would we need a solicitor? Couldn't it all be decided, like everything else, round Gwen's kitchen table? Or would you have to consult your Bishop again?'

Chris frowned as he considered the question. 'It's difficult. Personally, I agree that Gwen should decide. From what I gather, Barry's very well off – he was negotiating to buy a holiday villa on Lanzarote when they were on their honeymoon – so I'm sure she could afford to donate the sovereigns to the church. Has she seen Alicia's letter?'

'Well, it's all cross-written,' explained Heather, 'I can transcribe the relevant pages and hope she trusts me not to have invented it all. Then it's up to her what happens to it. Who was it said that money is the root of all evil?'

'That was...St Paul... but what he really said was that it was the love of money, not the money itself. Anyway, here we are, safely delivered back to Westhangar. Whoops – mustn't run over the dogs!'

It only took a few minutes for Heather to type out the key part of Alicia's letter and she took it across to the kitchen for Gwen and Barry to read at lunch.

'How did you get on with the old Bish this morning?' asked Kathie, 'Any embarrassing questions? Does he think you suitable to be a vicar's wife? Good thing he hasn't heard you swear when Cock o' the North wakes you up at five o'clock in the morning.'

'How do you know about that?' asked Heather, startled to think that her voice could carry all the way into the Hall. There was a burst of laughter round the table as Adrian explained that Sally had passed on her surprise at the colour and variety of her mother's language. In the midst of Heather's embarrassment, Gwen looked up from Alicia's letter.

'Oh, we must give the money to the church, it needs it badly,' she said, 'that was quite obviously Alicia's intention. That poor couple...I shall pay more respect towards their gravestones now.'

There was a short silence as they polished off their omelette and chips, then Elsie asked where Stewart was.

'He's at his house again,' said Kathie, 'don't save him any lunch, he's going to the pub for a sandwich.'

'On his own?' asked Gwen in pleased surprise. 'Can't remember when he last did that. He's a different man from what he was six months ago, all down to you, Heather and to you Kathie. Now,' she said, waving Alicia's letter in the air, 'come on, Barry, we're going to phone Chris and, if you all agree, tell him to start making a list of repairs needed for the church.'

'Who's coming to the village bonfire next month?' asked Elsie, two or three weeks later as they sat, once more, around the kitchen table. 'I usually bake a whole sack of potatoes, then we guzzle them while the fireworks go off. Bob and Harry do the honours, done it for years. Hope it don't rain, don't want damp squibs shootin' off all over the place,' then laughed heartily at her own joke.

'Will Sally be here for Guy Fawkes Night?' Adrian asked Heather, who nodded happily as the date coincided with her half-term holiday.

'And Charmian'll be here,' Elsie announced, 'used to bring her two boys but they say they're too old now for village fireworks. Don't think I'll ever be too grown up...and Dorrie hasn't even grown up proper yet, so she still loves 'em.'

'They've already started to build the bonfire on the Common,' said Adrian, 'I think they're going to put Arthur Scargill on top this year. They couldn't get Mrs Grierson to volunteer.'

'You're far too rude about that lady,' reproved Gwen, 'I'll have you know she provides most of the fireworks *and* the sack of potatoes. She's a good Christian woman and don't you forget it.'

As they were drinking their coffee, Gwen turned to Heather and brought up the subject of the Franklin family history.

'Goodness knows how you managed to discover all this,' she said with approval, 'makes so much more sense than when it was scattered about in bits and pieces and John always so secretive about it. Funny he didn't know anything about Alicia. To think that that trunk full of her undies and the jewels and gold had been sitting there under our noses ever since the 1850s! Now,' she continued, with another change of subject, 'when can we expect Sally to arrive? OK if she shares your rooms again?'

'If not, she can always share mine,' put in Adrian, quick as a flash, with a cheeky grin at Heather. 'And when are you and Chris going to get hitched? And who will marry you? A vicar can't marry himself, can he?'

This same question had occurred to Heather, but she hadn't had the chance to discuss it with him, so she merely shrugged and poured herself out another cup of tea.

'After the fireworks,' she said to Adrian, 'it'll only be a few weeks until Christmas and Sally will be here again, if that's OK by you, Gwen.' Gwen nodded emphatically.

When Heather returned to the study, her thoughts turned again to Mr Franklin's diary with his far too explicit description of their 'brilliant bang' in Athens. If she destroyed it, no-one would ever know – but the fact remained that it was the only piece of written evidence that could help to prove that Sally was his daughter. She recollected that she had mentioned something called DNA which would prove ones' parentage without doubt in the not-too-far distant future and she leaned back in her chair, her hands behind her head, deep in thought.

With luck, Gwen will live for at least another ten or even twenty years, she reasoned, and by then this DNA thing will surely have been developed sufficiently to be used as evidence of Sally's parentage. And until then it didn't really matter – so perhaps she *could* quietly dispose of the diary and evidence of the 'brilliant bang' could remain her secret for ever.

Sally arrived the day before Bonfire Night, bearing a box of rockets and they all trooped up to the Common to inspect the bonfire and admire the Guy. He didn't bear the slightest resemblance to Arthur Scargill but was a fine sight in more of Mr Franklin's old clothes and a straw hat that Gwen and Barry had brought back from the Canary Islands, then decided neither of them liked it.

'Hope he's got a rocket in his hat,' said Sally, 'it's traditional, you know!'

'In his hat, his hands and in all his pockets,' said Barry, looking as excited as a schoolboy, 'so keep well back when the flames reach him.'

Chris arrived just as they were about to leave but he thrust a dozen large flares at Adrian, some stakes and a length of rope and Heather, Kathie and Stewart helped arrange them at a safe distance from the fire.

'Charmian and I'll be bringing over a whole load of sausages, ready-cooked and bread rolls, ready buttered,' explained Chris, 'and there'll be a beer tent and Pepsi-Cola for the kids. Beginning to feel like a kid myself!'

'Me too,' agreed Heather, 'haven't been to a Guy Fawkes Night for years!'

'And Charmian says if you've got time would you like to come to the Vicarage this afternoon to see what changes you'd like to make? About three o'clock,' then hardly waiting for her to reply, he dashed off back to the village again.

'Makes you exhausted just to see him,' commented Kathie, turning to Heather with a broad wink, 'hope you'll find the energy to keep up with him in your married life.' In a more leisurely fashion they all trooped home, arriving just in time to enjoy Elsie's home-made vegetable soup and crusty rolls.

Shortly before three, Kathie and Sally took the horses out for their exercise and Heather strolled over to the Vicarage to be greeted with enthusiasm by Charmian, armed with sheets of paint-colours, swatches of material and furniture catalogues.

'It's the living-room that's in most dire need of a makeover,' she said, leading Heather by the arm and indicating the sagging sofa and worn-out arms of the armchairs. 'Men are hopeless when it comes to soft furnishings, don't you agree?'

Luckily, Charmian didn't expect an answer as Heather would have been embarrassed to confess that Jerome had been fastidious about such things and their house had been a picture of elegance and good taste. But she had to admit that the Vicarage sitting-room décor had seen better days.

'What's the budget?' she asked Charmian shyly, 'don't want it to look so much like Buckingham Palace that we can't sit on the chairs.'

Charmian patted her hand. 'Chris has given me a rough idea so I've ticked a few items in here,' she indicated the brochures, 'so anything you choose will be fine. By the way, my dear, he's already replaced the bed; like to have a quick peep at it before he comes back and see what you think?'

'Think I recognise this bed,' Heather reassured Charmian, as she gazed on the one they'd seen in Winchester, a slight smile twisting her lips, 'but...whenever I get into it... I shall always think of the Bishop!'

They clutched each other laughing, until they heard the front door shut and Chris's footsteps on the stairs and looked at each other like naughty schoolchildren caught stealing sweets from the corner shop. Chris glanced from one to the other then back to Heather.

'Been doing a Goldilocks?' he asked with a mischievous grin, patting the bedspread invitingly, 'can we hop in now, just to make sure?'

'Tut, tut,' said Charmian reprovingly, leading Heather firmly to the door, 'you'd never guess my brother had taken Holy Orders, would you?'

'Sometimes I wish I hadn't,' they both heard him murmur disconsolately as they headed down the stairs and into the living-room where they spent a delicious hour matching wall-paint to chair-covers before heading into the kitchen to choose some more modern appliances there.

'You will come and stay often after we're married, won't you?' Heather urged Charmian, 'Even though I'll be working up at Westhangar, it would be good to have someone like you to keep me on the straight and narrow. Don't want to make too many mistakes!'

'Whatever you do I'm sure will be OK with Chris – he's totally besotted, you know,' Charmian added, her voice softening, 'and in his dear old-fashioned way he thanks

God every day that you came to Selborne. I, too...I was beginning to worry that he'd never find anyone to love and love him.'

'Bit like Stewart and Kathie,' murmured Heather and at Charmian's start of surprise she explained that they were planning to move in together as soon as his house was ready. 'And now,' she continued, 'I'd better go back and carry on with the Walled Garden...the work never ends with gardens. And thanks for all your advice.'

Later that day before supper, she and Sally went for a stroll through the village and across the fields and caught up on each other's news. It was after a lengthy pause that Sally suddenly slowed and ventured, 'Oh, by the way, Mum, hope you won't be upset but...'

Oh, here we go, thought Heather, she's going to tell me she's pregnant... keep calm, offer support and reassurance....

'But,' continued Sally, looking nervously at her mother, 'Barry has a farmer friend, a former colleague, in New Zealand who's looking for a young man to help on his sheep-farm for a couple of years until his own son grows up a bit...a wonderful opportunity, he calls it...and Adrian's longing to go but only if I'll go with him.'

Almost weak with relief, Heather turned and gave her daughter a tight, delighted hug. 'But of course you must go with him,' she said, 'New Zealand! I'd have given my back teeth for that opportunity when I was your age!'

'Thank goodness!' said Sally, 'I was afraid you might throw a wobbly and burst into floods of tears. You obviously can't wait to get rid of me.'

'I shall hate saying goodbye,' admitted Heather, 'and might just sniff a little – any idea how Gwen will take the news?'

'I think Barry has already convinced her that it would be useful for Adrian to work with sheep, coupled with his experience with cattle in Brazil, so I don't think she'll weep for more than a month or two.'

The question that Heather was dying to ask but trying her best not to was in fact answered by Sally in the very next breath.

'So...we were wondering whether we should get married straightaway and go out as a married couple – gosh, that makes me sound really old!'

'So, when you say 'we', I presume you and Adrian have discussed it and both agreed?'

Sally nodded, suddenly serious. 'And we also wondered whether we could have a double wedding with you and Chris...here...sometime in the New Year. We'd be flying out to New Zealand about the end of January.'

'Goodness! It's a lot to take in! But I know Chris is getting...well, impatient for want of a better word and so am I. He's already bought a huge new double bed!'

'So, you never got round to having your test run?' Sally teased and they made their way back to Westhangar slowly, their minds full of thoughts and plans.

The Guy Fawkes party had been scheduled to begin early so the Westhangar group assembled in the courtyard at about 5.30 p.m. Heather ran up to her room a few minutes beforehand and slipped something into the depths of her jacket pocket, racing down again to join the others. Just as they were about to set off, however, Adrian sidled up to her and whispered a few words, then approached Sally and did likewise. As they reached the road, Adrian and Heather waved goodbye to the rest of the party and headed up the road towards the Zig-Zag.

'It's now or never,' said Adrian, 'what with you getting married to Chris and Sally and I off to Australia...the last chance for me to be your brother. Come on, let's see if we can race the others and be at the bonfire before them.'

Leading his future mother-in-law behind him, Adrian raced up the road and together they zigged and zagged in the half dark, dodging sticks and brambles arriving at the Wishing Stone breathless, gasping and laughing.

'I thought you might have forgotten that promise,' Heather said, clutching onto the Stone for support, 'and now, I suppose, we ought to make a wish.'

'Tell you what,' said Adrian when they had circled the Stone three times, 'I'll make a wish for you and you make one for me – then one day we'll be able to tell each other if they came true!'

'Adrian – you're a genius. Right, I'm going to shut my eyes – and don't you dare run off without me!'

In spite of their dash up the Hangar, the whole Westhangar contingent arrived at the bonfire at much the same time. Chris and Charmian joined them after a few minutes and Chris slipped his arms around Heather's waist, as they watched Bob and Harry take one of the flares and thrust it into the bottom of the huge pile of dead wood, broken pallets and bits of old furniture. They all cheered as the flames quickly reached the top, setting off Guy Fawkes's rockets which flew in alarming directions. Doris jumped up and down in ecstasy, clapping her mittened hands and all the village children waved sparklers about shrieking, trying to spell out their names against the dark sky. Thrusting her hand into her jacket pocket, Heather surreptitiously drew out Mr Franklin's diary and threw it into the centre of the fire, relieved to see it catch alight and disintegrate before her eyes, gone...gone for good. Turning to face Chris, they caught each other's eye in a long look. No words were needed, and they missed the first minute or two of Bob and Harry's firework display as they indulged in a close, clinging embrace.

The next few days of Sally's half-term holiday passed in a flurry of plans and discussions. Chris found a moment to tell Heather that the Bishop had hinted to him that he would be most honoured to be asked to conduct the double wedding next year – and that was far too much of an honour to be refused. Sally was to be married in traditional white with two former school-friends as bridesmaids, while Heather settled on a full-length dress in pale-blue and silver brocade, matching shoes and a close-fitting, feathery hat. As they were all discussing the coming weddings round the lunch-table, just before Sally had to return to school, Heather's eyes fell on Doris, her cheeks very pink, gasping with anticipation.

'And you, Doris,' she said, providentially reminded just in time, 'and Elsie if she wants to, will be *my* bridesmaids. After Christmas we'll go on a shopping spree to Winchester to choose your dresses, so get your thinking caps on.'

'We'd like to ask Stewart to be Chris's best man,' Heather told Kathie quietly as they left the lunch table, 'do you think he'd be...?'

'You bet!' replied Kathie, 'I'll bully him into agreeing if necessary. No really, he'd be thrilled, although don't expect him to show it. He might even make a speech. Gosh, who'd have thought this time last year that we'd all be in for such excitement! Pity we can't have Champion and Conker and Dizzy and Dotty to follow you all up the aisle.'

Gwen and Barry arrived from their lunch at the pub just in time to say goodbye to Sally. She and Adrian had decided to announce their engagement formally on Christmas Day and the whole Westhangar family and staff stood in the drive to watch Heather drive her off to the station, Adrian running down the drive until they were out of sight.

Later, as Heather made her way back to the stables, Gwen caught up with her just as she was about to go up her stairs.

'News this morning from Mr Grundy,' she said breathlessly, 'after consulting with some of his colleagues in London, it's agreed that the emerald necklace-set is mine after all...and the value of the gold sovereigns will be donated to the church.' At Heather's gasp of pleasure, Gwen put her hand on Heather's arm. 'Now keep this under your hat,' she said, glancing round the courtyard to ensure they were alone. 'I'll need you to fetch the jewellery from the bank soon, as I intend to give it to your daughter as a wedding present...so that she can wear it on her wedding-day...no arguments...that's my decision!' and leaving

Heather speechless with astonishment, she picked her way across the courtyard and went back into the house.

There was much to do over the next few weeks, work-permits for Adrian and Sally, new passports, vaccinations, airline tickets, more clothes to buy...and she and Chris, and Gwen and Barry promised to visit the young couple sometime in the coming year. The only sober faces around the Christmas dinner table were those of Elsie and especially Doris, who found it impossible to believe that it was safe to fly half-way across the world and live in a foreign country for two whole years without coming to frightful harm. They cheered up, however, as the turkey, sprouts and roast potatoes went down, crackers were pulled, the paper hats donned and the well-worn jokes read out and all laughed as Chris, exhausted after his busy round of school Nativity plays, Christingle, carol services, Midnight Mass, Morning service and his midday visit to the Alton Hospital, fell asleep with his head on Heather's shoulder...and snored!

She nudged him awake just in time to see Gwen put out the kitchen lights as Elsie brought in the huge Christmas pudding ablaze with flickering blue flames, setting the sprig of holly on top on fire. Afterwards Stewart, tears starting from his eyes, poured the port and proposed the toast to 'Absent Friends' reducing them all to shared tears too. Handing round and opening presents took up the greater part of the rest of the day with just an interval for them to gather in the rarely used drawing-room to watch Her Majesty's Christmas message. Doris was heard to mutter darkly, 'bet she don't help with the washin' up,' before they dispersed, some to rest, Kathie and Stewart to exercise the horses, others to walk off their huge lunch with a gentle stroll in the twilight, accompanied by Dizzy and Dotty, up and down the village street.

They'd arranged to meet again for a light supper and slice of Christmas cake – and copious cups of tea – in the drawing room and seven o'clock found them grouped around the fire, somehow managing to find room for turkey sandwiches and warm mince pies. Gwen disappeared for a few minutes, then reappeared bearing a long thin box and tapped on the marble mantelpiece for silence.

'Today is no ordinary Christmas Day,' she said solemnly, 'as it's the day on which my dear Adrian and dearest Sally have officially become engaged to be married – so next year they'll be enjoying their Christmas dinner on the other side of the world while we're all still fast asleep!' A burst of mingled sighs and applause greeted this announcement, as she continued. 'You'll also remember that Heather's painstaking efforts to decipher Alicia Franklin's letter led to two things. The first was that evil thieves had stolen Alicia and her husband's hard-won nuggets of gold. But the second thing was finding...,' she paused dramatically as she opened the box to display the emerald and diamond necklace, '...this set of most beautiful jewellery.'

As they all craned forward to gasp and admire the flashing, sparkling jewels, even though most of them had seen it before, Gwen worked herself round behind Sally's chair and fastening the necklace round her neck, faced her to give her a kiss on both cheeks to noisy cheers and clapping. Sally blushed scarlet, incoherent for the first time in her life with delighted shock and surprise.

'So now, Chris,' said Gwen, as everybody searched for their cameras again, 'would you call this a God-given miracle – or just a lucky chance?'

'Both,' Chris said, 'both! And now, at the risk of embarrassing you all, I'd like to bless these two young – and very lucky – people ... and to wish them all the luck in the world. They may not find gold in New Zealand but largely owing to my clever fiancée here,' and he pulled Heather towards him in a close hug, 'they have found each other, found their real fathers and – excuse the awful pun – I hope they will soon found a family that will, once more, settle here as owners and guardians of Westhangar Hall for many years to come.'

As they all began to sing 'For they are jolly good fellows,' Doris burst into noisy tears, Dizzy and Dotty – permitted to enter the drawing room as a special favour – lifted their heads and howled (with delight, everyone agreed) and all lost count of the number of times they embraced each other, laughing and crying at the same time.

Five weeks later they gathered once more in the courtyard on a frosty, sunny morning to wave good-bye to Mr and Mrs Adrian Franklin as they prepared to be driven to Heathrow by Barry and Gwen, Heather only just managing to hold back her tears at the sight of her daughter disappearing down the drive. *New Zealand was so far away!* Chris hugged her close, Kathie and Stewart gripped each other's hands while Elsie and Doris waved until their arms ached.

'Well, Mrs Garland,' Chris said when the sound of the car engine had ceased, 'a new year, new beginnings, new plans... would it be *very* wicked if we went and tested that lovely new bed again?'

'Again? At this time of day?' replied Heather, trying to look shocked. 'Could you wait another ten minutes? There's one place even more important than the bedroom that I need to see first.'

Waving to Kathie and Stewart as they headed towards the stables, she led Chris across the crisp, white grass and pushed open the door to the Walled Garden, gazing round it in awe. Every branch of every tree, every shrub, plant and blade of grass, even the chalet gleamed with deep fringes of rime. As they watched, entranced, the winter sun rose above the walls and turned each drop of melting frost into tiny, sparkling rainbows.

'Utter magic,' Heather heard Chris whisper, 'I shan't forget this moment for the rest of my life. And the rest of my life is going to be magic... with you by my side.'

Three months later they sat again in the Walled Garden after their day's work was done and listened to the almost deafening songs of the birds as the sun went down. Heather was glad that she and Stewart had agreed to allow one section of the garden to remain undisturbed as she, Bob and Harry had counted at least half-a-dozen nests in the thicket behind the chalet, blackbirds and chaffinches mostly, with a family of bluetits quite at home in the bird-box beside one of the chalet-windows. And the swallows had returned to the stables.

'I've been here a whole year,' mused Heather, 'never imagined when I arrived that within twelve months both Sally and I would be married...still can't believe it sometimes.'

'I hope you'll never regret it,' Chris murmured as they prepared to leave for home, 'I don't think Mrs Grierson would be too happy if both my wives upped and left me and as for the Bishop...!'

Heather chuckled and slipped her arm into his as they wandered slowly down the drive. She wondered whether she should tell him. No...it was a little too soon...she'd wait another two or three weeks, just to be sure. Then all they'd have to do would be to tell Mrs Johnson at the Post Office and in no time at all, the whole village would be rejoicing with them.

About the Author

Jane Preston was born in Manchester in 1939 but grew up in rural Hampshire. After leaving University, she embarked on a year or two of travel and met her husband John whilst both were working in Iran. Four years in Iraq followed, then three years in Abu Dhabi by which time three children had been added to the family. They settled in Hertfordshire for twenty years, then decided to retire to Dorset and Jane drew on her knowledge of the Middle East to write five romantic novels. Two books of non-fiction followed, family histories inspired by her part-time jobs in Hertfordshire and Norfolk.

Lockdown in 2020 and 2021 gave her the time and opportunity to return to fiction with *The Walled Garden,* setting the book in her favourite part of Hampshire and drawing on her vivid childhood memories.

Lightning Source UK Ltd.
Milton Keynes UK
UKHW010106060921
390023UK00001B/39